Bookkeeping on Your Hom

Windcrest®/ McGraw-Hill

New York   San Francisco   Washington, D.C.   Auckland   Bogotá
Caracas   Lisbon   London   Madrid   Mexico City   Milan
Montreal   New Delhi   San Juan   Singapore
Sydney   Tokyo   Toronto

–Based PC

Linda Stern

To Ken,
Ben and Laura,
and Mom

FIRST EDITION
FIRST PRINTING

©1993 by **Windcrest Books**, an imprint of TAB Books.
TAB Books is a division of McGraw-Hill, Inc.
The name "Windcrest" is a registered trademark of TAB Books.

Library of Congress Cataloging-in-Publication Data
Stern, Linda.
   Bookkeeping on your home-based PC / Linda Stern.
     p.   cm.
   Includes index.
   ISBN 0-8306-4305-2   ISBN 0-8306-4304-4 (pbk.)
   1. Bookkeeping. 2. Home-based businesses. I. Title.
HF5635.S836 1993
   657'.2—dc20   93-15875
                                    CIP

Editorial team: Lori Flaherty, Supervising Editor
Theresa Burke, Book Editor
Joann Woy, Indexer
Production team: Katherine G. Brown, Director
Tina M. Sourbeir, Coding
Patsy D. Harne, Layout
Lorie L. White, Proofreading
Design team: Jaclyn J. Boone, Designer
Brian Allison, Associate Designer
Cover design: Lori E. Schlosser

EPC1

Notices

ACT!™	Contact Software International
Apple®	Apple Computer, Inc.
CompuServe®	CompuServe Inc.
IBM PC®	International Business Machines Corp.
Lotus 1-2-3®	Lotus Development Corp.
Macintosh®	Apple Computer, Inc.
Managing Your Money®	Micro Education Corp. of America
MasterCard®	MasterCard International Inc.
Microsoft Excel®	Microsoft Corp.
MS-DOS®	Microsoft Corp.
Navigator™	NEC Corp.
Norton Utilities®	Peter Norton Computing
PCAnywhere™	Dynamic Microprocessor Associates, Inc.
PC/Computing®	Ziff Communications Co.
PC Tools™	Central Point Software
PRODIGY™	Prodigy Services Co.
Quicken®	Intuit Corp.
Rolodex®	Insilco Corp.
Tapcis®	Support Group, Inc.
Timeslips®	North Edge Software Corp.
Windows®	Microsoft Corp.
Yellow Pages™	Yellow Pages, Inc.

All other product names are trademarks or registered trademarks of their respective owners.

Other books in the series

The Entrepreneurial PC Series brings the hottest new work-at-home options and essential information and advice to the new breed of PC-based home business owners—information they can use.

Health Service Businesses on Your Home-Based PC, Benzel, (4327)

The Entrepreneurial PC, David, (4483)

The Information Broker's Handbook, Rugge/Glossbrenner, (4104)

Information for Sale: How to Start and Operate Your Own Data Research Service, Everett/Crowe, (3057)

Contents

Appendices

Acknowledgments

Even when only one person's name appears on the cover, a book is necessarily a group effort. Therefore, a very big and heartfelt thank you to the following people.

Ken Norkin, who provided professional advice, art, expertise, companionship, laundry services, and a big husbandly shoulder to fall asleep on when I finished my day's work.

Paul and Sarah Edwards, who brought me into the world of books and who always seem to have time to share a little more advice and expertise, no matter how busy they are.

Brad Schepp, who was unfailingly friendly, calm, professional, and persistent throughout the book acquisition and editing processing.

Lisa Black, who cheerfully handled my petty questions of the day (which were the publishing equivalent of "Will this be on the midterm?") when it was time to submit an unwieldy manuscript.

Rick Benzel, my book-writing buddy, who was always willing to share the tricks of the trade, even when *he* was on a deadline.

IBM Corporation, who graciously (and without any strings attached) lent me the computer system upon which the software mentioned in this book was tested.

Fred Steingold, author of *The Legal Guide for Starting & Running a Small Business*, for always sharing his top-notch legal and marketing expertise whenever I called.

The many bookkeepers, accountants, tax preparers, and other professionals who agreed to be interveiwed for this book, even though there was nothing in it for them. Thank you to those of you whose names appear in these pages, and those who chose to remain anonymous.

And a special thank you to Ingrid Landskron, the All-in-1 Bookeeper of Mahwah, New Jersey, who agreed to be interviewed time and again, who refused to call collect, and who graciously allowed me to reprint much of her own promotional material.

Neil Taslitz of the Backcare Corp., who provided technical information, good sources, nice conversation, dinner, and enough inspiration for me to finally start sitting right.

Stephen Sahlien, of the International Associations of Professional Bookkeepers, who overcame initial reluctance and a frantic work schedule to generously share his wealth of bookkeeping anecdotes and data.

Mark Thorson and Open Systems, Inc., for coming through in a last-minute hurry with information about their accounting program, Harmony.

Tim Baca and Lacerte Software, for allowing me a quick and thorough tour of their comprehensive tax preparer software systems.

Matt Hightshoe, who has a bright future as an artist or businessman, or both, should he choose.

Ben and Laura, who put up with far more fishsticks and chicken nuggets than anyone should have to and never complained.

And Mom, who understood when I said, "Please don't visit until *after* Thanksgiving. I'll be writing my book until then."

Preface

I hope you are wearing your pajamas. That's how I picture you—comfortably clothed, sitting at the kitchen table, a cup of coffee or glass of lemonade in front of you. Looking over this book and thinking, "I'd sure like to start every day like this instead of rushing off to an office."

You can make it work. The shift to self-employment, small businesses, computers, and the fast motion of information all converges on the need for people with bookkeeping skills. It's a field that can offer you individual freedom, respectability, and an income that can go well beyond basic comfort if you're willing to work hard.

If you like to work with numbers, but don't have much experience, this book will show you how to train yourself and get outside training. If you know all there is to know about debits and credits, but view self-employment with trepidation, this book will walk you through the steps to take to run your own business.

Bookkeeping is a tried-and-true enterprise that shows no signs of decline and every sign of expanding to meet the 90s marketplace. You can make yourself a part of it.

I'd like to tell you a little bit about myself. We have a lot in common—I *wrote* much of this book in my pajamas! I've been self-employed and working out of my home for six years, and have been through many of the small business stages I wrote about in this book. I've had to establish a home office, buy equipment, amass clients, advertise my services, file sole-proprietor taxes, discipline myself to follow a work-at-home schedule, set my rates, raise my rates, collect from slow-pay (and no-pay) customers, establish a filing system, upgrade my computer, upgrade my software, invest in a fax machine, invest in a modem, lust after a fancy laptop that I couldn't afford, deal with a hard disk crash, change my phone system twice, budget for the ebb-and-flow of irregular earnings, and meet all of the rest of the challenges that come with the convenient and soul-satisfying work-at-home lifestyle.

What I have not had to do is keep books, except for my own rudimentary ones. I am a journalist, not a bookkeeper. However, I do have some special credentials for writing a bookkeeping book. I've built the bulk of my career writing about financial planning and accounting. I've covered tax legislation in Washington, financial planning issues for Reuters news service, and small-business finance for *Home Office Computing* magazine. I've immersed myself in financial and accounting issues, logged many hours in front of computerized accounting systems, and interviewed many of you in financial fields. I'm an outsider, but one who has developed an awareness of the issues particular to bookkeeping and accounting professions.

All of this means that you'll hear a variety of voices throughout this book. On the home front, telling you how to set up your office or deal with your kids and neighbors, it's me talking, with healthy input from the dozens of bookkeepers and other home-based businesspeople I've interviewed. When we get into the particulars of the bookkeeping business, you will be hearing the bookkeepers' voices of experience. For technical matters relating to office design, equipment, and tax issues, I've drawn upon the advice of experts, who are credited throughout the book and on the acknowledgments page.

As for the lists of software, please accept my apologies for their failure to be comprehensive. Hundreds of accounting, payroll, and tax programs are on the market, and they come, go, get acquired, change names, and leave the field with frightening frequency. If I've left off a favorite program, let me know. I'll try to catch up with it for the next edition.

Finally, the SEX part. (Every book has one, right?) I've used *he* and *her* and *his* and *hers* interchangeably in an effort to keep readers of both sexes included throughout the book. Though it's conventional, using only male pronouns doesn't work, especially in a book by a female author about bookkeepers, a largely female profession.

That's all for now. It's time to get dressed and get down to work.

With best wishes for a brilliant new career,

Linda Stern

Introduction

Think of this book as your turnkey book. With it, you can start a bookkeeping business from scratch—organizing your finances, marketing for clients, setting up your office, buying accounting software, and doing everything else to become a bona fide self-employed, work-at-home bookkeeper.

Your instincts and sense of timing are sound. The bookkeeping business is strong, and the 1990s seem designed for those of us who love the thought of independence and working where we live. It's an era in which we'll all make our own way and our own security.

The book is designed so it is part resource guide, part checklist, and part tutorial. Some days you might want to browse, be introspective and thoughtful, so anecdotes and self-guided assessments are provided throughout. On other days, you might need data fast, so lists of the resources you need—along with current addresses and telephone numbers—are provided as well.

Some days you might simply want to look at pictures, so many are included. We learn by seeing, and the many examples of software screens and accounting reports should help you plan your own purchases. The flow-charts and graphs were designed to guide you through your decision making.

You do not need to read this book from beginning to end, or even read the entire book. You can pick and choose the chapters that you need most. Skimming through each chapter will give you a feel for the bookkeeping business and lifestyle, especially if it includes a quick read of chapters 1 and 3. A reasonable second step is to then go through the book once more, looking for all the software companies, trade groups, and newsletter publishers, and then calling for their brochures, catalogues, and demo disks. That way, your office can be as messy as mine is today, as I complete the manuscript for this book!

If you already know manual bookkeeping, you may never even need to look at chapter 7. Some of the chapters at the end of the book—on extra services you can provide—might be of more interest once you've set up basic bookkeeping.

Some of the questions you'll find answered in this book are:

- What's the market for bookkeeping today? What's the business like?
- Are you cut out to be a bookkeeper?
- Where can you get training, including via correspondence courses?
- What's the day-to-day life of a self-employed bookkeeper really like?

- How can you set up an efficient, healthy, and cozy office?
- What kind of equipment will you need?
- What type of computer should you select?
- What software will run your office for you?
- How can you qualify for the home- office deduction?
- What do backaches have to do with bookkeepers?
- What are the legal pitfalls of starting a business?
- Should you incorporate?
- Is a bookkeeping franchise for you?
- What are the fundamentals of traditional double-entry bookkeeping?
- How can you pick the best accounting software for your business?
- What are today's most popular software programs?
- How can you build a business identity and corporate image?
- What are the best ways to market your business?
- How can you win new clients and keep your existing clients coming back?
- What are the special financial considerations of a business owner?
- How can you protect your own retirement?
- What taxes will you have to pay? Are there special requirements for the self-employed?
- How much should you charge, and how much does everyone else charge?
- How do you use a modem to get the most out of on-line communications?
- What are the best on-line services for bookkeepers?
- What are some tips and tactics from bookkeepers around the country?
- What trade groups should you join?
- What publications should you buy?
- How do you add payrolls to your business?
- How do you add tax preparation to your business?
- How do you make extra money above and beyond that from your bookkeeping business?

Finally, don't forget the checklist at the very end of this book. It will guide you through the business-building process from start to middle. I'd say start to finish, but you might as well learn your first entrepreneurial lesson here in the Introduction—you're never finished!

1 Bookkeeping: A good choice

More than 20 million small businesses currently exist in America, and hundreds more open their doors each *hour*. The owners of these businesses all have one thing in common: they might not know you, but they certainly need you.

Each of these businesses must maintain financial records, and for most, it's a chore the owners of these businesses would rather avoid. These owners need clear records of their own sales and costs to run their businesses. They need records of their expenses and income to pay their taxes. They are probably too busy painting houses, selling clothing, making widgets, or seeing clients, however, to bother with the paperwork. Some of them aren't even that busy, but they'd rather spend their time making cold calls to insurance salesmen than face their own accounting systems.

Paying someone—like you—to handle their bookkeeping is one of the smartest business decisions a business owner can make. It allows the owner to concentrate on the business. "I make a lot of money per hour. I can certainly afford $40 an hour to hire a bookkeeper so I don't have to bother learning Excel [a spreadsheet program] or any of the rest of it," says Beth Chapin, a successful Connecticut public relations executive who credits her independent bookkeeper with saving her many hours and even more dollars.

Setting up your own bookkeeping business to service all the Beth Chapins of the world is one of the smartest business decisions you can make. Bookkeeping and accounting are among today's hottest fields, and with good reason: startup costs are minimal, profit potential is high, and the market is steadily growing. At the same time, new computer systems and software programs take the drudgery out of bookkeeping and make it a business you can do in your own home, on your own schedule, in your own way. (And in your own pajamas, if you want to!)

Think of it this way: accepting $40 an hour to protect Chapin and her colleagues from the horrors of Excel is the least you can do for your fellow entrepreneurs. It's not only a promising new career, it's a real public service!

Advantages of a bookkeeping business

Acquiring bookkeeping skills (or honing those learned in the pre-computer age) will position you for the 1990s and beyond. As the numbers of independent businesses burgeon, the need for solid financial records grows as well. Companies need to have their financial records in order, too: it's not an optional service. Bookkeeping thus tends to be somewhat recession-resistant.

Many practitioners report that they enjoy bookkeeping because it is interesting and fun (stereotypes of eye-shaded figures hunched over dreary ledgers to the contrary). Bookkeepers meet different types of clients and learn from the inside how many businesses are run. Bookkeepers begin to recognize the statistical signs of trouble and can tell by looking at a balance sheet or cash flow report how well a company is managed or whether problems might exist. A bookkeeping business can be an end in itself or a stepping-stone to a business consultancy practice.

Bookkeepers enjoy the challenging number-crunching aspect of the work, too. Taking a shoebox full of receipts and invoices and turning it into a neat set of informative reports with everything in its proper place and everything balanced carries its own satisfaction. It's similar to doing a serious Sunday crossword puzzle or mastering the game of chess.

A bookkeeping career is one you can feel good about—you're providing a valuable and honest service to clients who depend on you. You're delivering real value for their money. As FIG. 1-1 shows, a bookkeeper makes order out of chaos.

Bookkeeping is also a practical profession for people with personal lives because it's easily expanded or trimmed to fit the amount of work desired. If you intend to keep your business part-time, you can limit your clients; if you're energized to be busy, busy, busy and rich, rich, rich, you can fill your time with clients, hire helpers, and work long but financially rewarding hours.

1-1
*A good bookkeeper
creates order of chaos.*
Matt Hightshoe

The praises of self-employment have been well sung in recent years, and with good reason. As the large corporations grow increasingly leaner and meaner with each recessionary wave, more and more working Americans are learning no real security exists in any job.

Work for yourself, the experts now say, and you can make your own security. Amass a series of clients, and if one goes under, one goes under. Spend 40 hours a week and 20 years on one company's payroll, and your family's livelihood can be jeopardized when that company has problems (or just decides it doesn't need you anymore).

"In the future, you have to look within for the security you used to get at work," says Dave Corbett, President of New Directions, a Boston career consulting firm. "People are going to be more self-reliant and make money without being in the corporate world."

Leaving the corporate world has all of the advantages you've probably already considered. You can run a successful bookkeeping business out of your home. You can be your own boss, and use the software and equipment you like best. You can take off in the middle of the day if you need to go to

Working for yourself: The new security

the doctor's office or the bank, and you can get letterhead with your own name on it. You can work in blue jeans or sweats. And most importantly for many of the people who work for themselves, you can do work you are proud of and get all the credit when things go right. You can make it on your own terms. You can build your own security.

If you're willing to put in the hours and the energy, you can also make more money than you ever would on somebody else's payroll. At hourly rates of $25 to $50, a full-time bookkeeper working by herself can easily make $25,000 to $50,000 a year, by billing at an average rate of 20 hours a week and taking two weeks of vacation per year. If she adds helpers to key in information, she can double or even triple those figures.

On the other hand

All of the preceding isn't to say that anything goes when running your own bookkeeping business. You *can* work your own schedule, but if you are never around when clients need you, your clients will find someone who is. You *can* take vacations without clearing your schedule with bosses or coworkers, but if you disappear during tax season, so will some of your business. You can operate your practice at home to better meld your professional and personal life, but you can't realistically run a serious business while the baby sleeps. Anyone who tries to tell you that has probably never had a baby NOR run a business.

Financial facts of self-employment

The finances of self-employment present a balanced ledger as well. On the positive side, you'll get good tax breaks for contributing to a retirement plan, maintaining a home (or outside) office, and buying your own health insurance. You probably can take sizable tax deductions for all your business expenses, too, including the cost of your computer, the business use of your car, and any work done to fix up a home office.

Don't forget, however, that you get these deductions because you are paying for these items. When you work for yourself, you really do have to buy your own health insurance, maintain your own office, and create your own retirement plan. In chapter 11, you'll learn how to build these expenses into your fees, but for now, remember that self-employment is exhilarating and freeing, but not cost-free.

The pleasures of part-time

You can, of course, ease into entrepreneurship by setting up your bookkeeping business while still working full-time, and moonlight as a bookkeeper for a while. You can also limit your hours to part-time if you have other responsibilities (and income) so you don't want or need a full-time business. Once you develop the necessary skills, you can also limit your business by limiting the number of clients you have or the number of tasks you perform for them.

Many bookkeeping clients appreciate the opportunity to meet during nonbusiness hours, too. Thus, what might appear to be an inconvenient schedule of night and weekend work in other occupations can prove an advantageous niche in the bookkeeping business.

Retirees considering second careers and parents juggling family demands while earning income can find rewards in developing a bookkeeping business. These people can curtail their hours to fit their schedules and then expand their hours as they find the time and inclination to do more.

"There's no limit"

On the other hand, if those are dollar signs in your eyes, note that just about every bookkeeper interviewed for this book made a point that "there's no limit" to the amount of money you can make if you're willing to work hard, expand your services, and hire helpers. Bookkeeping is tangential to many business tasks that you can develop and sell to future clients. You can boost your income considerably by offering tax preparation payroll services, or computer consulting. First, however, let's answer the question of what bookkeeping is exactly?

What is bookkeeping, anyway?

Put simply, bookkeeping is the science of recording history. It is the physical recordkeeping of someone's transactions as they relate to assets, liabilities, income, and expenses.

Bookkeeping differs from accounting in that bookkeeping includes less analysis and advice. A small business owner might call an accountant or attorney to learn whether it's better to buy or lease his copier and when to make the down payment on his (partially deductible) car. But once the business owner cut the deal, he would call a bookkeeper to keep track of his lease or interest payments.

Bookkeeping basics

As an independent bookkeeper, you will most likely be called upon to perform some or all of the following functions for your clients:

- Record business transactions of money coming in and going out.
- Tally income and expenses and balance accounts.
- Prepare regular financial statements that show profits and losses and assets and liabilities.
- Reconcile bank account statements.
- Prepare statements that compare key figures in standard ratios, such as sales-to-assets, profits-to-assets, and debt-to-net-worth.
- Organize financial records for easier year-end tax filing.
- Process and pay quarterly estimated and payroll taxes.
- Examine vendor invoices and bills and write checks to pay them.

- Create profit center records and report profits and losses by product line or service.
- Maintain inventory records.
- And last and least favored, clean up your client's sloppy shoebox recordkeeping system.

In addition to the preceding standard duties, you might find yourself performing the following:

- Making bank deposits.
- Computing, recording, writing, and paying your clients' payroll checks.
- Preparing preliminary tax returns.
- Offering money saving and organizing suggestions.
- Creating an accounting system for your clients.

Bookkeeping versus accounting

Douglas Perreault, a certified public accountant in Tampa, Florida, and a consistently well-informed source of financial information, offers this definition: "Bookkeeping can be looked at as a science in that once the decision is made on how an event should be recorded, there's little deviation on how to record it . . . But accounting is the art of interpreting what the numbers mean that have been recorded by the bookkeeper. It is the art of properly determining the classification of an item on the financial statements."

The difference between bookkeeping and accounting is a very fuzzy line, but also a legal one.

In most states, you can call yourself an *accountant* or offer *accounting services* without being a certified public accountant, or CPA. In other states you cannot. Check your state's licensing requirements before naming your business. Practically speaking, however, most accountants spend some of their time doing bookkeeping, and many bookkeepers are often asked to make accounting recommendations and do. The best guidance here is to use your own judgment. Don't claim to be an accountant if you are uncomfortable going beyond the traditional recording duties of the bookkeeping profession. Don't limit yourself unnecessarily, either. If you're willing to keep up with current tax trends and stick your neck out occasionally by giving some advice, you can go beyond the traditional confines of the bookkeeping business.

What you cannot do, if you are not a CPA, is conduct a certified independent audit for submission to the Securities and Exchange Commission or a court of law. That, however, still leaves plenty for you to do.

"A lot of people seemed to think that unless you have a CPA you are worthless," says Karen Wetmore, who built a successful bookkeeping and consulting business in Boston in just four years. "But my clients think otherwise." The distinction between accounting and bookkeeping has changed, too, and today's software has helped blur the line. This software has removed much of the tedium from the traditional bookkeeper's job and made the typical CPA's analysis easier.

In the past, bookkeepers entered the daily financial activities in the books, and accountants summarized and analyzed them to produce financial statements. Today, sometimes all it takes is the push of a button to provide a level of analysis that would have once taken hours of an accountant's time.

Bookkeepers can often do analysis now that was once reserved for accountants because many bookkeepers have the same basic training as accountants—college-level courses and on-the-job training. In the past, someone became a bookkeeper through courses taken in high school. Today, many people become bookkeepers by going to college and getting an Associate's degree or even a Bachelor's degree in accounting.

Starting a business

How do most bookkeeping businesses get started? Here's one story. "The first thing you have to do is work for a company that goes belly-up," says a Delaware-based bookkeeper. "The second thing you have to do is be over 55 and not be able to get a job. The rest just came easy." This bookkeeper currently runs a *part-time* bookkeeping business out of his home office that earns him over $50,000 a year, and he's happy as can be. "I really love it," he summarizes.

The point is that adversity can be the mother of a brand-new career. Many of today's established bookkeepers started, as did the Delaware bookkeeper, after they were forced into a career decision by the loss of a job or by the need to earn money while caring for young children. Others left jobs voluntarily because they wanted to make their own way in the world and believed bookkeeping offered them the best opportunity to build a successful, self-employed lifestyle.

Most people also bring some bookkeeping experience to the table. The Delaware man was working as a comptroller for an auto dealership—he started doing the books for private customers on a free-lance basis when he realized what was happening at the showroom. Others work as office managers or bookkeepers for independent businesses, where they learn the basics of bookkeeping for at least one type of company. Still others, noting their own affinity for numbers and details, take bookkeeping courses or.work for another bookkeeper while they learn the basics until they feel secure enough to hang their own professional shingle outside their office.

Working as an apprentice first can be the best way to train. While the job route can deliver more hands-on experience, it can also limit your knowledge to only one type of company.

Still others just do it. They buy the software and learn how to keep books by practicing on their family finances and their friends' small and easy businesses. These people build a clientele by word of mouth, advancing to more complicated accounting work as they develop the expertise, and taking fill-in courses when they find gaps in their knowledge.

Love your computer!

At first, you might think the boom in affordable, powerful personal computers and accounting software might impede your ability to offer bookkeeping services. After all, can't most people just buy a program like *Managing Your Money* or *Quicken* and do all their bookkeeping themselves?

Nothing could be further from the truth! In the first place, as noted at the beginning of this chapter, many small business owners don't have the time or the inclination to be bothered with their own accounting. In the second place, if these owners aren't financially savvy, they might not have the expertise to select the best program or keep their records in the most meaningful and useful format.

The availability of personal computers can do more for your business than create a generation of befuddled and stressed-out entrepreneurs for your client pool, however. Your computer enables you to be more efficient and more professional than any previous generation of bookkeepers. Automatic calculations allow you to work fast and service more clients for greater financial rewards. Desktop publishing enables you to do most of your own marketing and makes beautiful financial reports a snap. Online services enable you to put your fingers on information fast (and also enable you to work on site at clients' offices while sending information back to your own computer.) Databases enable you to track clients and prospects for quicker collections and greater sales.

In the following chapters, you'll learn how to do all this and more on your personal computer, the best business partner a work-at-home entrepreneur could have.

2 Bookkeepers are made, not born

Do you have what it takes to be a successful, self-employed, work-at-home bookkeeper? It requires both traits and techniques. You need to be born with the right traits. You can always learn techniques. Take Mary Olcott Greiner, who runs Mary's Bookkeeping Service in Arlington, Virginia. If there were such a thing as a born bookkeeper, it would be Mary, who started bookkeeping in 1953 with a nice clean ledger book, a clunky adding machine, and beautiful handwriting.

"All I do is record history, that's what I feel comfortable doing," she says. She always had a feel for keeping books. "I knew that you never change anything, and I was methodical," she says. Mary has the traits of a bookkeeper. She's naturally organized, methodical, and math smart. And, after 30 years in the business, she's learned a lot of techniques.

Mary can operate most accounting and tax filing software on both Apple and IBM-compatible computers. She can tailor spreadsheets and database programs to answer all her accounting questions. She can hire good help and weed out less-than-desirable clients. She can network for new clients and use her new fax machine to increase her productivity. She can not only budget her time at home but also the limited space in her home office.

As you read this chapter, think about whether you have the traits that make a good bookkeeper. You can worry about the techniques later. Once you've set your goal, you can pick up training and expertise in many places. The self-assessment in this chapter consists of three parts:

- Do you have what it takes to be a bookkeeper?
- Do you have to have what it takes to be self-employed?

And, if you intend to set this business up in your home:

- Do you have to have what it takes to be a home-based business owner?

Work-at-home wisdom

Without seeming too flip, the main attribute you need when working at home is a good sense of humor. So when you are talking to a potential client on the phone, for example, and your child picks up the extension and says, "Mommy, Ben hit me!" and then Ben picks up the other extension and says, "No I didn't, she kicked me first!" you'll be able to complete the phone call with grace and aplomb before you hang up and scream at your kids.

Much of what you need to succeed at home is self-evident. Following is a brief checklist of success factors.

Discipline   Some people just can't make themselves work when surrounded by their books, hobbies, or family responsibilities. You really must be able to walk past the dirty kitchen and the good television show to get to your office and do your job.

A happy home life   Working at home can stress family relationships, especially in the beginning when laundry, dishes, and other responsibilities get renegotiated. If you are going to work out of your home, at the very least you should enjoy being there.

Family respect   Your spouse and children need to understand that, even if you are wearing your bedroom slippers and sitting in the den, you are at work. Make sure that they will support your business by not disturbing your business area, by answering the phone politely and taking good messages (if you are sharing a personal and business phone line), and by staying quiet when you are talking on the phone. Devote at least one night to discussing these types of work-at-home issues with your family before you begin.

The ability to say No nicely   You must be able to say "No" to neighbors who think that, because you are there anyway, you could look after their child for a few hours or interrupt what you are doing to let the refrigerator repairman into their home (and then supervise him). Or, to PTA moms and dads who say, "Well, you're home, why don't you call all the third-grade parents about the bake sale?" You must even say "No" to good friends who call or drop in in the middle of the day, just to chat.

A babysitter   By now, the promise that you can work while the baby sleeps has become widespread enough to be one of the three great lies. If you have very young children, you will need to arrange childcare during your working hours.

Grace under pressure   Your personal life will sometimes slip over into your business life. These situations are when that sense of humor comes into play. If you stay cool and collected, react professionally, and remain unapologetic, you'll weather those storms nicely.

Knowing how to conduct business   Most of us learn "business manners" during our first jobs. If you've never worked in an office setting before, you'll need to work extra hard to create and keep a businesslike image.

Enjoying your own company   Working at home, even for people with spouses, children, neighbors, and friends, can be lonely. Furthermore, some people do their best work only when surrounded by coworkers against whom they can bounce off ideas and questions. Be honest about whether you could be productive and happy spending most of every day by yourself. If you are single and live alone, you may find working at home too much "aloneness," even for a person who thrives in solitude.

Willingness to spend money   Just because you are saving money on rent and intend to be frugal, you cannot run a home-based business "for free." You need to realize that you now must buy all the trappings of office life for yourself.

Many studies have been conducted to discern the key attributes of the entrepreneur. These studies have found that successful self-employed people have many traits in common, but one seems to supersede the others: successful self-employed people are proactive.

Self-employment success factors

Proactivity means you make things happen, you don't wait for them to happen by themselves. Think about the last time you expected a repair-person at your house. Did you take a day off from work and wait and wait and wait? Or, did you call early in the morning and say, "I'm on a tight schedule. What time shall I meet you at the house?" *That's* proactive.

Proactivity serves you well when you are running your own bookkeeping business. If business is slow, you pick up the phone and call your clients (or a list of prospective clients) to stir things up. If business is too busy, you buy the equipment, software, or help you need to get more accomplished during the same hours. If you need certain IRS forms before you can process a batch of work, you call, write, or drive wherever you must to get those forms as quickly as possible. *You* make it happen.

Beyond proactivity, many other personality traits signal success in self-employment. How many of those mentioned next do you have?

Enjoyment of work   You have to enjoy it! When you are building a business (even an at-home, part-time business), your work will consume many of your waking hours. Everyone gets frazzled, but true entrepreneurs would rather be at their desks than anywhere else.

Decision-making ability   Make that a *fast* decision-making ability. You will make dozens of decisions every week, and they won't all be good ones. The ability, however, to look at the facts, make a decision, and act on that decision is crucial. If you feel stressed by too many choices or beat yourself up over bad decisions of the past, you'll need to train yourself to become more authoritative.

Adaptability   The rules of bookkeeping might be constant, but the market is an ever-changing universe. You'll need to keep up with the changing needs of clients, new computer programs, and clients who call at the last minute to change their report requests. And these examples don't even include the changing whims of Congress and the IRS!

Self-confidence   You need to rely on yourself, you need to like yourself, and you need to trust yourself if you expect your clients to do the same. Learn from your mistakes, but take them in stride.

Financial smarts   You don't need to be a Wall Street-trained money manager, but you do need to have a concept for and an appreciation of the bottom line. Remember, when running a business, you must be profit-oriented.

Stress tolerance   Working for yourself always causes more stress than working for someone else. It can be a more satisfying stress because it's not the powerless stress of working for an unpleasant boss or an insecure company. Things do go wrong and they will go wrong, and *you* will be solely responsible. You'll also have to survive through very trying deadlines and even more trying times of not enough work.

Self-awareness   Like everyone else, you have strengths and weaknesses. If you play to your strengths and seek outside help to compensate for your weaknesses, you'll be ahead of most of us. The most successful business owners hire help—employees, consultants, advisors, or contractors—to compensate for the owners' weaknesses.

Sales ability   You can forget the smiling, handshaking used car salesman that the word *salesmanship* brings to mind. At some basic level, however, you must be convinced of your value and be able to convince others of it if you are to survive self-employment. Some very modest people have made it as independent business owners, but it helps if you have persuasive abilities.

In your heart of hearts, you probably already know if you will be a good bookkeeper. "It's not like someone who hates math and can't operate a calculator will wake up one day and say, `Gee, I think I'll open a bookkeeping business,'" chides Wanda Walter of The Company Clerk in Lanham, Maryland. "You already know by the activities you enjoy."

Maybe you're keen on puzzles, or have become good with a calculator. Maybe you enjoy organizing your family's financial records. Or maybe you just like math. A good bookkeeper does not need to be someone who ALWAYS keeps everything in its place and ALWAYS boasts precision in every aspect of life. A good bookkeeper *does* need a flair for numbers, an appreciation of order in certain tasks, and an ability to be abstract.

The people who fail at bookkeeping tend to not have a sense of abstract logic. "They just don't get certain concepts," says Walters, "like why you do a certain step, why you want to reconcile an account, or what difference a certain entry made in the first place."

Doug Perreault adds, "Many people find it hard to understand that you debit cash to increase it. They usually say, `NO!, I want to credit my account!'" Here's a brief test: if you already understand why you debit your cash account when you get money, you probably are a bookkeeper or accountant already. If, however, you are willing to accept on faith that the definition of *debit* is closer to "left" than to "minus" and *credit* is closer to "right," rather than "plus," you are well on your way. You can learn the rest!

You can always learn accounting, computer operation, and business skills. But to be a bookkeeper, what you need to get started, besides the qualities listed in FIG. 2-1, is the following:

What a bookkeeper needs

Trustworthiness

Some people don't even let their spouses balance their checkbooks until the marriage has lasted a few years. If prospective clients are going to choose you out of the yellow pages and hand over the particulars of their financial lives, you must be worthy of their trust. This trust goes beyond discretion; these people are trusting you to be all of the other things on this list as well: honest, accurate, careful, professional, helpful, and (in more than a few cases) kind. To a business client with a mountain of receipts and a swamp of an accounting system, a new bookkeeper is like a cross between an Eagle Scout and the Coast Guard. Create your own pledge here.

Discretion

Money is the source of more concern and competitive stress than anything else in the modern world (and probably the ancient world, too). More than anything else, your clients need to know that the details of their finances will remain totally private with you. Particularly in small towns, the last thing clients want to hear is details about their finances from your other clients. Sometimes, details can slip out unintended.

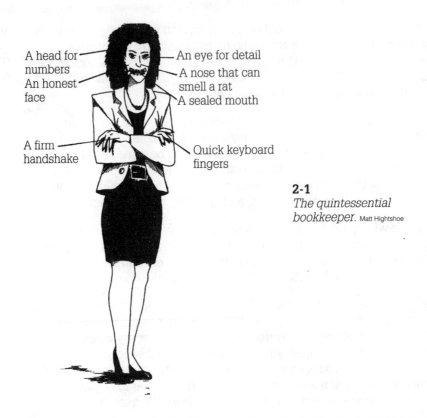

A head for numbers
An honest face

An eye for detail
A nose that can smell a rat
A sealed mouth

A firm handshake

Quick keyboard fingers

2-1
The quintessential bookkeeper. Matt Hightshoe

Saying to one of your clients, "I have another client who is a bricklayer, and he always takes a big deduction for his annual trip to the Tahitian Bricklayers conference, even though he then skips all the educational sessions," may sound anonymous enough, but it isn't. A good bookkeeper might notice business hints that can be passed on from one client to another, but those hints must be provided only in the most general of terms. It should be second nature not to leave records open on your desk while meeting with clients, as well as never discussing one client with another. Many potential clients could become offended when you discuss another client with them, even if you don't mention names.

A head for numbers

Someday, you'll be balancing a set of books and, when you run the monthly totals, you'll realize that you are $22.14 off. It really helps if you can say, "Wait a minute! I remember seeing that number somewhere! I think it was a bank charge for new checks that must not have been entered."

Wanda Walters claims that the best employee she ever had was a woman who was neither well-educated nor experienced. "But she remembered every number she ever saw and could make a calculator hum," according to Wanda. If you have this innate sense of math, it will make your job easier and your work possibly better. You'll be able to spot mistakes more quickly and conceptualize big-picture trends as well for your clients.

An eye for detail   An eye for detail does not mean you have to be a picky personality. If, however, you think of yourself as a broadbrush idea person, you probably don't belong in the bookkeeping business. Accounting is a series of details, and it has a logic all its own. You have to be able to spend your days in those details—sorting, recording, reviewing, and noting when details seem out of place. It very much matters if you make a mistake. A cavalier attitude about columns, decimal points, and tax categories will hurt both you and your clients. Don't be like the woman I knew who, applying for a job in the accounting department of a major retailer, told the interviewer, "I always get millions and billions mixed up," and then wondered why she didn't get the job.

Social ability

Social ability is where being kind matters. You not only need sales ability to win clients over initially, you have to put your clients at ease through friendliness and small talk. You need the ability to ask questions (such as "What did you do with the $10,000 your mother gave you to start the company?") that your clients might find personal or discomforting. You need to be able to discuss overdrawn bank balances, negative cash flows, and seriously sick balance sheets with gentleness and grace. It's a myth that you can't be both a numbers person and a people person. If you are to be successful as a self-employed bookkeeper, you have to be both.

Computer affinity

Today's accounting, bookkeeping, tax reporting, and payroll businesses are strictly computer businesses, and the better you are with a keyboard and mouse, the better you will do in business. You don't have to understand programming or even MS-DOS, but it helps a lot if you like using or even playing around on computers. Once your business starts to move, you'll be spending much of your time in front of a computer screen; if you find interfacing with a computer difficult, you probably won't be happy in these professions.

Logic power

Bookkeeping is like playing with puzzles. Do you reconcile your own bank account? If your account doesn't balance, do you just shrug off the difference and trust the bank's numbers? Or do you spend as long as it takes to get the ledger even? Double-entry bookkeeping, masked as it is by many of today's user-friendly software packages, has a logic of its own, and you should be able to follow it.

Honesty

Before you plug in your computer, hang up your shingle, or get your first client, know this: some potential client will present figures that don't look right. Or, someone will ask you to fudge the details on a tax return. Or create two sets of books. Draw your lines now, before you set up that business phone number, and life will be easier for you and those clients. A bookkeeper who veers too close to the edge is just waiting for disaster to strike.

Knowledge of bookkeeping

The most important attribute is mentioned last, of course. You can't be a bookkeeper (at least not for very long) if you can't keep books. The good news is, while you can't train yourself to be detail-oriented, math-proficient, or even honest, you can train yourself to do accounting. If you have the personal attributes of a good bookkeeper, there are many places to learn the details.

How people become bookkeepers

This section describes some of the various ways to learn bookkeeping. One of them is right for you. See the sidebar for a quick self-assessment to see where your strengths and weaknesses are.

Self-assessment quiz

Nobody has it all. If you take a few minutes to reread this chapter, keeping your own strengths and weaknesses in mind, you'll be able to attack those areas that need work while you are learning bookkeeping skills and printing your business cards. Use this form to plan your attack.

Home-based business issues

Weaknesses

_____
_____
_____

Strengths

_____
_____
_____

To improve on my weaknesses, I'll:

_____
_____

Self-employment issues

Weaknesses

_____
_____

Strengths

_____

_____

_____

To improve on my weaknesses, I'll:

_____

_____

_____

Bookkeeping issues

Weaknesses

_____

_____

_____

Strengths

_____

_____

_____

To improve on my weaknesses, I'll:

_____

_____

_____

On-the-job training

Many bookkeepers learn their skills when they are hired to keep someone's books, or to help someone keep books. There are advantages and disadvantages to on-the-job training. It's a good way to learn, because you'll learn real bookkeeping in real situations while in the real business world. You won't be just memorizing classroom accounting rules that don't seem to apply to the real world.

"I started bookkeeping when I was hired to do the books for a construction company," says Mary Olcott Greiner. "The payroll was really complicated; there were 40 people that needed to be paid every week at different rates and on different jobs. By the time I left there, I could do it all."

The disadvantage to on-the-job training is that it can be self-limiting. If you do bookkeeping for your church, for example, you might never learn how to depreciate construction equipment or levy sales taxes, both of which you might need to know for potential clients.

Mentors

I had a friend who was working for an accountant, and he needed help," says Beth Roll, a California bookkeeper. "When I lost my job he started using me. I learned enough at it to open my own business." A big advantage exists in learning from a mentor. You learn the real stuff—the way real bookkeepers and accountants work with and for their clients. Asking a more experienced professional to teach you the basics of bookkeeping is asking a lot, but if you're willing to supplement your hands-on experience with accounting books or courses, you can really go far.

Back to school

"I was working for another bookkeeper who was teaching me to help her maintain her computerized clients. It was a good way for me to start and understand what she was doing," says Karen Wetmore, a Boston bookkeeper. "But I needed more, so I went back to school and received a Bachelor's degree in accounting, and then went back again and received a degree in business administration."

Karen is more highly educated than you need to be to start a bookkeeping business, but knowledge never hurts, and Karen is using her expertise to perform management consulting assignments for her clients. Most colleges and junior colleges offer bookkeeping and accounting courses, and you can take these courses individually as refreshers or to fill in knowledge gaps as your business expands.

How long does it take to get from ground zero to a proficiency good enough to let you hang out your shingle? If you have a knack for basic bookkeeping, you can learn it as you go with a good, simple computer program and a workbook, and can be ready to take on small, straightforward business clients in just a few months. More typically, it takes a year or two to complete a series of bookkeeping or accounting courses.

Some people learn best when alone with written materials rather than in a classroom. If you fit this description, you can order the software, corner the market in accounting textbooks, hide in your bedroom for a few months, and come out with a working knowledge of bookkeeping. You can volunteer to keep the books for your PTA, religious group, or neighborhood organization. Or, you can take a correspondence course (See the section at the end of this chapter about specific correspondence courses for bookkeepers) to pick up the basic as well as advanced accounting skills you'll need to start.

Training for bookkeepers

If you really don't have any background in bookkeeping or need to learn specific skills, you'll find the following correspondence courses helpful:

Contemporary Bookkeeping and Accounting
McGraw Hill's NRI School of Home-Based Businesses
McGraw-Hill Continuing Education Center
4401 Connecticut Avenue, NW
Washington, DC 20008
(202) 244-1600

The NRI school offers a comprehensive package of bookkeeping and home-based business management courses. The entire package costs $995 and includes a computer and basic business software that is good enough, according to Training Development Director David Dasenbrock, for simple small-business accounting, but does not include extras like inventory control or payroll. Students who later start their own business might find they need more sophisticated software later.

The program includes 32 lessons, 20 of which are bookkeeping and accounting and 12 of which concern general issues of running a home-based business. The lessons all include self-scoring multiple-choice tests. The program also includes seven action-learning kits, in which students are led step-by-step through bookkeeping and small business startup exercises. The learning kits are then mailed back to the instructors for grading and review.

You can proceed at your own pace, according to Dasenbrock. Most students, however, take about 16 to 18 months to complete the course and pay their fee monthly over that time period. If you already have a computer, you can receive the software and take the course for less. The business management lessons, covering topics such as advertising, legal issues, and marketing, are not specific to bookkeeping and accounting but are generic lessons and part of several different NRI home-based business courses. The 32 lessons of the program are:

Becoming a Home-Based Entrepreneur
Business and the Balance Sheet
Measuring Financial Performance
Preparing a Balance Sheet
Preparing an Income Statement
Starting Your Home-Based Business
Keeping Business Records
Your Business and the Law
The Business Plan
Developing a Marketing Plan
Advertising that Gets Results
Setting Up the Books
Setting Up Special Journals
Preparing a Trial Balance
Understanding Cash Flow
Accounting for Inventory
Accounting for Plant and Equipment
Accounting for Liabilities and Equity
Keeping Payroll and Income Tax Records
Building Customer Confidence
Managing Your Time
Charting the Growth of Your Business
Your Computer: The Ultimate Business Tool
Setting Up the General Ledger on Your Computer

Entering Data into Your Computer
Preserving Records of Your Data Entry
Producing Financial Statements with Your Computer
Managing Accounts Receivable with Your Computer
Managing Accounts Payable with Your Computer
Preparing Payroll and Tax Forms with Your Computer
Budgeting and Forecasting with Your Computer
Interpreting Financial Statements with Your Computer

The seven action learning kits are:
Completing a Simple Balance Sheet and Income Statement
Drafting a Business Plan of Your Own
Preparing a Trial Balance
Getting to Know Your Computer
Practice Set I: Transaction Entry with Your General Ledger Software
Practice Set II: Using Your General Ledger and Spreadsheet Software for Specialized Functions
Practice Set III: Budgeting with Your Spreadsheet Software

Bookkeeping Home-Study Courses

The American Institute of Professional Bookkeepers (AIPB)
6001 Montrose Road, Suite 207
Rockville, MD 20872
(301) 770-7300

This professional association offers six home-study courses and is developing more all the time. Each course is $39 and includes 9 to 11 sections that can be completed in 15 to 20 minutes each. Each section includes two to three pages of explanatory material with on-the-job examples and illustrative problems, followed by a double quiz that tests what you've just learned and retests key points. Each course comes with an optional open-book exam. Earn a grade of at least 64 percent and the association will send you a certificate of completion to hang on your wall. (A complete description of the other services offered by AIPB appears in chapter 13.) The six home-study courses from AIPB are:

Mastering Financial Statement Analysis
Mastering Payroll I
Mastering Payroll II
Mastering Adjusting Entries
Mastering Depreciation
Mastering Collections

Here's an example of the sections within a course. These are the nine sections in the first course, Mastering Financial Statement Analysis:

What financial ratios can do for you
Evaluating a firm's ability to pay its short-term obligations

Measuring the liquidity (ability to turn into cash) of a firm's assets
Seeing how efficiently a firm operates
Sizing up ability to service debt
Quickly see how a company is doing in terms of its return on investment
More tools that let you evaluate company performance
Evaluating a firm's performance in comparison to its industry
Mastering stock market ratios (optional)

Accounting Program

United States Department of Agriculture
Graduate School Correspondence Programs
Room 1114, South Agriculture Building
14th Street and Independence Avenues, SW
Washington, DC 20250
(202) 720-7123

The Agriculture Department's graduate school is a nonprofit organization
that was established in 1921 to help farmers develop career advancement
opportunities or just learn to run their farms better. The program now offers 3
Principles of Accounting courses and 16 electives. While no degrees are
awarded, the program does provide a certificate of accomplishment for
students who complete 24 credit hours (approximately 9 to 12 courses) of the
program. The course fees range from $186 to $303, and include books,
assignments, and tests that are graded by faculty members. Some
scholarships are available.

Most of the courses have 11 lessons and are quite comprehensive. Some are
focused on specific accounting requirements, such as federal government
accounting or rural electrification authority bookkeeping. The more general
courses include the following:

Principles of Accounting I: Basic Principles
Principles of Accounting II: Financial Accounting
Principles of Accounting III: Managerial Accounting
Cost Accounting I: Job Order Cost Accounting
Cost Accounting II: Process Cost Accounting
Cost Accounting III: A Management Tool
Internal Auditing, Elementary and Advanced

American Institute of Certified Public Accountants (AICPA)

1211 Avenue of the Americas
New York, NY 10036-8775
(800) 862-4272

The AICPA offers a full complement of refresher and continuing education
courses aimed at practicing CPAs, but many of which are open to the public.
Be prepared for a higher level of discourse and a greater level of detail—don't
expect any introductions to debits and credits here.

Hundreds of courses are offered in every state of the country, ranging from Preparing Financial Statements for Nonpublic Entities to Estate Planning for the Small Business Owner to Working Through Complex 1040s. Some of the courses require other courses or auditing experience as prerequisites, while others are aimed at newcomers and have no preregistration requirements.

National Society of Public Accountants (NSPA)

1010 North Fairfax Street
Alexandria, VA 22314-1574
(703) 549-6400

The NSPA offers a series of self-directed courses in textbook, computer disk, audio cassette, and videotape formats. Included are basic and sophisticated courses in all areas of accounting, including cash flows, bankruptcy, auditing, pensions, small businesses, and family businesses. A second series of courses discusses taxation in depth, and special programs are offered on computer applications and management issues. For nonmembers, the courses typically cost $140 to $225.

3 A day in the life of a bookkeeper

What does the everyday life of a self-employed bookkeeper consist of? You might think every day is the same—client meetings, stacks of reports, screens filled with numbers—but, in fact, bookkeeping follows the rules of most other businesses: there are days, and there are days. In other words, good days that are really great, and bad days that are so bad, you wonder why you're doing what you're doing.

Let's experience a bad day and a good day in the life of a bookkeeper in this chapter. Yes, our character here is a composite, but no, she is not a work of fiction. The type of things that happen to her have happened to the bookkeepers interviewed for this book. And not just the *types* of things, the actual things. Such as the smoking computer screen and the client with the gym bag.

A bad day

A bad day starts when the phone wakes you instead of the chirping birds or the smell of brewing coffee. It's your client, Juan Titnow, and he's calling at 7 o'clock in the morning in a frenzied state. "Carol! I'm in a panic here! I know I told you I was going to take care of all the day-to-day recordkeeping, but the third girl in a month just walked off the job, and I think she made a mess. I'm supposed to go to the bank tomorrow to renew my line of credit, and I can't find a damn thing. Can you come over and help me straighten this out? Now?"

"Gee, that's terrible. I can't come right now because I'm meeting with another client this morning," you say (if you have any self-respect at all). How about if I come by at 5?"

"Five? I'm supposed to go to a cocktail party at five!" says Juan. "OK. I'll meet you here with the keys. But I'll have to leave 15 minutes after you get here. You'll be on our own."

Hang up the phone, get up, and dress for the day. If you're smart, you'll shower now, while you've got the chance. Go to the kitchen, where you then experience the personal complications of a work-at-home bad day. Choose from this list:

1. Your child feels sick, her eyes are red, and you suspect an outbreak of pinkeye. Pinkeye is not particularly serious, but so contagious that if you send her to school you'll be shamed for life.
2. Either your sink, your toilet, or both are backed up and overflowing.
3. You look at the calendar and remember your mother is arriving for a visit today.
4. All of the above.

You then say to yourself, "Well, that's why I work at home! Good thing I'm here." And you stand tall, take appropriate action, pour a cup of coffee, and head for your office. Which is a mess. You remember last night's marathon session with your new general ledger program. You stayed up until past midnight setting up new charts of accounts for your clients. You can't even bill them for the time spent—it's not their fault you decided to discard the software you were using for this new full-featured program.

You set about cleaning your office, and despite the interruptions, (your sick daughter, the plumber, the phone calls from office supply stores and banks that now have your name from business mailing lists and want to sell you paperclips and credit cards) you're at your desk ready to reconcile bank statements by 10 o'clock. Only those statements just don't want to reconcile.

At 11:30, you are still working on the same account, and your records still show that your client, Alice Verrgotten, has $273.42 more than the bank is willing to say she has. So you've put in a call to her, but her secretary says she's "in a meeting." If the past is any predictor of the future, the meeting will continue into next week, and you'll have to call her repeatedly until then to reach her.

Just as you are hanging up from that call to her secretary, the doorbell rings. It's Harry Dallweiss, another client, with two gym bags. One has his tennis shoes, running clothes, and a tennis racket sticking out the side. The other appears to be stuffed with papers—receipts, invoices, canceled checks, and check stubs. Yes! It's time for his quarterly review. "Could you please go through this mess and have the reports by Tuesday? Thanks, Carol. You're a lifesaver!" he says.

You turn back to the $273.42 in Alice's accounts (or, more accurately, NOT in her accounts) and check her bank statement again. Wait a minute . . . you see checks clearing that are out of sequence with the ones in your records, and that are not entered in her register. And doesn't Alice always withdraw money from the automatic teller machine and forget about it? You try to call her office again and find out whether she started writing checks from a separate book, gave some checks to one of her employees, went to the automatic teller machine, or WHAT she did with the $273.42, but you're not sure how to ask her diplomatically. Especially the part about how she'll start bouncing checks any day now if she doesn't find another $273.42 to deposit. You almost feel relieved when her secretary says she's in another meeting.

Forget lunch. At 1 o'clock in the afternoon, you take a break, make a cup of tea for your sick daughter, look around the kitchen that your mother will inspect in just a few hours, and decide to use your lunch break to review your own receivables and update your invoices. You are dipping lower than you'd like into your business account to make your monthly phone bill and computer payments, and you have two clients that have owed you money for almost three months now. Those clients are always in meetings, too.

You then send out reminder invoices, pause to let the plumber in, and come back to find your computer smoking. "Yes," says a real-life bookkeeper who had this experience. "My screen actually burned up right in front of my eyes." You unplug the computer, call your computer service center, and resolve to spend the rest of the day organizing your office, making appointments, and doing all the other busy work kinds of things you can do without a computer. But then the phone rings.

"Okay Carol, sorry I was in all those meetings," says Alice. "Why don't you call up that register now and we'll go over it? I'm leaving tomorrow morning for two weeks in Europe."

"Well," you mumble. "It seems like my system is down."

"Oh," says Alice in meaningful overtones.

"But wait . . . Did you use any extra checkbooks last month? Do you have any ATM withdrawals that you didn't tell me about?"

"Oh, probably. You know me!" says Alice. "I do remember leaving my checkbook home one night and just taking an extra book of checks out of my desk to pay my printer. Why don't I look through my wallet and call you back when I get home from my trip?" Another hanging thread, another half hour passes. Then the phone rings again.

"Carol. What did you do to my records?" barks Ann Gryell. "I don't pay you to screw up my files!"

"What do you mean? What's the problem?" you say calmly.

"Well, you show my professional services account up by $700 last year! And my salary expenses account is down. It doesn't make any sense to me; I think I'm paying more than ever in salaries. This is the third month in a row you've done this."

"Why don't I pull your files right now and check it out?" you suggest, reaching for the file as the plumber yells into your office. "THAT'LL BE IT MA'AM. SEEMS THERE WAS A SOCK STUCK IN YOUR TOILET. IT'LL COST YOU $125. BUT I DIDN'T CHARGE YOU FOR THE EXTRA RUBBER GASKET I HAD TO USE."

"Well, maybe I'd better check it out and call you back," you tell Ann.

Which you do. You pay the plumber, walk him to the door, and pick up your mail. Which includes no checks, but an overdraft report on the one client who has his bank statements sent directly to you and a letter from Ken Dredspirit, one of your genuinely nice clients. "I am sorry to have to discontinue your service, Carol. In the current recession, however, we have had to pull our company back and lay off most of our employees. My wife will be keeping the books from now on. I'll call next week to pick up our records."

"I'll worry about that tomorrow," you say, pop a tape in the VCR for your sick (but mainly bored) daughter, and start looking at Ann's files. Didn't she fire a staff accountant a couple of months ago, about the same time she hired you to start keeping her books? The professional services is probably your fee, and the drop in salaries is because she is no longer paying a staff accountant. You call her back, pleased to report another mystery solved. "Well, actually, I have hired another accountant," Ann says. "Didn't I tell you? You've been wonderful, but it seemed easier to keep someone on staff. So just send me a final bill, and good luck to you."

Losing a client is bad enough, and losing two in the same day is worse. When you have to call them, however, so that they can tell you they're gone, that seems the worst of all. Just as you are about to close up shop for the day, the phone rings one more time. What the heck, you might as well answer it. How much worse can it get?

It's Cary Onalot, your most hysterical client. "Carol! What are you doing October 3? I'm being audited! What did we do wrong? Why did they pick me? Is this fair? Can you go for me? Can't I just tell them I gave you all the information and you'll deal with it? It's not my fault if you posted things to the wrong account! What should I do now? When can you come over here?"

How about next year, you think irritably, but remember that Cary is so hysterical he's the last person who would have cheated on his taxes. An audit isn't any fun, you reassure him, but you're sure he's done nothing wrong. And, you'll be able to supply plenty of documentation to his accountant. "Well," he says, more quietly now. "I'm not sure you actually got *all* the documentation."

It's almost four o'clock in the afternoon now, and you promised a new client prospect you would see him at his office today. Maybe you'll swing by on your way to Juan's office. You call a neighborhood teenager, beg her to sit with your daughter for a couple of hours until your husband gets home, and head out the door.

"Here's the deal," says the potential client, Ben Darules, whose office you finally find on the far side of town in an industrial park you've circled for half an hour. "I don't believe in income taxes. They're unconstitutional! Why should I have to give the Government all my money? For what? I'm willing to pay top dollar, but I want you to keep my books so that I never show any income. Can you do it for me?"

Actually, you say to yourself, you're rather glad to encounter Mr. Darules. He's such an extreme and unusual case, it provides release, and you can't wait to get back to your car and start shrieking. For now, you say "Sorry, I'm not the bookkeeper you're looking for," and speed off to Juan's office.

"Enough is enough," you tell Juan. Without going into details, you let him know that you can't possibly sit in his office all night and sort through the piles of papers his last "girl" left. You will, however, be happy to gather them all up, bring them to your home office, and work late into the night on his behalf. Anxious to get to his cocktail party, he agrees, and you're almost home-free.

When you get home, your mother is sitting in the kitchen drinking tea with your daughter (who is now wearing two extra sweaters). Mom is also eyeing you suspiciously. "She's SICK," your mom says. "Where were you?"

"Out at a client's. Emergency," you say.

"I wish you would tell me why you stay in this business," your mother then says. "It seems kind of frustrating. Is it worth it?"

"NO! IT'S NOT WORTH IT! I DON'T HAVE ANY IDEA WHY I DO IT!" is what you are either thinking or saying, depending on your relationship with your mother, and how bad you really feel.

The rest of the evening passes uneventfully. Grandmother, husband, and daughter watch television, and you can hear the sound of laughter waft down to your office, where you are working over Juan's files (by hand) well into the wee hours. When you tiptoe to bed, you find a copy of *Bookkeeping On Your Home-Based PC* on your pillow, where you left it last night. You pick the book up, toss it across the room, hit a lamp, and break the lightbulb.

"Fine. Serves me right. I'll pick up the broken glass in the morning, on my way to the Career Development Center," you think as you drift off to sleep. (Note to my readers: I hope you're still with me here, because that really was as bad as it gets, and far worse than it almost always is. Don't forget, there are the good days to look forward to, too)

A good day

Sometimes the phone wakes you up on a good day, too. "Carol? Sorry to call so early. This is Rae Wardingclient. I have four tickets to the ballgame tonight, and I can't use them. Do you want them? I know it's been a hectic month and you've done a lot to keep me organized and to meet all my deadlines."

"Sure, I'd love to take them," you say, thinking that a great way to entertain your mother (who is still here) just fell into your lap. "Thanks very much." Before you can get to the shower, your daughter bounces into your room, happy, energetic, and cleareyed. *And* in her school clothes. You shower and dress in business clothes yourself, because this morning you are going to a client's office. By the time you get to the kitchen, your mother has made coffee, and you have a few minutes to sit and chat.

"It is so nice that you work at home," she says. (Most likely in a conciliatory tone, because she's afraid you're still crazed from the night before.) "How many other parents these days can be home for their kids when they stay home from school? You're doing a great job."

You're feeling better already, even if you are still a little tired. You drop your daughter off at school and head for Max Iteasy's office, where you've promised to go over last month's reports with him.

"Why do you think my overhead is so high?" he asks.

"Well, I've been thinking about that. And to tell you the truth, your company seems to spend a lot more on supplies than many others of your size," you answer. "Do you think you have someone stealing supplies? Or maybe just buying far more than you need?"

"Well that's good to know," Max says. "You really have a good eye for what all the numbers really mean. I'll check into the supplies. How is it going otherwise?" You always like talking to Max; he treats you like an equal and has passed on some of his better business tips to you. As the conversation ends, he says, "I wanted to let you know that a friend of mine, Maury Zee, is looking for a bookkeeper. I gave him your number, so he might be calling you within the next couple of days."

You thank Max, and head for Gwen Straight's flower shop to pick up her monthly paperwork. It's always a pleasure to visit Gwen. The place smells so good, and she's disorganized but nice, and fun to chat with, too. "Carol! I used the organizer you gave me. It works great," Gwen says, and hands you a neat accordion file filled with receipts, invoices, and hand-printed forms. "I just recorded all the checks the way you said, and it made my month much less crazy. Here . . . take some gladiolas."

On the way home, you stop at the bank and the grocery store, feeling upbeat about the freedom you have to schedule your day. "Maybe I'll even meet a friend for lunch next week," you think. By the time you get home, it *is* lunchtime, and your mother is chatting with the computer service people, who have replaced your burned-out screen just in time for you to get to your afternoon's work.

You grab a sandwich and head for your office. You have four messages on the answering machine. Maury Zee called, saying he's "heard terrific things about you" and wants to know when you can start. There's a second call from a prospect who says he got your most recent direct-mail letter and needs a bookkeeper who understands the construction business. There's also a message from Juan Titnow. "Carol, thanks a million. We got the credit line, thanks to you. And I'm done with these office temps. Why don't you just keep up all my books and bill me monthly? I'll send over a letter." The last call is from an accounting student at a nearby university. "I need to make some extra money this semester," she says. "Do you need any part-time help?" Hmmm, you ponder.

You put in three solid hours sitting in front of your screen and entering data. The data is as clean as yesterday's was messy. The process goes quickly; you're starting to get the hang of this new software now. The statements balance, the invoices print without a hitch, and you feel totally productive.

At three o'clock in the afternoon, the phone rings. It's Frank Endfair, the activities chairman of the local chamber of commerce to which you belong. "We were thinking of having a lunch next month on the 16th to discuss what businesses need to know about managing their finances," he says. "Do you think you can be the speaker?" It sounds like a great opportunity to put your name out to a lot of prospects at once, so you happily commit to the speaking engagement.

You've been productive enough for one day and decide to turn off your computer and quit early. You'll spend a couple of hours being with your family and getting ready for the ballgame. On the way into the kitchen, you pick up the mail, which includes two long-awaited checks and your monthly financial newsletter, just in time for a quick browse.

It's such a nice day out, you decide to go for a walk. You and your mother walk over to the bus stop, where you meet your daughter and head home for a three-generation cup of tea. As you sip your tea, you think, "This is not bad at all."

A real day

Of course, a real day in the life of a work-at-home bookkeeper is a little from column A and a little from column B. Life is seldom as dramatic or black and white as the examples given here. Here's a last bit of encouraging news, however. If you lay the groundwork right, you're less likely to have a day in which everything goes wrong and more likely to have one in which everything goes right.

The reason is because you can make your own luck: by keeping your equipment maintained and having a handy computer repairman on call; by prescreening clients and refusing to let them walk all over you; by taking the time to do your work calmly and correctly, and by following many of the other tips you'll pick up in this book. Most of all, you can make your own luck by allowing yourself to take the few really awful days in stride, realizing that sometimes bad days happen to good people, and it really isn't *you*.

4 Home sweet office

"You never told me that Bill's son played soccer," my eight-year-old son said to me one day when I walked in the door after a business appointment. "Who the heck is Bill?" I thought to myself, as a looked at the phone message my son had carefully written. "Bill" turned out to be Dr. William Mucketymuck, the president of a midwestern research company, whom I was trying to reach for days to interview for a magazine story I'd been writing. While I was out and my son was answering the phone, Dr. Mucketymuck struck up a friendly conversation that led quickly to my son's and his son's soccer careers. Initially, I felt unprofessional and embarrassed when I returned his call. But my son had broken the ice for me. To this day, "Bill" remains one of my best professional sources and business contacts.

That story basically sums up the pros and cons of working at home. There's a lot you can (and should) do to appear and really be professional. Home IS more informal than the corporate environment, however, and sometimes your personal life will seep in around the edges of your home-based business. When that happens, it can and will turn some prospects off. (My personal theory for that situation is that those people are jealous of you.)

More likely, aspects of your personal life will encourage other prospects. Clients who like the way you can integrate your personal and professional life, who appreciate that you don't have high overheads built into your fees, and who, on occasion, will connect with your kid, your cat, or your stamp collection and become a valuable business contact or even a lifelong friend.

Such a nice place to work

You probably can already imagine the many advantages of working from the home. You can be there during the day, when deliveries are made and kids get sent home sick. You can hold down your costs and even take tax breaks for the space you use. You can totally meld the activities in your life—go down to the office after dinner for a couple of hours of catching up; take a break in the middle of the day to weed your garden; work in your sweat pants. You don't have to commute. You can eat fresh food out of the refrigerator instead of buying expensive downtown lunches or eating stale brown-bag food. You can stay cozy in your own nest. Working from home is a great life, and as 27 million Americans have already chosen it for all of the preceding reasons.

The bad news

The previous section has a flip side, of course. Proximity to the refrigerator can add unwanted pounds. Friends and relatives who fail to distinguish between work hours and play hours can interrupt regularly and even appear highly insulted if you spurn their midday visits to get back to work. Neighbors can take advantage of your availability by using your house as a convenient delivery point and using you as an emergency babysitter and carpooler. The proximity of your work, while a convenience, can lead you to a life where you work all the time. You can develop a lifestyle in which you are always working, the answering machine is never on, and the computer is never off. The proximity of your personal life can also distract you from your job, leading you into a pattern of interrupting your paying business to clean out the closets, empty the dishwasher, mow the lawn, or (oh, no!) watch daytime TV. You have to avoid these work-at-home distractions (Fig. 4-1).

Most of these disadvantages can be controlled through firm self-discipline on your part. Stay on a regular schedule, remain firm with friends and family, and train yourself to walk past the kitchen with your eyes closed so you can get to your computer early. Organize yourself as you would in any outside job or business, and buy the extras you need, such as an answering service staffed by adults, for example, to stay professional and on top of things. Organize your surroundings to support your endeavors. Your first order of business, of course, is setting up a serious home office.

The "look"

A good home office will make you feel efficient when business is up and consoled when business is down. It should be well organized and equipped to offer speed and efficiency when you are buried under work. It should also offer enough personal touches of comfort for solace you when you're not.

When you are really busy (during tax season, for example) you need an office that will run like a pit crew. Your chair should be comfortable, your desk

4-1
When your office is at home, ignore those personal distractions and get to work. Matt Hightshoe

clear, and your files organized and handy. You'll need a well-lit work surface and every tool within reach. When work is slow, you'll want a couple of photos or posters or special objects that are pleasing to the eye and spirit. Maybe they will remind you of why you're working at home in the first place. You'll want your office to reflect you.

Separation

Several important reasons exist for truly keeping your office separate from your personal family space, and tax considerations, while valid, are not the most vital. The most important reasons are little kids who will put quarters in your disk drives so they can play video games; older kids who will sit, feet on your desk, talking to their high school buddies for hours while you try to get work done; or out-of-town relatives who take up residence in your office/guest room during the holiday season, sleep late, go to bed early, and hang their pantyhose over your fax machine. If you are to be a professional, you need professional space free of distractions and interference from other family members.

Then, of course, there IS the matter of the home-office deduction. It can offer considerable financial savings and is available only to offices kept wholly separate from your personal life.

A really great office

Use the following guidelines to create your perfect office at home.

Start with an empty room   The best way to set up a home office is to empty the chosen room completely and start from scratch. Ideally, you should have a room of your own. Many people use basement family rooms or spare bedrooms. You can, if you must, use part of a room. If you are feeling flush and can afford it, consider constructing part or all of your office anew: you can remake an unused garage, refinish an attic, or install new lighting and heating in a basement. The cost of this construction, when done to establish or improve a legitimate home office, is all deductible. Up to $10,000 of the cost can be deductible for the tax year in which you've spent the money.

Repaint your office, too—you never know when you will get the opportunity to paint it again! Use light colors to reflect light or dark colors or wood if you want an especially cozy effect. Select a decor that you like. If you are carpeting the office, find out whether the carpet you've selected has antistatic properties—you don't want to shock yourself every time you shift in your chair and go back to your keyboard!

Cover your windows and add lights   Your windows need to be covered for other reasons besides not wanting neighbors looking in when you are working at night. You don't want bright sunlight glare to interfere with your ability to focus on your work. You also don't want to spend all of your time daydreaming and looking out the window. Window coverings don't have to be expensive decorator shades or sophisticated gray blinds that look totally businesslike.

It's almost impossible to get optimum lighting in a home office, but look on the bright side: you don't have to work under extensive panels of fluorescents, either. Pick lighting you like, avoiding bright lights right in front of where you expect your desk to be (they'll shine in your eyes) or directly behind your desk location (they'll reflect on your computer screen).

Recessed ceiling lights around the room, to illuminate bookshelves, file cabinets, and other office equipment are more helpful than a central bright light source. You can always add spot lamps later. Try putting halogen bulbs in your regular light sockets—they emit a crisp, white light; last longer; and use less energy.

Wire it   If possible, you should have your computer on a separate circuit. While the room is empty, have an electrician put some extra outlets around the walls—you never know when you'll want to rearrange the furniture, add a copying machine, or install a second computer.

Add phone lines   If money is really tight, you can get by on your family phone, but you'll be much happier if you can add a separate business line. If you can afford it, add a third line that you can dedicate to your fax machine and computer modem.

Get your chair   "Absolutely, the first, most important piece of furniture in an office is the chair," says Neil Taslitz, president of The Backcare Corporation in Chicago and a leading expert on ergonomics. "The chair is the foundation for everything else."

You will spend many, many hours in your chair. If it doesn't support you correctly, you will end up with backaches and pains in the neck. A good chair, according to Taslitz, has what is called a "five-star base" that looks like its name sounds. A chair with only four base appendages can easily flip you out of it. A good chair is balanced to support your back and ride with you when you tilt forward to do close work as well as lean back to put your feet up and talk on the phone. A good chair is adjustable in many ways: total height, backrest height, angle, and strength. If the front edge is turned up a bit, it will hold you in it. Finally, if your carpet holds static, find a chair with static-reducing casters.

Taslitz suggests buying a chair from someone who will let you use the chair for a week or two and then return it if you don't like it. Many chairs feel comfortable for two minutes in the furniture store. Spend eight hours in one, for five continuous days, and all of its peculiarities will become apparent. See the exhibit on ergonomics for more information.

Bookkeepers used to be recognizable, along with writers, by the knobby bumps on their index fingers from gripping their pencils too long and hard. Today, bookkeepers rarely grip pencils, but do find themselves leaning over keyboards and computer screens for hours at a time. Knobby fingers have given way to shoulder pains, wrist disorders, and other problems known as *cumulative trauma disorders* or *repetitive motion syndromes*. Besides these problems, there has been talk recently of increased vision problems from spending too much time focused on a screen that's only about two feet away from you.

If you give them some attention while designing your office, you can avoid a lot of trouble later. You can protect your body from the pains associated with sitting in front of a computer for hours by taking a few simple precautions. Don't make the mistake of thinking you're immune because your day is varied. According to Neil Taslitz, president of the Backcare Corporation in Chicago, professionals can sit for hours and not even realize it when they are on deadline with a big project. For your health, take the following precautions:

- Get an adjustable footrest or adjust your chair to a height that allows you to have your feet flat on the floor.
- Adjust your computer monitor about 16 to 28 inches from your face and just slightly below eye level.

Ergonomics

- Place your keyboard so that your wrists are straight and forearms parallel to the floor. Ideally, your keyboard should be lower than your desk height.
- Consider investing in a wrist support pad, such as the one shown in FIG. 4-2 that tucks under your keyboard.
- As you work, adopt these habits: Get up once every hour and stretch your back, neck, arms, wrists, and fingers. Walk outside and focus on the horizon. Look around. Take some deep fresh air breaths. Remember why you work at home!

4-2
An ergonomic wrist pad can do a lot to protect your wrists on the days you spend hours keying in data. The Backcare Corp., Chicago

Add a desk Surprisingly, the desk is one of the least important pieces of office furniture. You need a good work surface, but some people today substitute a table and companion chest of drawers instead of the all-in-one desk. Having a desk without a top middle drawer allows you to use a chair with good arm supports (you won't crash into the drawer with the arm supports). Avoiding that drawer also allows you to clamp a lower keyboard holder onto the desk without blocking the drawer. That being said, I use a big old clunky wooden desk with a long middle drawer. It's probably not ergonomic, but I like it.

A good file cabinet   If you've skimped on your desk, use whatever extra cash you have to get a good, well-balanced file cabinet. You don't want to have to tug at the drawers to open them or have to push mightily to shut them. You also don't want a file cabinet that threatens to tilt over on top of you whenever you open one of the drawers.

The office extras   Think about the way you work and any other furniture you'll need. A tall bookshelf for computer manuals, tax references, and other books is a big help. Or, a separate table for your computer printer and fax machine. Note that many bookkeepers work with more than one printer—a laser printer for business correspondence and a dot-matrix printer for multiple-part forms.

When configuring your office, think about your own work style. Do you like a clean, clear work surface on which you take out one project at a time? Or do you like to keep most of your reference books, equipment, and files all around you? Do you hate having your back to the door? Do you pace a lot? Lay your office out with your own rhythms in mind. Taslitz says the best arrangement, if you can set it up, is a semicircular one that puts you at the center of the computer keyboard, a writing surface, your reference materials, and any regularly used supplies.

Once you start working in your office, you might find that parts of it don't work. Change them! Unless you've had a carpenter install your office and furniture as a built-in module, you can move the furniture all around until you find the arrangement that makes you comfortable.

The home-office deduction

The Internal Revenue Service has good news and bad news for those of us who take a tax deduction for a home office. The bad news is that we must file a special form with our tax returns that flags us as home-office deductors. This form is one that the service estimates takes one-and-a-half hours to comprehend, calculate, and complete, as well as has you walking around your home with a yardstick, looking up old real estate tax records, and figuring out how much your property would be worth without your house.

The good news is that, despite the attention-getting form, there's some evidence that the home-office deduction is not the audit bait it once was. The sharp growth of legitimate home-based businesses have made this deduction much less fruitful for audits. We all really are running businesses from our homes!

IRS Income Tax Form 8829, "Expenses for Business Use of Your Home" walks you through the calculations, step by step, simplifying and clarifying the home-office rules to the point where the deduction may actually be easier to take than it was in the years before 1991, when there was no special deduction form. Figure 4-3 shows you this form.

You are "rightfully entitled" to a home-office deduction if your space passes this test: it must be used exclusively either as a principal place of business or as a place where you regularly meet clients, patients, or customers. Your space does not have to be a separate room, but can be a distinct area of a room, as long as that area is set apart and reserved exclusively for your business.

4-3
IRS form 8829.

Form **8829**

Department of the Treasury
Internal Revenue Service (5)

Expenses for Business Use of Your Home
► File with Schedule C (Form 1040). Use a separate Form 8829 for each home you used for business during the year.
► See instructions on back.

OMB No. 1545-1266

1992

Attachment Sequence No. **66**

Name(s) of proprietor(s)

Your social security number

Part I Part of Your Home Used for Business

1	Area used exclusively for business (see instructions). Include area that does not meet exclusive use test and either used for inventory storage or regularly used as part of a day-care facility	1
2	Total area of home	2
3	Divide line 1 by line 2. Enter the result as a percentage	3 ___ %

● For day-care facilities not used exclusively for business, also complete lines 4–6.
● All others, skip lines 4–6 and enter the amount from line 3 on line 7.

4	Multiply days used for day care during year by hours used per day	4 ___ hr.
5	Total hours available for use during the year (366 days × 24 hours). See instructions	5 8,784 hr.
6	Divide line 4 by line 5. Enter the result as a decimal amount	6 .
7	Business percentage. For day-care facilities not used exclusively for business, multiply line 6 by line 3 (enter the result as a percentage). All others, enter the amount from line 3 ►	7 ___ %

Part II Figure Your Allowable Deduction

8 Enter the amount from Schedule C, line 29, **plus** any net gain or (loss) derived from the business use of your home and shown on Schedule D or Form 4797. If more than one place of business, see instructions 8

See instructions for columns (a) and (b) before completing lines 9–20.

		(a) Direct expenses	(b) Indirect expenses	
9	Casualty losses. See instructions	9		
10	Deductible mortgage interest. See instructions	10		
11	Real estate taxes. See instructions	11		
12	Add lines 9, 10, and 11	12		
13	Multiply line 12, column (b) by line 7		13	14
14	Add line 12, column (a) and line 13			15
15	Subtract line 14 from line 8. If zero or less, enter -0-			
16	Excess mortgage interest. See instructions	16		
17	Insurance	17		
18	Repairs and maintenance	18		
19	Utilities	19		
20	Other expenses. See instructions	20		
21	Add lines 16 through 20	21		
22	Multiply line 21, column (b) by line 7		22	
23	Carryover of operating expenses from 1991 Form 8829, line 41		23	
24	Add line 21 in column (a), line 22, and line 23			24
25	Allowable operating expenses. Enter the **smaller** of line 15 or line 24			25
26	Limit on excess casualty losses and depreciation. Subtract line 25 from line 15			26
27	Excess casualty losses. See instructions		27	
28	Depreciation of your home from Part III below		28	
29	Carryover of excess casualty losses and depreciation from 1991 Form 8829, line 42		29	
30	Add lines 27 through 29			30
31	Allowable excess casualty losses and depreciation. Enter the **smaller** of line 26 or line 30			31
32	Add lines 14, 25, and 31			32
33	Casualty loss portion, if any, from lines 14 and 31. Carry amount to **Form 4684**, Section B			33
34	Allowable expenses for business use of your home. Subtract line 33 from line 32. Enter here and on Schedule C, line 30. If your home was used for more than one business, see instructions ►			34

Part III Depreciation of Your Home

35	Enter the **smaller** of your home's adjusted basis or its fair market value. See instructions	35
36	Value of land included on line 35	36
37	Basis of building. Subtract line 36 from line 35	37
38	Business basis of building. Multiply line 37 by line 7	38
39	Depreciation percentage. See instructions	39 ___ %
40	Depreciation allowable. Multiply line 38 by line 39. Enter here and on line 28 above. See instructions	40

Part IV Carryover of Unallowed Expenses to 1993

41	Operating expenses. Subtract line 25 from line 24. If less than zero, enter -0-	41
42	Excess casualty losses and depreciation. Subtract line 31 from line 30. If less than zero, enter -0-	42

For Paperwork Reduction Act Notice, see back of form.   Cat. No. 13232M   Form **8829** (1992)

Does this mean that you are not allowed to pay personal bills while sitting on your desk? Or keep the computer game Tetris on your computer? A stickler would say yes, but a more practical person would note that even corporate employees sometimes bring their bills to work or play a fast computer game on their coffee break. Such a practical person would also point out that, if you do get selected for one of the IRS's scarce on-site home audits, you'll have ample time to cleanse your office of offending paraphernalia before the auditor arrives.

This does NOT mean that you should run your home office out of an actively used family room or guest room, or that you should take a writeoff for the kitchen table. The fact that doing so jeopardizes the legality of the home-office deduction is secondary; what's primary is that it is very hard to run a profitable business in a room that isn't set up and always available to you as a specific place of business.

Once you've met the legitimacy test, you can deduct a prorated portion of your mortgage interest, home maintenance, insurance, and utilities. In addition, if you own your home, you can deduct a portion of your home's value; depreciating it every year that you use your home office. If you rent your home, a prorated portion of your rent is deductible. Tally this up, and your home office can save you thousands of dollars a year in taxes. Note, too, that those items that are deductible in more than one place (such as real-estate taxes and a prorated share of home mortgage interest, which you can take against your business income or on your personal 1040 form) are worth more as a home-office deduction against your business taxes because they offset self-employment taxes as well as regular income taxes. See the exhibit about the only time when you *don't* want to take the home-office deduction. Here are the mechanics of the home-office deduction:

Measure your office   You need to determine the percent of your home used for your business. While the IRS says you can use square feet, number of rooms, or "any other reasonable method" of comparing your office space to the total space available in your home, the agency auditors seem most comfortable with the square footage test.

Separate your land value from your home value   To determine the basis for figuring out the proper amount of depreciation for your home, you must separate the home's land value from its building value; only a percentage of the building value is deductible.

Take all of the related deductions   Your home office entitles you to a prorated portion of depreciation, rent, utilities (except phone service), mortgage interest, and property taxes, as well as any furniture or furnishings (down to the drapes and carpets) that you install to fix up your office.

Construction   If you've been thinking of construction, go for it. You can deduct the costs of building a new office, converting an attic or garage, installing recessed lighting, building in bookshelves, or any other setup work to create your home office. As a small business, up to $10,000 of that cost could be deductible in the year that you do the work.

Deductions for portions of a room   You can take a deduction if your home office is only a portion of a room—a desk in the corner of your bedroom, for example. If that's all the space you can spare for your home office, do all you can to keep that area separate. If you don't like the fabric screen approach, pile file boxes around you or stick a tape line on the floor to keep other family members away.

Be too legit to hit   The more exclusive your office is, the better. Take pictures of your home-office, or keep a schematic of your floor plan (with home-office dimensions) on file in case of an audit.

Think twice about incorporating   For some inexplicable reason, the home-office deduction is available only to sole proprietors and not one-person corporations or partners of partnerships.

The computer can be a catch-22   While you are theoretically allowed to prorate a computer and deduct its percentage of use for business, if your family has been using your computer to play math games or store recipes, even if that computer is in your home office, it could fail the "exclusive home-office test." Consider buying an inexpensive back-up computer as a family computer and keep it out of your office, which is not as prohibitive as it sounds. You'll have your business hard drive to yourself, and if it crashes, you still have the backup computer in the kitchen to use in a pinch.

Don't put games on your business computer   Chances are, the IRS auditor will never even peek at your hard drive. But games will ruin your profitability nevertheless. Take it from someone who knows.

When NOT to take the home office deduction

Don't take the home office deduction if you intend to sell your home within the next year. If you have depreciated a portion of your home as a business expense, and you then sell your house for a gain, you must pay a capital-gains tax on that portion of the home that you depreciated, and you cannot "roll over" that capital gain into your next house. Of course, this law does not affect renters. If you rent your home, you are in the clearest position to benefit from the home office deduction and can continue to deduct rent, utilities, and insurance until the day you move.

If you are a homeowner who intends to sell your home and you have been claiming the home-office deduction, just do not claim it during the year of the sale. Aggressive accountants argue that doing that is enough to stop the recapture of past depreciation for deductions taken in previous years.

Someone could probably devote a book the size of this one to answer the question of whether you should lease or buy your equipment. Practically speaking, however, the fundamental equipment needed for a start-up bookkeeping business is inexpensive enough to buy and impractical to rent. If you don't have the money on hand to buy your first computer system, finance it by using your home-equity line or put the computer on a credit card.

Because the equipment you're buying is business equipment used for business purposes, the interest you pay while paying off the credit card will be fully deductible, and the equipment itself used to generate money for you. In this instance, credit card purchasing is more acceptable than usual. Don't even try to get a business bank loan for your computer equipment. Most banks don't lend at all to start-ups; they want to see results before they'll lend you money.

How much money will you need to get started? Think between $3,000 and $10,000, depending on how extensive and high-end you want your equipment to be.

Buy the best computer you can afford. It doesn't take a top-of-the-line computer to run most accounting programs these days—number crunching is one of the most basic computer skills. Eventually, however, you'll want speed, and will get impatient with how slow some the lower-priced models are. As your business grows, you will want to use your computer for more and more tasks. The computer is not an item you'll want to replace very often, and you'll be surprised by how quickly you can outgrow a low-level product.

The computer

Before buying a computer, consider which type of computer environment you want. A *computer environment* basically means deciding between the most common MS-DOS command-based operating system of IBM and IBM-compatible computers and the typically "user-friendly" environment of the pulldown menus and point-and-click operation of the Macintosh.

People who want an IBM-compatible computer and the user-friendly interface can now use Windows, a program that acts as a navigational layer between the computer's operating system and the user. Be aware, however, that the broadest range of accounting programs are those available for the IBM-compatible MS-DOS environment. Some programs won't work with Windows, although most software manufacturers are rushing to market with comparable accounting-for-windows formats. Figure 4-4 gives you an idea of what type of computer you should buy.

The hard drive   When it comes to hard drives, the bigger the better. David Lawrence, a computer consultant who operates a Washington, DC, area business under the name of "Dr. Mac," points out that hard drives are meant

*This flowchart can help
you choose the right
computer system, but you
won't be unhappy if you
buy the best you
can afford.*

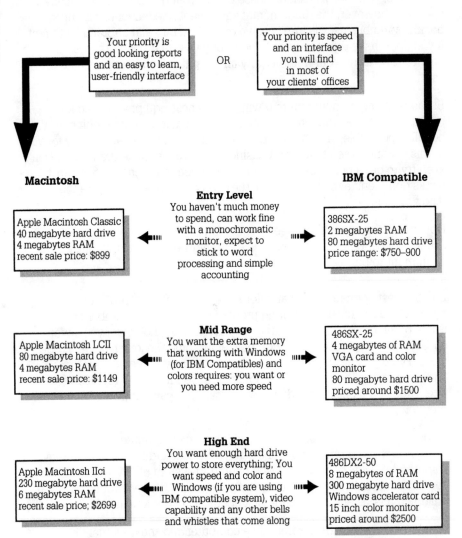

Which Computer Is For You?

Your priority is
good looking reports
and an easy to learn,
user-friendly interface

OR

Your priority is speed
and an interface
you will find
in most of
your clients' offices

Macintosh

IBM Compatible

Entry Level
You haven't much money
to spend, can work fine
with a monochromatic
monitor, expect to
stick to word
processing and simple
accounting

Apple Macintosh Classic
40 megabyte hard drive
4 megabytes RAM
recent sale price: $899

386SX-25
2 megabytes RAM
80 megabytes hard drive
price range: $750–900

Mid Range
You want the extra memory
that working with Windows
(for IBM Compatibles) and
colors requires: you want or
you need more speed

Apple Macintosh LCII
80 megabyte hard drive
4 megabytes RAM
recent sale price: $1149

486SX-25
4 megabytes of RAM
VGA card and color
monitor
80 megabyte hard drive
priced around $1500

High End
You want enough hard drive
power to store everything; You
want speed and color and
Windows (if you are using
IBM compatible system), video
capability and any other bells
and whistles that come along

Apple Macintosh IIci
230 megabyte hard drive
6 megabytes RAM
recent sale price; $2699

486DX2-50
8 megabytes of RAM
300 megabyte hard drive
Windows accelerator card
15 inch color monitor
priced around $2500

to hold your daily work and all of your key programs. Unfortunately,
sometimes the easier a program is to use, the more complicated its behind-
the-scenes functioning, and thus the more memory it will occupy on your
hard drive. A hard drive should have a minimum capacity of 80 megabytes.

The printer   Many bookkeeping professionals find they use more than one
printer: A dot matrix printer is used for multiple-part forms that require
impact printing on the paper, and a laser printer is used for professional-
quality letters. In today's climate, you can find a good laser printer for less

than $1000. Try a few before you buy one, and consider these issues before selecting the right one for you:

- Does the printer feed envelopes easily and neatly, without crushing the envelope or getting it caught in your paper track?
- How fast is the printer? Try it with a spreadsheet and detailed report, if you can. If you'll be doing any graphics, make sure you try to print a graphic to see how long it takes.
- Will it print a variety of fonts? If you intend to create your own reports and sales material (such as letterhead, brochures, and flyers) on your computer, you want it to print a clean and sharp image.
- What needs to be replaced on the printer, how often, and how much does it cost? Some printers require you to replace an entire internal cartridge as frequently as once a year if you are a heavy user. Those cartridges can cost $250 or more, too. That's not necessarily bad—a replaceable cartridge can keep the inside of your printer clean and running well for a long time. But don't forget to add replacement costs into your estimate for how much the printer costs.

The modem   Get a modem and learn how to use it! (Chapter 12 describes why.) A modem allows you to transfer files to your computer from a client's office, call online services for technical accounting and tax information, network with fellow bookkeepers around the country, and dial into your clients' computers from your home office. A fax/modem (along with a fax card inserted into the computer) allows you to send faxes directly from your computer to somebody else's fax machine or receive their faxes on your computer. A good quality, 2400-baud modem (that's medium fast) will cost approximately $90, or $125 if it has fax capabilities. Boost the modem speed up to 9600 baud (very fast) and you will spend $275 for the modem, or $325 for fax capabilities.

The laptop   You don't really need a laptop computer to run your business, but you'll want one. Especially in the bookkeeping profession, when you might spend a good part of your week working on site at your clients' offices. You can take your laptop with you, work "in the field" all day, and then pop the floppy disk into your computer at home the next morning when you are ready to start posting transactions and printing reports. Some people run their entire businesses on a laptop alone, but it's not recommended: laptop screens are generally not as big nor sharp as screens on desktop computers. When your business involves ledgers and spreadsheets, the last thing you want is a weak screen image or a fuzzy display.

It's also a good idea to have a laptop as your second computer (when you are ready to purchase a second one), so that if your computer breaks down you don't lose workdays waiting for it to be fixed or hunting in a panic for a rental computer to use in the interim.

"I would especially love to have a laptop computer during tax season," says Mahwah, New Jersey, bookkeeper Ingrid Landskron. "I could take it to visit my clients, sit down with them, enter the rough data into my computer and say, 'OK, this is your bottom line.' Then I could take it back home to fill in all the forms without rekeying the information."

The calculator

A bookkeeper's friend is her calculator. You'll want one that has a tape printout, so that you can review the calculation to make sure the numbers were keyed in correctly, without double checking all the calculations. Consider the readout—a liquid crystal display will be easiest to read in a bright room and use the least amount of power, a fluorescent readout will be bright in minimal light but subject to glare. Today's calculators can be quite sophisticated—financial calculators will run investment calculations, such as future value of an investment or bond yields, automatically. Most bookkeepers, however, report that they don't use these features; they save the fancy computations for their computers. You can get a very good calculator with printing ability for well under $100.

The phone

Phones are available in all qualities and prices but there's a minimum level you shouldn't go below for a business phone. Your phone should sound crystal clear and loud or your clients and potential clients will be anxious to get you off the phone. If you are going to have more than one line into your home, such as a separate business and personal line, you'll want a phone that can answer both lines from your desk. If you are installing a separate business line that runs only to your desk, you might want to get a phone with an answering machine built-in.

The phone service   Phone service is an expensive convenience. You'll have to decide, in planning your budget, just how much money you want to spend for just how much convenience. Consider how the phone rings in your home office, for example. What happens when your business line rings in your downstairs office and you are up in the kitchen? Do you run like crazy to answer it, let it ring off the hook, or let an answering service or phone mail system answer? Or, do you simply answer it in the kitchen, because you are paying for all lines to run to all phones in your house?

When you aren't there, how do you ensure that your phone gets answered? Answering machines sometimes break down, or require you to listen to lengthy tapes just to get to one message. New phone mail systems (including services run by many local phone companies) allow you to sift through messages, saving and deleting specific ones. They also enable you to direct phone calls to more than one mailbox, which you will need if you are sharing a line with your teenage daughter, for example. These systems also route calls directly to phone mail when you are already speaking on your line. Call waiting, which is slightly cheaper than phone mail services, allows you to catch every call that comes in (unless three come in at the same time), but it is also a disruption that many clients and business people find unsettling.

You will want a fax machine—take it from someone who hated them herself until she bought one. Fax machines save huge amounts of time and effort, make information available to you in an instant, and (not the least of its advantages) allow you to win clients who wouldn't respect you if you didn't have a fax machine. Some of the features you'll want in a fax are the following:

The facsimile (fax) machine

- A document feeder that sends 10 pages automatically, rather than requiring you to handfeed each page through.
- An automatic paper cutter, so your faxes don't hang in streams all over your floor that you then must cut apart, page by page.
- Broadcast features that let you fax the same message to multiple locations automatically. Think about how easy it is to be able to just fax a quick tax reminder to all of your clients at once.
- A fax-phone switch that allows you to use the fax line as a voice line.

You can get a solid, multifeatured fax for about $600 or a basic model for as little as $350. Besides having the features mentioned previously, you need to make two big decisions regarding your fax. These decisions depend largely on how much faxing you will do. The first is plain paper or thermal paper, and the other is dedicated line or shared line. See the next two sidebars for how to make your decisions.

Plain paper is nicer—and cheaper—than thermal fax paper. The paper is not slippery, so you can write on it without destroying your pens. It also lasts longer and reads cleaner. A plain-paper fax can double as a copier, because the copies look as good and last as long as those of a real copier machine. You still have to feed pages through a fax machine to copy them, however, so you can't use it to copy items such as pages in a book.

Plain paper vs. thermal paper

Plain paper faxes are a luxury. You can expect to pay at least $1000 more for a plain-paper fax than for a thermal one with comparable features. You'll have to decide whether it's worth it. If you decide that it is, console yourself with the fact that you'll save money on paper over the years.

A dedicated fax line is a luxury, but one you could quickly learn to appreciate. If you try to put too much business activity on one line— computer modem communications, faxes, and your business voice calls— your current clients, as well as your prospects, will constantly receive busy signals. Also, your electronic submissions will be regularly interrupted by Call Waiting.

A dedicated line vs. a shared line

My husband and I have three phone lines, one for his business voice calls, one for mine, and a third for data. The fax machine and each of our modems is hooked up to the data line. This system allows us to fax or modem work to clients while talking to them on the phone, or receive phone calls while conducting online research.

If you decide to share a phone line between your voice and fax, you'll need a machine with a fax-voice switch, and you'll need a system to answer the phone when you're not at your office. Some faxes are equipped with built-in answering machines that answer the line by voice and instruct the sender to follow certain instructions if they want to send a fax or leave a voice message.

Don't forget that you can save money (and space) if you purchase a combination fax/modem and fax card for your computer.

The copier

If your copying needs are frequently one-page or single-copy, you might find it worthwhile to invest in a copy machine for your office, especially if you don't live near a commercial copy shop. (Library machines tend to be more expensive per copy—about 15 cents each instead of 6 cents at a copy shop.) Many home-based businesspeople find copying machines one of the least cost-effective pieces of equipment, however, especially if you can consolidate your copying needs and go to the copy shop once a day or twice per week.

Supplies

One of the best things about self-employment is office supplies. For any former student who always envied the teacher's supply cabinet, today's office superstores are just as fun. Don't share office supplies with your family, however. Buy your own stapler and ruler, tape dispenser, pencils, pens, and file folders. If you keep your own, they will always be in your desk when you need them. See the sidebar for some of the extra supplies that others have found useful in their home-office setting.

Office supplies suggestions

❑ Wall-mounted "hot files" or other hanging plastic bins. Keep folders of work in progress, finances to be filed, papers to be copied at the copy shop, and other frequently used files somewhere that is always visible.

❑ Hanging-file folders and regular folding-file folders (otherwise known as manila folders). The ideal filing system involves one regular-file folder inside one hanging-file folder for every category in your file system. When you need to look at a file, pull out the inside folder and leave the hanging file in the drawer to keep its space.

❑ A literature organizer for your flyers, forms, and letterhead. In a pinch, a cardboard shoe organizer works well.

- ❏ A tape player or radio. On some days, you'll be filing papers, cleaning your office, and doing busy work and will appreciate the musical background. You might also want to listen to training tapes or technical tapes that explain your software.

- ❏ A three-ring bound notebook with plastic sheets for business cards to store your professional associates' cards. You might remember meeting someone at a seminar that you'd like to contact, but have forgotten his name. These flat sheets allow you to visually glance through all the cards to jog your memory rather than forcing you to go through an alphabetized card file.

- ❏ A postage meter. A meter will earn its price quickly by allowing you to reduce mailing costs and trips to the post office. Just weigh the material you send out and buy your stamps in a variety of prices.

- ❏ A letter opener. People sending correspondence about their money tend to pack it (and tape it) more securely than a typical letter or package. You'll want the quick-slice ability.

A software library

The truth is, even though I don't like to admit it, you really don't *need* a lot of software to run a bookkeeping business. (Of course, you do need a superior, comprehensive, and user-friendly accounting program, which is the subject of chapter 8.) Beth Roll, who runs a highly successful bookkeeping service out of Marina Del Rey, California, claims not to use anything except accounting, networking, and communications programs and has never really had any need for word processing software. At the other extreme, of course, is the software-driven office. Only the top of the line in each category will do, and the entrepreneur in this office spends most of her time installing software, reading computer magazines, and talking to technical support staffs around the country.

In the happiest of mediums, you will have a full complement of any software you need to run your business easily and efficiently. Here are some suggestions for the type of programs you might find useful. Note that there are tradeoffs between general-purpose software and specially targeted programs. You can do just about anything with a good database program, for example, if you're willing to learn to use it and use it consistently. You can also achieve the same results as a database, however, by buying a freestanding mailing list or contact management program, without the many hours of frustration reading database manuals and learning the program.

An integrated package

The typical integrated software package includes a word processor, a spreadsheet, a database, a communications program, and some graphical features. Don't underestimate integrated software just because it's all bundled together and sells for under $200. The components can be more than sophisticated enough for most independent business needs. In fact, you can run a business for years without ever needing anything but an integrated package (I did). You can write letters to clients, dial up bulletin boards, prepare profit and loss statements, design your letterhead, and keep track of your business contacts all with an integrated package. Two popular integrated packages are Microsoft Works and Claris Works.

A dedicated communications program

If you regularly go online with one information service or bulletin board, you might find it worth the price to buy a communications package targeted to that service or bulletin board. The service Prodigy, for example, comes bundled with its own computer software, and you can access the bulletin board CompuServe without special software, but using the software packages Tapcis or Navigator allows you to get in and out of CompuServe quicker, saving you connect charges. You can also set up a generic communications program to "talk" to just about any other computer through your modem, if you don't think you need a dedicated program.

A backup system

You can invest in a tape-based backup system for your computer or simply use a utilities program that quickly performs manual backups of your hard disk to floppy disks. You can, of course, not buy any special software and just back up your system manually, using your computer's operating system to copy all your work to floppy disks at the end of every work session. Regardless of which method you choose, you *must* back up.

Spreadsheet software

Despite the sophistication of today's accounting programs, many bookkeepers report that they like having a spreadsheet for customizing reports or doing calculations that might not match their accounting software's parameters. Two popular spreadsheet software packages are Excel by Microsoft and Lotus 1-2-3 by Lotus Development Corporation.

Word processing software

If you don't have an integrated program, you need a word processor to write letters to clients and potential clients, design your own ads, and address envelopes. Even a basic word processor delivers far more power than you really need. I'm a *writer* and I've never used anything beyond the word processor that comes with the integrated package Microsoft Works.

Time billing software

A program such as Timeslips III, by Timeslips Corporation allows you to track the hours spent on your computer. You can key in a client, along with the billing information, and then let Timeslips know as you are starting that client's job. If you get interrupted or quit working on that client's account, you simply stop the program's counter. At the end of the month, week, year, or project, the program states how much time you've spent on various projects and prints out invoices at the rates you've preset for the hours you've worked.

The industry leader of contact management software, ACT!, by Contact Software International, enables you to keep complete records of every contact you have with potential or existing clients. If, for example, you send letters to everyone in your local Chamber of Commerce and enter that information in ACT!, the program can prompt you to call them all back in 10 days. Then, as you make your follow-up calls, you can enter notes about each prospect into the program. The program keeps up with you, spitting out a To Do list every day if you want, listing those clients who are due reports or calls, or those prospects that you most want to contact. If you want to remember that Betty Brown's boys are Bill and Bob, and Bobby Black's birthday is June 12, you can enter all that information in your contact management software.

Contact management software

Of course, you can set up your own contact management database, even using the database program of an integrated software package, although these methods won't be as full-featured as a dedicated program.

A *memory resident* program means that you can access that program anytime, even if you're already working in another program; in the Macintosh environment this type of program is called a *desk accessory*. A good memory-resident financial calculator can be quite inexpensive, and you'll use it all the time, mostly for fun. You can use it to teach your clients about the time value of money or help them plan their future mortgage payment schedule. You might also want to load up your memory resident library with a spell checker, calendar, clock, phone dialer, envelope printer, and other conveniences.

Memory resident software

Do you want to keep your calendar on the computer? You might not, but having an extra calendar available on-screen can help you plan. Reminder software, which you can get free or almost free as shareware (*shareware* is software available for download from bulletin boards or sold inexpensively on disk collections) beeps or flashes to remind you of important dates and deadlines. Reminder software is a personal favorite—I haven't missed a birthday or meeting since I loaded it.

A calendar or reminder notice

Even if you don't file tax returns for your clients, a program like Personal Tax Planner can let them know with a few keystrokes (okay, maybe more than just a few keystrokes, but very fast) what their tax bill is likely to be in the current year. You can run tax projections for your clients to help them decide how to time year-end contributions, equipment purchases, and retirement deposits. This software is very inexpensive, very easy to use, and likely to provide extra value for your bookkeeping clients.

Tax planning software

OCR software Optical character recognition (OCR) software allows you to scan into your computer forms such as financial reports and checkbook registers, and then massage the data into shape in word processing or financial management programs. OCR software is still a little labor intensive—it doesn't always work great, and, if you intend to scan in financial facts, you need it to work great. This software is getting better all the time, however, and will someday be able to save you hours at the keyboard.

Utilities Utilities are the programs that help you manage your computer better. Most utilities come bundled together in group programs, although every program doesn't feature every utility. Two popular packages are Norton Utilities and PC Tools. Some of the functions utilities software can perform include:

- Find files you've buried on your hard drive and forgotten.
- Help boot up your computer if your hard drive is acting sluggish.
- Undelete accidentally deleted files.
- Reclaim damaged disks.
- Clean and reorganize your hard disk.
- Secure files with password entries.
- Allow you to preview fonts.
- Protect your computer against viruses.
- Automatically save your work.

5 Right from the start: Legally

"I'm doing what most accountants do; I've got more experience than most of them, but I don't have any letters after my name," recounts one home-based bookkeeper who ran afoul of his state's regulations after he had been in business for more than a year. "Since I was doing accounting work, I called myself an accountant, which you are allowed to do in many states, but not mine. Somebody complained to the state licensing authorities—I'm guessing it was one of my competitors who has been jealous of my success—and I had to change all of materials. I had to print up new business cards, new stationary, and change my ads. I'm frustrated now because the average person on the street can look at my ads and not really understand what I can do for them. It's been a big, huge headache."

Working from your home does not protect you from the same start-up headaches and legal hoops through which most companies must jump. In fact, working from your home might add a few hoops in the form of zoning problems or neighbors who don't want to live next to businesses. In setting up your own bookkeeping practice, you need to resolve a number of legal issues, including:

- Local zoning laws.
- The form of your business.
- State and federal licensing requirements.
- Protecting the name of your business.
- Insuring your business.
- Taxation.

There are worse ways to spend a couple of hours (and a couple of hundred dollars) than getting start-up advice from an attorney who already knows the ropes. If you do talk to an attorney, make sure she knows specifically about home-based businesses. Get recommendations from other home-based businesspeople who are happy with their lawyers, and ask your lawyer up front if she's guided businesses similar to yours through establishment. If, however, you have more time than money, you can learn most of the basics yourself.

Zoning requirements

It seems unfair, but many communities are working against the national trend of home-based businesses by passing new rules that prohibit them when millions of Americans are seeing the advantages of working at home. Neighbors are perhaps concerned that parking problems might ensue if clients formed a steady stream to your door (don't we all wish!). Or, they might worry about the appearance of the neighborhood if your business started looking too much like a business, including neon signs and a paved front yard. Or, your neighbors might simply be people who are afraid of something new. Older local zoning laws do prohibit businesses in residential areas, but many of these are a throwback to another era, when "business" meant manufacturing or retail, both of which imply a much greater disruption in a neighborhood setting.

Even if you have zoning ordinances where you live, they might not restrict you from running a home-based bookkeeping business. They might, however, limit certain aspects of your business, such as parking activity. Many bookkeepers get around parking restrictions by visiting clients at the clients' offices, rather than asking clients to come to the bookkeeper. This approach serves two functions at once, as clients who are hiring bookkeepers tend to be time-squeezed anyway and view on-site visits from their bookkeepers as a value-added service.

Zoning laws might also restrict the size of the business you have at home, the number of employees, or even the percentage of your house that you use to run your business. Don't judge these rules too harshly: they might do you a favor, too. Often, home-based businesses build to a size that is no longer contained within the spare bedroom. Those businesses start to take over the lives of these people, room by room and closet by closet. (I know one entrepreneur who keeps his copier and fax in his kitchen, his computer on the dining room table, and his employees in the house's two bedrooms). Others businesses get to a point where they have several employees and more than three desks and the owners know it's time to go office-space shopping. Another common zoning rule restricts the number, size, and appearance of any signs you post outside your home. Most home-based bookkeepers aren't counting on drive-by trade, however, and need no signs whatsoever to run a profitable business.

To determine your own zoning situation, call both your city and your county zoning boards because both might have rules that apply. Ask which zone your home is in; whether businesses are allowed, and what restrictions are placed on those businesses. If local laws do prohibit you from operating your business, you can seek a variance or waiver. Or, (you didn't read this here) you can consider operating anyway. Particularly if you go out to visit clients, your bookkeeping business will be low impact enough that it won't disturb your neighbors or the ambiance of your neighborhood. And if you have a good relationship with your neighbors, it's unlikely that anyone will take the trouble or the time to report you.

Don't forget, too, that if you live in a planned community or cooperative building, they have their own rules and restrictions on the conduct of business at home. In these instances, it is especially worth cultivating sympathetic neighbors.

Your business format

You have several choices of your business format, but, practically speaking, most independent, one-person, work-at-home service businesses opt for "sole-proprietor" status.

Sole proprietorship

As a sole proprietor, your business expenses and income are reported as part of your personal income tax package. You *are* the company, and the company is you. A sole proprietorship is the simplest to create. In many states, if you are operating under your own name, you don't have to do anything until tax time. You don't have to see a lawyer, draw up technical documents, or find backers.

Sole-proprietor status allows you to deduct your business expenses, set up a tax-deferred retirement program, and get a tax write-off for using your home office. Sole proprietorship, however, doesn't offer you any immunity from personal liability for the debts or misdeeds of your company. As you'll soon see, though, there really isn't a structure that does protect you when you are a one-man (or woman) business. A major advantage to sole proprietorship is that it allows you to deduct depreciation and expenses for your home office. That's a tax break that can be worth thousands of dollars a year and is unavailable to incorporated businesses.

Partnership

A partnership is similar to a sole proprietorship except that there is more than one owner of the business. Several of the bookkeepers interviewed for this book did work with partners; they found it easier to get their business started when they could split the work. In some cases, one partner does the bulk of the bookkeeping while the other handles the clients. You may find a partner that is better at marketing than you and can run the office and leave you free to do the accounting. Mary Olcott Greiner of Arlington, Virginia, for example, works with a partner who specializes in taxes. Mary does the monthly bookkeeping, her partner does the tax preparation and payments.

Corporation

Several forms of incorporation are available to businesses, even small businesses, but look before you leap. The traditional advantages of incorporation—broader deductibility for fringe benefits and liability limits—are not as solidly available as you might think. And the costs of incorporating can be high.

A classic C corporation can provide tax advantages. You can set your corporate fiscal year as different from your personal tax year and use the different dates to shift income to later periods. Money kept in the corporation is not taxed as income to you, but the corporation itself is taxed on profits, and then you are taxed on your salary income. If you don't distribute the income from the corporation carefully, then, you can end up paying more in taxes instead of less. S corporations—more typically used by small businesses—allow you to pass through corporate income and pay taxes on it at the same rate as your personal income. But an S corporation causes you to lose one of the bigger benefits of incorporating—full deductibility of fringe benefits. Fringes such as health insurance and life insurance, which are deductible for corporate employees, are not deductible for owners of S corporations. The main reason most small businesspeople choose incorporation is because they believe it provides immunity from lawsuits. This idea, however, is a myth. In a one-person company, the only real immunity is a solid liability insurance policy.

"The world has wised up to the corporate entrepreneur hiding behind the corporate veil," write attorneys Robert A. Esperti and Reeno L. Peterson, in *Incorporating Your Talents: A Guide to the One-Person Corporation* (McGraw-Hill, Inc., 1984). "It is sad that so many people believe so strongly in a limited liability that rarely exists."

Licensing requirements

You might be required to register your business in your state, county, or municipality. Many localities don't care, but some do. Repeat your zoning phone calls, but ask about business licenses this time. If you must file a business license, expect the costs to be minimal. Expect, too, for your name to be sold to entrepreneurs who use direct mail to sell to listed businesses. If it hasn't already, the junk mail will start soon.

Because you are in a financial profession, your state might have special licensing requirements. Depending on how much education you have in accounting, you might find that you fit into a special class of accountants who are not CPAs but who still can (or must) get special state licenses and meet continuous education or service requirements. Every state has a board of accountancy (appendix A provides a state-by-state list). Write to your state board for a complete list of the requirements for accountants, CPAs, and bookkeepers in your state.

You really don't have much to worry about protecting the name of your business unless your name happens to be H.R. Block or Price Waterhouse. While business name trademarks are crucial and proprietary, the standards of exclusivity and protection are less stringent for small local businesses (especially service businesses) than they are for nationally known companies or nationally distributed products.

You can, of course, establish a business under your own name without jumping through any legal hoops. You might decide, however, to pick a different or descriptive name for your business, such as "Seven Day Bookkeeping Service," for example. Chapter 9 describes how to pick a good business name that can help you get clients. Once you've settled on a name for your business, you might be required to register the name with your state or county as an assumed name or a "doing business as" name, as in Linda Stern, DBA Seven Day Bookkeeping Service.

If you take these steps, make sure nobody else starts operating a bookkeeping service with the same name as yours. If they do, gently let them know that you're already using that name. If you are concerned that clients looking for you will go to them instead, you can take legal action to keep the other company from using your company name.

There are limits, however. Don't expect to get far in court if your company name is strictly generic and descriptive, such as "Joe's Professional Bookkeeping Service." If Moe wants to go into business across the street, you most likely won't be able to keep him from using the same words on his business cards.

Insuring your business might be the scariest topic of this book, and of your business start-up. Not only do you have to think of the dark side and imagine all the things that can go wrong with your bookkeeping business, you have to talk to insurance salespeople!

Before buying a business insurance package, take a minute to think about the risks involved. Don't assume your homeowners insurance covers an additional $10,000 in business equipment that you never mentioned to your agent until *after* the fire. Don't assume your clients are your friends and won't sue you if you make mistakes because they'll know your intentions were honorable.

Realize that liability is the one area where you might prefer not to call yourself an accountant. The past few years have seen such a rash of lawsuits against independent auditors that the American Institute of CPAs calls it "an epidemic of litigation that is threatening the independent auditing function and financial reporting system" of the United States. CPAs are sued with regularity because they (1) prepare audits of companies that later develop problems and blame the auditors; (2) miss tax deadlines or make costly mistakes on tax returns; (3) take responsibility for managing somebody's money and find themselves in charge of a failed portfolio; (4) give bad business or investment advice (or give good advice that the client misinterprets, misuses, or just rues at some later date); and (5) give managerial advice that can go bad.

Contrast that with this statement by Stephen Sahlein, copresident of the American Institute of Professional Bookkeepers: "I cannot think of any instances where a bookkeeper was held liable for an error, and I don't know of any cases where a bookkeeper was sued just for keeping books." Of course, as Sahlein points out, the more you do for your clients the more you risk. And tax-preparing bookkeepers have their own legal issues, which are explained in depth in chapter 15.

For the most part, your insurance needs are limited, though not insignificant. You probably need the following types of insurance:

- Property insurance.
- Liability insurance.
- Expanded business liability, including errors and omissions insurance.

Don't forget personal insurance either. If you are supporting your family (even if you are the supplemental and not the primary breadwinner) you need life insurance and disability insurance as well. If you can't get health insurance through a spouse or other family member, you will also need to think of health insurance.

Taxation

Chapter 11 covers income tax issues thoroughly. Be aware, however, that you might encounter certain other business tax requirements. You must pay self-employment taxes (Social Security and Medicare) on top of your regular income taxes. You will also need to learn how to pay quarterly estimated taxes on the income you expect to have every year because you don't have a third-party employer withholding and paying the taxes for you. Some counties and municipalities levy special business taxes that you cannot escape as a home-based business. Besides the aforementioned licensing fees, these could include asset-based taxes, such as property taxes on the computers, desks, and fax machines that your business owns.

Until now, most service organizations did not worry much about sales taxes. Unless you sold a product, you didn't have to collect the state's share from your clients and customers. Hard times, however, are forcing states to go further with service taxes and, in the future, you might find yourself assessing and passing through taxes to your state for the services you perform. Most service-representing trade associations are fighting these laws nationwide, and the first one passed, in Florida, was rolled back after much opposition. Watch this issue carefully!

A fine line always exists between not going far enough and going too far when you talk about legal issues. You can obsess about getting every "i" dotted and "t" crossed and every eventuality covered and never actually do any business. For a good overview of the specifics of small business law, read *The Legal Guide for Starting & Running A Small Business* (1992, Nolo Press) by Fred Steingold. Nolo's an attorney who specializes in small businesses and explains everything you need to know in great detail, but with an approachable, open style.

Read the sidebar for quick tips on the legal issues of starting your business.

Zoning Don't let zoning inquiries delay the start-up of your business. Continue to establish your business and assume that you will not meet any barriers to bookkeeping. If you do, you can deal with these barriers as an already-existing business.

To incorporate or not If you are on your own, start out as a sole proprietor. You can always incorporate later.

Names Browse through the yellow and white pages of your local phone book after you pick your business name. If you don't see it in the phone book, chances are it's yours to use.

Insurance Call the insurance company that sold you your homeowner's policy and see how much of business insurance can be piggybacked onto your personal plan. Chances are, given the limited nature of your business, you can obtain an inexpensive business rider that covers your business equipment as well as basic liability insurance, which protects you in the case of, say, a client slipping on your steps and breaking his leg while delivering a monthly package of receipts.

Most bookkeepers interviewed for this book operated without errors and omissions policies in insurance, which can be costly and, according to Sahlien, are seldom used. If you get property and liability coverage, you can take your time looking for a more full-featured business liability policy if you prefer to err on the side of caution.

The last word on legal issues

Quick start tips

6 To franchise or not to franchise

If you are new to bookkeeping, new to self-employment, new to your local business community, or you just need a hand to hold, you might want to consider buying into a national franchise rather than starting a business on your own. A good bookkeeping/accounting business franchise can give you moral support as well as practical guidance for your business. It can support your marketing efforts with national advertising, answer your technical questions with tax and accounting experts, and provide you with a computer, software, and business forms. It can also cost you an arm and a leg, so tread carefully!

Roger Goodeve of Windham, Vermont, has been a General Business Services (GBS) franchisee for 18 years. What started as a bookkeeping business for Goodeve is now a comprehensive home-based business advisory/tax preparation service that charges $90 per hour, and Goodeve gives all the credit to GBS. "I don't think I could have set this business up and started on my own," he says. "GBS gave me a business of my own, but in which I was not alone. It gave me the format to run my business, taught me how to go out and get clients, and taught me about what kind of service the clients needed.

"The really important things it gave me," Goodeve continues, (he tends to gush when questioned about GBS) "was tax preparation and tax research and advisory departments that gave me answers to technical questions. The final thing it still gives me is the synergy that comes from being part of a group. We GBS franchisees in Vermont, New Hampshire, and Maine meet just about every month."

All this support comes at a substantial price. To buy into a GBS franchise today, you need a $25,000, up-front franchise fee, and you must demonstrate that you have $25,000 more for start-up equipment and working capital. Once in business, you then must pay GBS annual royalties of 10 percent on your first $120,000 in billings and 1 percent on billings over that.

Not everyone thinks it's worth it. Joe Latin, a Kensington, Maryland accountant and tax preparer, originally bought into the GBS franchise hoping it would help set up his business and draw new clients. He was disappointed in the results. "It was a fine franchising idea, but they just didn't do a good job, and a lot of people left them."

In fact, so many people left GBS that the company found itself in chapter 11 bankruptcy reorganization. In mid-1992, the firm was sold to LGC, Inc., a subsidiary of a large Canadian firm. LGC is breathing new life into the franchises with a proprietary electronic network, a marketing plan for franchisees, greater hands-on service, and an outreach program. Latin concedes that the new GBS is doing many things right, but has found that, with his own expertise and his membership in several professional associations, he didn't need the hand-holding or continuing royalty costs. You can buy a lot of tax advice for $25,000 up-front and $12,000 a year, he points out.

Cost/benefit analysis

There are advantages to aligning with a national franchise. Just performing the market research you should do before signing up with any franchise will give you a much better idea of the local market for bookkeeping, even if you ultimately decide to go it alone. A national franchiser can offer valuable networking opportunities with others in your field, as well as support in the business management issues that arise when running your own office. See the sidebar for the largest bookkeeping franchises.

Major bookkeeping franchises

The following franchisers are the major ones in the bookkeeping/accounting and business services fields. If you are seriously considering franchises, research *all* of them before making your selection.

AFTE Business Analyst
2180 North Loop West
Suite 300
Houston, TX 77018
(713) 957-1592

AFTE provides a training program and software to enable someone with no bookkeeping background to get started. Franchise fee is $4000.

Advantage Payroll Services
800 Center Street
Auburn, ME 04210
(800) 323-9648

Advantage's central mainframe computer processes payroll information for you via your personal computer.

General Business Services
7134 Columbia Gateway Drive
Columbia, MD 21046
(410) 290-1040

GBS franchisees offer tax planning and financial management services as well as bookkeeping.

Comprehensive Business Services
1925 Palomar Oaks Way, #115
Carlsbad, CA 92008
(800) 323-9000

CBS franchisees take a 21-week training program on accounting and practice management.

E.K. Williams & Co.
8774 Yates Drive, Suite 210
Westminster, CO 80030
(800) 255-2359

Broader than bookkeeping, these franchisees are set up to offer many business management services, including recordkeeping systems and computer consulting. Franchise fee is $25,000.

Triple Check Income Tax Service
Triple Check Business Services
727 South Main Street
Burbank, CA 91506
(818) 840-9078

Triple Check has two different franchise programs: one for tax preparation and another for bookkeeping and other consulting services.

Risks are involved, but franchising today does not present the same out-and-out risk of scams that dogged the industry in the 1960s and early 1970s before the Federal Trade Commission regulated franchising in 1979. Enough bad deals and unsavory offers still exist out there, though, to make the buyer beware. Figure 6-1 presents a quick comparison of the advantages and disadvantages of going franchise.

Pros	Cons

Pros	Cons
■ Training on bookkeeping issues and on how to run your business.	■ Higher up-front expenses.
	■ Continuing royalty requirements.
■ Technical support on accounting questions.	■ Software use may be restricted.
■ Networking opportunities.	■ Lack of total freedom in how you run your business.
■ Continuing seminars in your field.	■ Bookkeeping is a field in which personal reputation counts; a national name might not help you win clients as much as word of mouth.
■ National advertising and marketing.	
■ A business identity that may attract customers.	
■ A proven business system that you know works.	
■ Possible tax filing assistance, electronic filing.	

6-1
Advantages and disadvantages of buying into a business service franchise.

Check it out If you are interested in franchising, play with the possibilities by requesting a sales kit from some of the franchiser companies listed in the sidebar. Make sure you request and receive a Uniform Franchise Offering Circular disclosure document, the federally mandated disclosure statement that includes details you must know before making a decision.

While considering the franchise alternatives, the companies will wine and dine you and treat you like you're very special. Regard the pre-investment period as seriously as you would any mate-selecting courting period, however. Will they still treat you special once you're married? Take the precautions described in the following subsections before you sign on any dotted lines. Finally, make sure you ask the questions listed in the sidebar before you sign up.

Ten questions to ask a franchiser

1. Will I have to use your software, your forms, journals, or other products?
2. How many franchisees do you have? What is their average length of affiliation with you?
3. How many franchisees (or what percentage) have you lost and how many (or what percentage) have you retained over a three- or five-year period?
4. How will you attract clients to me?
5. How well do you know the bookkeeping or accounting market, nationally and in my region?
6. What are the total start-up costs I will incur if I sign with you?

7. How can I terminate the arrangement if I decide I'd rather go it alone?
8. What type of training do you provide?
9. Do you have an ongoing technical support service for tax, finance, and accounting questions?
10. What is the average income of your franchisees *per franchise*?

Analyze personality—yours and theirs   Make sure you are the type of person to fare well under a franchise system. People who do best are those that are self-directed but do not chafe under advice, according to John Hayes, a Fort Washington, Pennsylvania franchising consultant. "If you consider yourself a real maverick, you should go off on your own and do it without a franchise relationship."

Carefully analyze the personality of the franchisers with whom you would be working. Never buy into a franchise without first visiting the home office and sitting down with the company's key contacts. Some franchisers may want to have little involvement with you, other than collecting royalties. Others will have extensive support networks that can train you to hire employees, keep books, attract business, and other such services. "If you find the people offensive for any reason, go elsewhere," says Hayes.

In analyzing the corporate culture of a potential franchise, find out how well the executives running the headquarters company know accounting and bookkeeping. Are they up to date on the market and the latest computerized accounting techniques? One of the first changes LGC made once it bought GBS was to eliminate any executives who didn't understand the franchisees from the top-heavy corporate headquarters. "All the senior people in this company have run these kinds of businesses themselves," says John Macdonald, executive vice president of franchise relations.

Think carefully about what you are buying   Franchisers can charge 10 percent or more in royalties for their business guidance and moral support, and an additional 2 percent or more for advertising. Up-front fees can run $25,000 or more, and that doesn't even include your own start-up costs of equipment, supplies, and cash to live on until you start making money. If the company in question offers a good name that will draw customers, that name can be worth the costs. If the company doesn't offer something like that, you might be better off starting your own business and buying your advice on an ad hoc basis from attorneys, consultants, and professional trade associations.

Study the *Uniform Franchise Offering Circular*   Study this document with a magnifying glass. Make sure your territory is protected; that your franchiser can't put another competitor a block (or even a mile) away. Don't sign a contract that forces you to sell the franchise back to the parent company for a predetermined fee if you want out. Be wary of companies that want you to buy costly forms and supplies from them, whether you need them or not. Review the company's failure rate.

Get references   Call some of the firm's other franchisees from different regions (who won't view you as a competitor, as some in your own area might) for a frank review of the pros and cons. Look in the phone book to see if any franchises are near you. Call these local franchises and find out whether they think there's room for one more or not. (If they all offer to sell to you, run for the exit!)

Hire an attorney   If you are serious about buying a franchise and you think you've found one that's right for you, hire a lawyer who specializes in franchise contracts to review yours and negotiate the deal for you. It could be the best money you ever spend.

The International Trade Association for Franchises   Finally, for more information about franchises, contact the International Franchise Association at the address provided. This group has a library of advice on how to find and select a franchise that will work for you. You can contact them at:

International Franchise Association
1350 New York Avenue, NW
Suite 900
Washington, DC 20005
(202) 628-8000

7 Bookkeeping fundamentals

> *"When you make the mistake of adding the date*
> *to the right side of the accounting statement,*
> *you must add it to the left side, too."*
>
> **— Accountant's maxim**

Double-entry bookkeeping has been around since the late fifteenth century when Leonardo da Vinci's friend, Luca Pacioli, first wrote about it in his *Summa de arithmetica, geometria, proportioni et proportionalita*. Many people still don't get it, however. The words *debit* and *credit* are used so loosely (and often so inaccurately) in colloquial speech that most people who are not accounting professionals do not understand the fact that these words just mean something like "left" and "right" and not "minus" and "plus." Stripped of its jargon, the fundamental fact of bookkeeping is this: Whenever a transaction occurs, money comes *from* somewhere and goes *to* somewhere. The purpose of double-entry bookkeeping is to ensure that records of both somewheres are kept, and that they match up.

Today, even accountants and bookkeepers are often shielded from true double-entry accounting by software that does it for them. A few years ago, you might have painstakingly recorded the same number in two different places to keep a ledger balanced. Today, even low-end checkbook programs force you to choose accounts to debit and credit for every transaction entered. Although you'll never see those words in many of the programs.

It's worth reviewing the fundamentals of bookkeeping and accounting here, even if you intend to spend your entire professional life guided by an all-knowing computer program. If you understand the why and wherefore of traditional double entry bookkeeping, you can better select a computer program and keep financial records in a manner that better fulfills the records' traditional purpose as well as your clients' needs.

Think of this chapter as a quick review of the basic concepts of bookkeeping. This chapter will not teach you accounting—that would take a whole other book (or series of books). If you aren't already an accounting professional, you can use one of the methods previously described in chapter 3 to train yourself for financial recordkeeping.

Accounting & financial reports

The purpose of accounting is to accumulate, organize, and report quantitative information about a business for a variety of reasons. End-users of accounting are the following:

- Business owners and their managers, who use the reports to make decisions about the conduct of the business.
- Lenders and suppliers, who use the reports to determine when the business is a worthwhile credit risk.
- Federal, state, and local tax authorities, who use the reports to determine appropriate tax liability.
- Investors or potential purchasers, who use the reports to determine the value of the company as an investment.

The only way that all these different users can find worth in the same reports is if the reports are standardized; therefore, a good set of financial books for a company carries standard information in standard formats.

Accounting standards

Bookkeeping standards come from many sources, including the Securities and Exchange Commission and the American Institute of Certified Public Accountants. Since the early 1970s, however, most have come from the Financial Accounting Standards Board (FASB), a widely recognized and respected independent board with more political clout than its name might suggest.

In the late 1980s, for example, the Board's requirement that companies account in current years for retirement promises of the future rocked corporate pension departments and caused investor consternation. What appeared a dull, dry accounting rule was actually a dramatic shift in business practices that many thought protected the pensions of future generations yet others believed ruined the balance sheets of the present.

In 1980, the FASB published *Qualitative Characteristics of Accounting Information*, which has become the basis for all accounting reports. Think about these requirements as you select reporting systems and organize data for clients. According to the FASB, accounting reports must be:

- useful
- relevant
- reliable
- verifiable
- user independent
- understandable
- comparable
- complete

Reports must be useful   They must be organized such that all users can understand and work with them.

Reports must be relevant   Financial reports must be directed at the questions end users most want answered.

Reports must be reliable   The work must be free from error and bias. Computer programs, of course, greatly reduce the chance of mathematical error, but good bookkeepers and accountants must also know how to correctly classify data to produce worthwhile reports. The lack of bias can be a selling point when promoting your services as an independent contractor: a business owner who keeps his own books might be tempted to let his love of his company overshadow the stark realities of his balance sheet.

Reports must be verifiable   Two (or more) accountants reviewing the same numbers must be able to reach the same conclusions.

Reports must be independent   Financial reports must be created without deference to the end-users. A business profit and loss statement prepared for a lender, for example, should be the same as that company's statement would be were it prepared for the company's owner or the Internal Revenue Service. Different results for different users is not only unethical and a violation of FASB standards, it makes the information less useful to other end-users.

Reports must be understandable   Much of your skill as an independent bookkeeper depends on your ability to explain "what it all means" to your clients. Many people can't read a balance sheet or ledger; clarity of design and simplicity of textual explanation will be great selling points for your business.

Reports must be timely   A quarterly statement that arrives more than a quarter late is not much help; financial reports must be developed and delivered quickly enough to be useful. This requirement will put pressure on you as you manage your practice: many clients will want their monthly statements prepared as early as possible in the following month; they will all want year-end reports generated as soon as possible in the new tax season. In some cases, such as for estimated income taxes and payroll taxes, failure to deliver timely information can be penalized by government fines.

Reports must be comparable   Investors know that financial statements must be comparable. If a company splits its stock, for example, it often generates "split-adjusted" financial reports so the firm's followers can compare pre-split and post-split results. Similarly, results from more than one firm must be made on the same basis, and results within a firm must be reported consistently so that end-users can compare one period with another.

Reports must be complete   A balance sheet listing assets but no liabilities wouldn't be of much use. Solid financial reports include all the financial activities of the firm during the period covered. All relevant information about a company's financial picture should be included in its financial reports.

Conventions & concepts

In addition to the preceding characteristics that underlie good accounting work, certain concepts exist that all accountants and bookkeepers use to keep their work comparable and reliable. These universal concepts are:

- The stable dollar.
- The business entity.
- The continuing concern.
- The cost principle.

The stable dollar concept

The stable dollar concept is one in which all financial report writers and readers agree to pretend that the value of the dollar does not change. Of course, the value of a dollar *does* change, and an asset valued at $20,000 in 1965 and one valued at $20,000 today would probably have very different real, inflation-adjusted values. It would be almost impossible to prepare monthly statements and quarterly reports, however, if you had to constantly adjust your figures for U.S. inflation, as well as any fluctuations of U.S. currency on foreign markets. By agreeing to use the stable dollar concept, it is easier for accountants and bookkeepers to prepare and compare reports. Of course, you can always provide inflation-adjusted figures to clients who want to see how their asset values have held up.

The business entity concept

The business entity concept means that every business is treated as a separate entity, distinct from other businesses and its owners. The business entity concept can be difficult to enforce, especially when businesses are sole proprietorships, exclusively held by one person who commingles his money and assets with those of his company. It can be similarly difficult for the occasional entrepreneur who tries to run several businesses at once from the same office, borrowing from Peter Enterprises to pay Paul and Associates.

Ultimately, your clients will appreciate the business entity approach; it's the only way they can really find out how well their businesses are performing.

The continuing concern concept

Continuing concern simply means that you expect the business to keep running and keep needing the assets it bought. Therefore, those assets do not need to be reassessed (or revalued on the balance sheet) with their market values. Unless you are preparing financial statements for a business about to be sold, you continue to carry the assets on the books at their initial cost, minus the amount they've depreciated. The continuing concern concept works with the *cost principle*, which states that acquired assets be carried on the books at their cost value, rather than their market value or some other theoretical measure of their true worth.

Adequacy of accounting records

One of the questions to ask is whether your clients have enough of the right types of records. A list of records that SCORE, the Small Business Administration's Service Corp of Retired Executives, uses to evaluate company accounting systems is provided in the sidebar. You can use this list to evaluate your own accounting methods or to teach your clients about the types of records they should be keeping. Use it to ask potential clients whether they are getting all the information they want and need from their current bookkeeping system or service.

SCORE's accounting system evaluation

_____ Are monthly statements readily available?

_____ Does a complete accounting system exist?

_____ Does the present system involve excess posting?

_____ Would a combined journal-ledger system reduce the work of the system?

_____ Can the owner quickly tell the amounts owed by credit customers (is there an accounts receivable ledger of some type)?

_____ Can the owner quickly tell the balances owed to creditors (is there an accounts payable ledger of some type)?

_____ Can sales be divided into departments, chief lines of merchandise, or special items?

_____ Does the system provide a means of identifying the profitability of individual departments or lines of merchandise?

_____ Do the monthly adjustments include the proper charges for depreciation, amortization, and new inventories?

_____ What information, not currently or easily available, does the owner need?

_____ Does the company take advantage of purchase discounts? Do the records provide notice of discount periods?

_____ Do the procedures include regular aging of accounts receivable?

_____ Does the accounting system produce meaningful control reports?

Financial statements & journals

Financial statements are the backbone of your business. You are most likely already very familiar with them. If not, you will be!

The profit/ loss statement

Also known as the income statement, the profit/loss (P/L) statement is the most important report you provide for most businesses. It lists all of the company's income and then subtracts all of its expenses. The resulting dollar left at the bottom is the profit (or loss) that the company experienced. Many clients will want you to prepare a monthly or quarterly P/L statement; all of your clients will need one at the end of the year to prepare their taxes.

For single proprietors, a profit and loss statement can look a lot like the Internal Revenue Service's Schedule C. In fact, organizing your client's expenses into those categories specified on Schedule C (or Form 1065 if the business is a partnership) will save quite a bit of time during tax season. Figure 7-1 shows a very simple profit and loss statement. A more complicated one, based on the deductions listed in Schedule C, is shown in FIG. 7-2.

Smith and Daughters Public Relations

Profit/Loss Statement

7-1
Simple profit and loss statement.

Income

Sales revenues	$92,000.00
Interest income	$55.00
Total revenues	$92,055.00

Expenses

Salaries	$18,000.00
Office expenses	$15,124.00
Total expenses	$33,124.00

Net Income	$56,931.00

Smith and Daughters Public Relations

Profit/Loss Statement

Income

Sales revenues	$92,000.00
Other income	$55.00
Total income	$92,055.00

Expenses

Advertising	$1200.00
Bad debts	0.00
Car expenses	$980.00
Insurance	$459.00
Interest	240.00
Legal services	$1375.00
Professional services	$1995.00
Office expenses	$875.00
Rent	$4800.00
Repairs	$85.00
Supplies	$295.00
Taxes	$320.00
Travel	$2500.00
Salaries	$18,000.00
Total expenses	$33,124.00

Net Income $56,931.00

7-2
Detailed profit and loss statement based on Schedule C deductions.

A balance sheet is to a company what a net worth statement is to an individual. It measures what you own and subtracts what you owe. The balance sheet is a snapshot of a company's financial condition at any particular time. The balance sheet is also the heart of double-entry accounting. Each side equals the other. The central equation of a balance sheet is

The balance sheet

assets = liabilities + owner's equity

Assets include cash, equipment owned by the company, and money owed to the business (accounts receivable). Liabilities are any money the business owes others (accounts payable), including credit cards, loan balances, employee benefits, and taxes.

Most business owners like to see the balance sheet flipped: What do they really own? That equation looks like this:

$$\text{owner's equity} = \text{assets} - \text{liabilities}$$

Whenever an unequal change in assets and liabilities occurs, owner's equity changes.

The balance sheet and profit and loss statement work together. At the end of the year, assuming the owner adds no more money to the company and takes no more out, the change in "owner's equity" should equal the profit or loss that the business had. A simple balance sheet is shown in FIG. 7-3.

Smith and Daughters Public Relations

Balance Sheet

7-3
Simple balance sheet.

Assets		Equities & Liabilities	
Cash	$2400.00	Accounts Payable	$1200.00
Equipment	$2500.00	Paid-in capital	$3700.00
Total assets	$4900.00	Total equities	$4900.00

Journals

A bookkeeper enters every transaction into a journal, which is nothing more than a list of transactions. When a manual system is used, the bookkeeper might enter all transactions into one journal, or might keep separate journals for different business activities, such as a cash disbursements journal, an inventory journal, or a sales journal.

A journal consists of several accounts, each of which can be arranged as a "T" with the left side of the "T" for debits and the right side for credits. Any transaction entered into the journal must have a debit (Dr) and an offsetting credit (Cr). Put as simply as possible, debits are *increases* to asset and expense accounts and *decreases* to liability and equity accounts.

There are five types of T accounts: asset, liability, equity, income, and expense accounts. Asset T accounts, such as equipment or cash, look like the account shown in FIG. 7-4. Liability T accounts, such as accounts payable, look like the account shown in FIG. 7-5. Equity T accounts, such as paid-in capital, look like the account shown in FIG. 7-6. Income T accounts, such as sales, look like the account shown in FIG. 7-7. Finally, expense T accounts, such as rent, look like FIG. 7-8.

Equipment

Debit	Credit
Increase	Decrease
+	-

7-4
Asset "T" account.

Accounts Payable

Debit	Credit
Decrease	Increase
-	+

7-5
Liability "T" account.

Paid-in Capital

Debit	Credit
Decrease	Increase
-	+

7-6
Equity "T" account.

Sales

Debit	Credit
Decrease	Increase
-	+

7-7
Income "T" account.

Rent

Debit	Credit
Increase	Decrease
+	-

7-8
Expense "T" account.

Assume, for example, that a business owner takes $5,000 out of his pocket to start, or capitalize, the business. To record that in a ledger, you debit (increase) the cash account on the asset side by $5,000 and credit (increase) the paid-in capital account on the liability side by $5,000 as well.

If the owner then spends $2,000 from the company's new cash account to buy a computer, you increase (or debit) the equipment account by $2,000 and credit (or decrease) the cash account by the same amount.

He then buys $1,200 in software and puts it on his Mastercard reserved for business. You increase (debit) the supplies account and increase (credit) the accounts payable account.

Finally, the business owner makes a $250 payment on his Mastercard bill. The accounts payable account is decreased (debited) and the cash account is also decreased (credited). These transactions are shown in a simplified journal format in FIG. 7-9.

A more sophisticated journal, such as the ones in most computer programs (or on a really wide piece of paper) have dual debit and credit columns for each category (or account) of assets and liabilities.

The general ledger A bookkeeper using a manual system periodically copies journal transactions into a general ledger, called *posting*. The general ledger is where all the accounting information collected is brought together. In a manual system, the general ledger can have a separate page (or pages) for the different

	Debit	Credit
1. Owner pays $5,000 into company		
Cash	$5,000	
Paid-in capital		$5,000
2. Buys computer, pay cash		
Equipment	$2,000	
Cash		$2,000
3. Buys software, on credit card		
Supplies	$1,200	
Accounts payable		$1,200
4. Makes credit card payment		
Accounts payable	$250	
Cash		$250

7-9
Simplified journal.

account categories used in the ledger. The balance sheet and income statement are then created from the general ledger.

In today's computerized accounting systems, almost all of the preceding debiting and crediting occurs automatically. Most programs will not allow you to enter an unbalanced (single-entry) transaction, and most will automatically place transactions in their proper journals and then post the journal entries to the general ledger.

Of course, much more exists in accounting work, and the process gets much more complicated than described in this chapter. Assets purchased are used up, equipment is depreciated, and cash flow is tracked. The heart of it all remains the same, however. Transactions are entered by accounts into journals and then posted to ledgers, from whence balance sheets, profit and loss statements, and all other useful information flows.

Computerization & complications

8 Computerized accounting

Your accounting software package is your bread and butter, your silent partner, your office mate, and the heart of your business. Choose it as carefully as you would any of these. Invest the time and effort to find a program that does what you need in a way you enjoy. You can choose from an array of products (FIG. 8-1).

The good news about accounting software is that it has dropped dramatically in price. Even high-end programs are responding to market forces by dropping their costs to easily manageable levels. Peachtree Insight Accounting for the Macintosh, for example, was a series of five accounting modules offered for $395 each. Recently repackaged as a single, stand-alone program, Insight Accounting for the Macintosh lists for $395 retail and can be found for as low as $299 *with* a 30-day money-back guarantee. Lower-end programs, which still claim to have the accounting capabilities most small businesses need, can be found for $100 to $150. *PC Magazine* reports that software with accounting capabilities that cost $5,000 at the beginning of the 1980s now costs under $200.

At today's software prices, you can afford to audition and discard a program and then buy another if you didn't like the first. This statement is true not because you don't have anything better to do with your $100 bills, but because once you are in business, you will discover one thing worse than wasting money on software you don't like: wasting time.

8-1
The startup bookkeeper can choose from an array of accounting programs.
Matt Hightshoe

If you continue to use a program that is not quite right for you and your clients, you can end up spending many, many hours rekeying information from one program to another when you finally decide to change software. While many of the high-end accounting programs do have the ability to import data from other programs, some do not. Take advantage of any 30-day money-back guarantees to try software you aren't sure about. Go to local software stores and ask the salespeople to put different accounting programs on the screen for you. Really get a feel for a program before you start keying all of your clients' data into it. The leading accounting/bookkeeping packages are listed in the sidebar. The most popular packages are reviewed later in this chapter.

Leading accounting software packages

ACT 1 Plus Accounting
Cougar Mountain Software
PO Box 6886
Boise, ID 83707
(208) 344-2540

ACCPAC Simply Accounting
Computer Associates Intl., Inc.
One Computer Associates Plaza

Islandia, NY 11788-7000
(516) 342-5224

ACCPAC BP Accounting
Computer Associates Intl., Inc.
One Computer Associates Plaza
Islandia, NY 11788-7000
(516) 342-5224

Access To Platinum
Platinum Desktop Software Inc.
15615 Alton Pkwy, #300
Irvine, CA 92718
(800) 999-1891

DacEasy Accounting
DacEasy, Inc.
17950 Preston Road, #800
Dallas, TX 75252
(214) 248-0205

Pacioli 2000
M-USA Business Systems
15806 Midway Road
Dallas, TX 75244
(800) 933-6872

Profitwise
Solomon Software
PO Box 414
Findlay, Ohio 45839
(419) 424-0422

One-Write Plus
MECA Software
PO Box 912
Fairfield, CT 06430-9747
(800) 388-8000

Accountant Inc. (Macintosh only)
Softsync Inc.
800 SW 37th Ave., Bldg. 3770
Coral Gables, FL 33134
(305) 445-0903

Business Vision II
Business Vision Mngmnt. Systems Inc.

2600 Skymark, Bldg. #3
Mississauga, Ontario L4W5B2
(800) 563-2956

Peachtree Basic Accounting
Peachtree Software
1505 Pavilion Place
Norcross, GA 30093
(800) 247-3224

Peachtree Complete Accounting
Peachtree Software
1505 Pavilion Place
Norcross, GA 30093
(800) 247-3224

Peachtree Insight Accounting
for the Macintosh
Peachtree Software
1505 Pavilion Place
Norcross, GA 30093
(800) 247-3224

Peachtree Accounting for Windows
Peachtree Software
1505 Pavilion Place
Norcross, GA 30093
(800) 247-3224

Peachtree Accounting
for the Macintosh
Peachtree Software
1505 Pavilion Place
Norcross, GA 30093
(800) 247-3224

Managing Your Business
Management Information Software
3301 Gandy Blvd.
Tampa, FL 33611
(800) 825-5647

M.Y.O.B.
Teleware
300 Roundhill Drive
Rockaway, NJ 07866
(800) 322-6962

Bookkeeping by Teleware
300 Roundhill Drive
Rochaway, NJ 07866
(800) 322-6962

Harmony
Open Systems, Inc.
7626 Eden Prairie, MN 55344
(800) 328-2276

BusinessWorks
Manzanita Software Systems
2130 Professional Drive #230
Roseville, CA 95611
(916) 781-3880

Accounting software

Accounting packages can look different, operate differently, and be more or less complex, but they all have the same core modules, or sections: general ledger, accounts receivable, and accounts payable. They are also all based on traditional double-entry bookkeeping. Some hide the words *debit* and *credit* and automate the double-entry process; others display screens that look as much as possible like the traditional bookkeeper's ledgers, so that old-timers can feel at home.

All the accounting packages guide you through establishing a chart of accounts, some with an easier process than others. They all provide password protection to the separate accounts. Finally, they all allow you to produce basic balance sheet and profit/loss statements. That is where all similarity ends, however. Sheldon Needle, President of Computer Training Services, Inc., and an expert in analyzing accounting software at all levels, notes that the belief that "all accounting packages are pretty much alike" is one of the great myths of accounting software.

"Differences between systems involve capacity, ease of use, processing speed, documentation, price, and features," he writes in his *Guide to Small Business Accounting Software Priced Under $500* (1992, CTS). "For instance, two packages may be very similar, but one may calculate state income tax withholding for payroll and one may not. Or, one may charge interest to customers on overdue amounts for all accounts, while the other may not do it at all. It is crucial "that you select a system that meets your specific needs," Needle asserts. The last section of this chapter, which reviews accounting software, also describes CTS, Needle's company, in more detail.

A basic accounting program

This section guides you through the various parts of a basic accounting program.

Chart of accounts Just about every accounting program starts with the chart of accounts. This chart is the list of categories you will use to keep track of the sources and destinations of funds: the list of payers and payees. Every business has its own unique chart of accounts, with specific names of vendors and customers, bank account, numbers and addresses. Charts of accounts in similar businesses, however, are usually similar. Appendix B shows some sample charts of accounts for different businesses.

The general ledger The general ledger is the master record of every transaction that occurs in the business for which you are bookkeeping. It includes the chart of accounts, along with the activities for each account for a specified accounting period or the year to date. The key financial statements, including the balance sheet, the income and expense statement, and the trial balances, are drawn from the general ledger. Figure 8-2 shows a sample general ledger report from One-Write Plus Accounting.

8-2
Typical general ledger report from One-Write Plus Accounting.

```
12/16/92 AT 1:20PM                    THE KITE STORE                      PAGE 1
                                GENERAL  LEDGER  REPORT
                          FOR  THE  PERIOD  12/01/92  TO  12/31/92

    DATE      SOURCE        DESCRIPTION              DEBIT           CREDIT
    ----      ------        -----------              -----           ------
    1000 Checking account
                         *** BEGINNING BALANCE ***    6,788.33
    12/12/92  A/P CHK     1-1 #351 MONAD                                34.00
    12/13/92  A/R PMT     1-2 #554 BAKER                342.34
    12/15/92  CHKBK       COD Delivery                                  38.32
    12/15/92  CHKBK       Dec Rent                                   1,100.00
    12/15/92  CHKBK       Dec Tax Deposit                            1,730.23
    12/22/92  A/P CHK     1-2 #352 DENNIS                              150.00
    12/28/92  A/P CHK     1-2 #541 MONAD                                34.00
    12/31/92  A/P CHK     1-1 #672 BYRON                              238.00
    12/31/92  A/R PMT     1-1 BAKER                   1,430.00
                         --- UNPOSTED ITEMS ---                      1,875.00
                                                                   -----------
                         ***   ENDING BALANCE   ***                  3,961.12

    1010 Checking account #2
                         *** BEGINNING BALANCE ***    4,000.00
                                                     -----------
                         ***   ENDING BALANCE   ***   4,000.00

    1100 Accounts receivable
                         *** BEGINNING BALANCE ***   41,635.09
    12/15/92  A/R PMT     1-2 #554 BAKER                               342.34
    12/15/92  A/R INV     1-2 #231 REYNOLDS           3,243.24
    12/15/92  A/R INV     1-2 #672 BAKER                342.34
                         --- UNPOSTED ITEMS ---         457.00
                                                     -----------
                         ***   ENDING BALANCE   ***  45,335.33

    6300 Telephone expense
                         *** BEGINNING BALANCE ***    2,322.40
    12/15/92  A/P PMT     1-2 #678 TELEPHN              156.00
                                                     -----------
                         ***   ENDING BALANCE   ***   2,166.40

                                                     ===========    ===========
                         TOTAL CURRENT ACTIVITY      19,378.40       19,378.40
                                                     ===========    ===========
```

Regardless of how complex an accounting program gets, the general ledger remains at its heart. Figure 8-3 is a flowchart of Peachtree Complete Accounting and its modules. It shows how a typical accounting program is organized. As you can see, information flows to the general ledger.

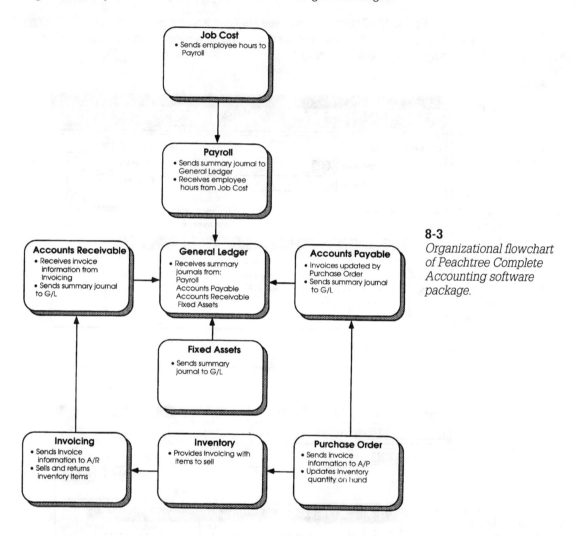

8-3
Organizational flowchart of Peachtree Complete Accounting software package.

Transactions and journals   As in traditional, paper-based accounting, transactions are entered in journals before they go to the general ledger. These journal entries are the typical screens for which you will work in most accounting programs, and the screens come in the form of checks, cash transactions, purchases, sales, payrolls, and other similar transactions. Each transaction is typically entered with a date, amount, account number, and description. Each has a "from" and a "to" category from the chart of accounts. The program tallies the various transactions in their proper journals.

In Peachtree Accounting for Windows, for example, the journal-entry screens all look similar, although they are tailored for the specific type of transaction they record. Figure 8-4 shows the cash receipts journal, FIG. 8-5 shows the purchase journal, and FIG. 8-6 shows the sales journal.

The Pacioli 2000 software package also has a standardized data entry screen, shown in FIG. 8-7. In this window, the program prompts you for the type of transaction you are entering.

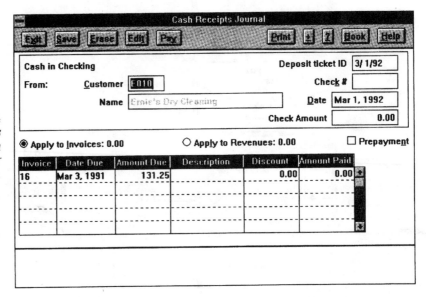

8-4

Sample cash receipts journal screen from Peachtree Accounting for Windows.

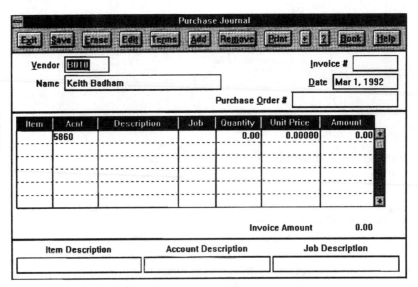

8-5

Sample purchase journal screen from Peachtree Accounting for Windows.

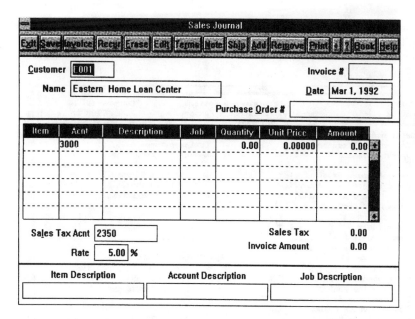

8-6
Sample sales journal screen from Peachtree Accounting for Windows

8-7
Typical transaction screen from Pacioli 2000 software package.

Posting   Moving the transactions from the journals to the general ledger updates the chart of accounts automatically.

Accounts receivable   The accounts receivable part of an accounting program keeps track of payments, sales, and money due to the business and prints invoices. It will generate reports of money owed by age of receivables, assess interest on late accounts, add sales taxes where appropriate, and provide discounts for quick payments when you provide the proper information. Peachtree Accounting provides many options for customizing invoices and reports. Figure 8-8 shows the first screen you see when you start the accounts receivable module.

8-8

Accounts receivable screen from Peachtree programs, which, like most others, allows users many options to customize invoices and accounts receivable reports.
Peachtree Complete Accounting

```
ARMAINTZ                    Maintain A/R Options        COMPANY ID: WD
11/30/92                 W.D. Peachtree & Company       GENERATION #: 11

General Module Options                  Service Charge Options
    Controller Password.....:               Customer Types........: 3
    Operator Password.......:               Amount or Percentage..: P
    Use Menus...............: Y             Min Amount............:      2.00
    Allow Changes/Deletions.: Y             Include Past Charges..: N
    Force Control Reports...: Y             Avg Daily/Ending Bal..: A
    Keep Historical Detail..: N             Service Chg Amts/Pcts
    Current G/L Period......: 11                Code 1.............:      6.00
    Post to General Ledger..: Y                 Code 2.............:     12.00
    Consolidate A/R Trans...: N                 Code 3.............:     18.00
    Check Credit Limit......: Y                 Code 4.............:     21.00
    Generation Number.......: 11
    Print Company Name......: Y          Age Analysis Options
    Print Titles............: Y             Age Period Length.....: 030
    Use Expanded Lookups....: N          Dunning Messages
    Auto Invoice Numbering..: Y             Extended Messages.: N
    Starting Invoice Number.: 23550         Period 1:
    Ending Invoice Number...: 999999        Period 2:
    Invoice Reset Number....:      1        Period 3:
                            Accept (Y/N)..:  Y
F1-Help                                 F8 - Undo                    C N
```

Accounts payable This part of the program keeps track of all the money the business owes by vendor and date. Many programs keep track of discounts available for early payments, or age invoices until just before they are due before prompting you to pay them. When you record a purchase, most programs allow you to specify in which tax-related category the item purchased belongs. Figure 8-9 shows the typical purchase screen from the One-Write Plus software package.

8-9

Accounts payable screen from One-Write Plus Accounting allows swift entries and automatic posting to appropriate expense categories.

Vendor information

Journal lines for recorded transactions

Checking account balance

Distribution columns

Record Purchases and Payments Screen

Account reconciliation   Computers reconcile bank accounts for you automatically! One of the most enjoyable parts of an accounting program, if you are accustomed to manual reconciliation of bank accounts, is this function. Most programs display an account activity screen and let you simply check off those items that have been returned and paid. Figure 8-10 shows the reconcile accounts screen from the M.Y.O.B. software package.

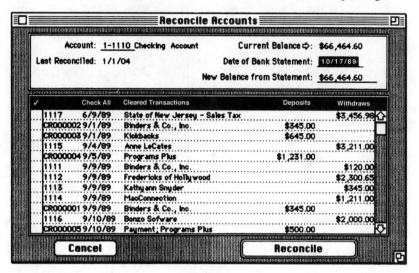

8-10
Bank account reconciliation screen from M.Y.O.B., in which you simply click on the transactions that have cleared and let the program do the rest.
Teleware, Inc.

Reports   The purpose of accounting is to record information accurately, and even the simplest program generates numerous reports—including trial balances, cash flow, balance sheet, income/expense reports, vendor lists, and customer lists. Often, the difference between the more- and less-sophisticated accounting programs is seen in the variety and specificity of reports they produce.

The reports menu screen from M.Y.O.B. shown in FIG. 8-11 allows the user to select from a variety of reports and then customize the selected reports. For example, the sidebar shows the breadth of reports that can be generated from ACCPAC BPI, a mid level accounting program available from Computer Associates. Appendix C shows some sample reports from the same package.

ACCPAC BPI is a full-featured but not top-of-the-line accounting program providing a lengthy list of reports that can be customized to fit your clients' needs. A list of the reports it produces is provided here. Note that most accounting programs generate similar reports, and this list is provided as a sample of the types of statements you'll be able to offer your clients.

ACCPAC BPI Report List

General Ledger Reports

Financial Reports
  Balance Sheet
  Income Statement
  Trial Balance
Transaction Detail Reports
  General Ledger
  General Journal
  Cash Disbursements Journal
  Receipts Journal
  Invoice Journal
  Merchandise Purchased Journal
  Cash Register Journal
  Customer Ledger
  Vendor Ledger
  Earnings Report
  Employee Information
Schedules
  Checkbooks
  Chart of Accounts
  Automatic Journal Entries
  Cash Register Prompts

Accounts Receivable

Transaction Detail Reports
  Receivables Aging Report
  Receivables Account Distribution
  Customer Analysis
  Category Analysis
  Billing Cycle Invoice
  Invoice Exceptions
Journals and Ledgers
  Customer Ledger
  Invoice Journal
  Receipts Journal
Schedules
  Billing Cycles

Payment Terms
  Invoice Journal Prompts
Listings
  Customers
  Automatic Charges
  Finance Charges
Special Forms
  Customer Statements
  Customer Invoices
  Customer Labels
  Customer Index Cards

Accounts Payable

Transaction Detail Reports
  Cash Requirements
  Payables Aging
  Check Selection
  Check Distribution
  Account Distribution
  Activity
  Vendor Status
Journals and Ledgers
  Vendor Ledger
  Voucher Journal
  Check Register
Listings
  Vendors
  Voucher Journal Prompts
  Other Cash Requirements
  Automatic Vouchers
Special Forms
  Checks
  Labels and Index Cards
  1099s

Four levels of accounting software

The universe of bookkeeping and accounting software can actually be divided into four basic levels, shown in FIG. 8-12. Level 1 doesn't include professional accounting software, and many industry experts see levels 2 and 3 converging. Level 4 programs tend to be highly specialized and individually tailored. "The low-end products are becoming very, very feature rich," notes David Duplessy of Computer Associates. "A couple of years ago, the products that would have been classified as mid-range are now considered basic."

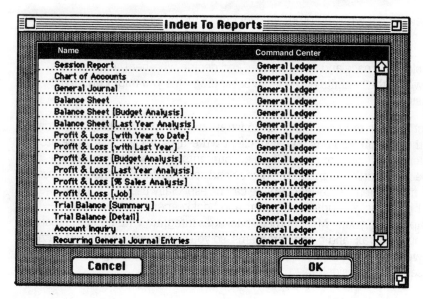

Name	Command Center
Session Report	General Ledger
Chart of Accounts	General Ledger
General Journal	General Ledger
Balance Sheet	General Ledger
Balance Sheet [Budget Analysis]	General Ledger
Balance Sheet [Last Year Analysis]	General Ledger
Profit & Loss [with Year to Date]	General Ledger
Profit & Loss [with Last Year]	General Ledger
Profit & Loss [Budget Analysis]	General Ledger
Profit & Loss [Last Year Analysis]	General Ledger
Profit & Loss [% Sales Analysis]	General Ledger
Profit & Loss [Job]	General Ledger
Trial Balance [Summary]	General Ledger
Trial Balance [Detail]	General Ledger
Account Inquiry	General Ledger
Recurring General Journal Entries	General Ledger

Cancel   OK

8-11
The M.Y.O.B. report menu offers a broad range of reports, which users can select and then customize further to fit their needs.
Teleware, Inc.

Top of the line

Modular in design for big businesses that have several products and departments that must be accounted for separately and together, and that can have highly specialized accounting needs. Can costs $900 or more for each module. Examples: *ACCPACC Plus, Solomon III.*

8-12
The four levels of accounting software have been downshifting: simple accounting packages now have the features only a mid-range program would have offered a couple of years ago.

Mid-range accounting

Offer greater flexibility in setting up accounts, performing job cost calculations, formatting reports and forms. Will include payroll and inventory modules. Examples: *ACCPACC BPI, Peachtree Complete Accounting, Pacioli.*

Simple accounting

Starter programs that are now as complex as most mid-range programs used to be. Are all-in-one programs that include accounts receivable, accounts payable and general ledger functions, but may not include payroll or inventory functions. Examples: *Bestbooks by Teleware, One-Write Plus, ACCPACC Simply Accounting.*

Personal accounting

Usually home budget-based, these programs include checkbook functions and are only suited for the most basic, cash-basis businesses. Examples: *Managing Your Money, Quicken.*

Client write-up software

A completely separate category of accounting software called *client write-up software* also exists. This software is aimed at bookkeeping and accounting professionals who keep records for many different clients and might need to jump back and forth among the records several times during the day.

It is difficult to generalize about how sophisticated this software is. Write-up software generally costs more than the low- or even mid-range accounting software but is less full-featured than the top-of-the-line programs.

In selecting a write-up program over one of the other programs discussed in this chapter, look first at the reports and calculations available to make sure that the software will deliver the information your clients need. Then consider the ease and speed of use, and decide whether these benefits outweigh the benefits of the more basic programs you might otherwise consider.

Most of these programs have demonstration software available, so you can try them before you buy. Because client write-up software is supposed to be easier and quicker for professional accountants and bookkeepers, it's especially worth looking at the demos and seeing which interface pleases you most. Client write-up software can be especially useful if you enlarge your business, add other computers and bookkeepers, and link their computers to yours. Most of these packages integrate with other full-featured accounting, tax, and payroll programs, so you can import and export data between them. A list of the more popular client write-up programs is presented in the sidebar.

Client write-up programs

CPA-11
Franklen Computer Systems
456 South Central Ave.
Glendale, CA 91204
(800) 821-1790

DataWrite
SCS Compute
1244 Powerscourt Drive #400
St. Louis, MO 63131
(800) 326-1040

LIBRA Client Write-Up
LIBRA Corp.
1954 East 7000 South
Salt Lake City, UT 84121
(800) 453-3827

Peachtree Client Write-Up
Peachtree Software
1505 Pavilion Place
Norcross, GA 30093
(800) 554-8900

PDS Client Accounting
Professional Design Systems
1975 Linden Blvd
Elmont, NY 11003

Solomon III
Solomon Software
1218 Commerce Parkway
PO Box 45839
Findlay, OH 45840
(800) 879-2767

Unilink Write-Up Plus
Unilink
460 East Pearl Street
PO Box 1635
Jackson Hole, WY 83001
(800) 456-8296

The Write-Up Solution II
Creative Solutions
7322 Newman Boulevard
Dexter, MI 48130
(313) 426-5860

Consider the following points when buying your software package:

- Interface
- Speed
- Navigation
- Number crunching ability
- Simplicity
- Extras
- Technical support
- Forms
- Upgradability

- Setup ease
- Cash accounting option
- Aging of accounts
- Open periods
- Custom invoicing
- Mailing list
- Word processing ability
- Automatic backup
- Automatic and batch processing.

These points are discussed in the following subsections. You can use the chart in FIG. 8-13 to rate the programs you're considering, according to your own list of requirements.

	Program 1:	Program 2:	Program 3:	Program 4:
Interface				
Speed				
Navigation				
Number-crunching abilities				
Ease-of-use				
Extras				
Technical support				
Forms needed				
Upgrade ease				
Setup ease				
Cash accounting				
Aging				
Open periods				
Custom invoicing				
Mailing list				
Word processing capabilities				
Auto-save and ease of backup				
Automatic and batch processing				

8-13
Accounting software evaluation guide to help you grade the programs you are considering.

The interface The interface between you and the program is a personal question best answered by your intuition, and is dealt with in more detail in chapter 4. In what type of environment are you happiest working? If you enjoy the ease of a mouse and "user-friendly" pull-down menus, compare Macintosh and Windows environments. If you want added speed and prefer the more technical feel of the traditional PC environment, stick with a DOS program. Relax in the knowledge that sophisticated accounting software has now been developed for every environment.

Speed   The faster the better! If you are not accustomed to working on today's personal computers, you may think every program runs fast. Once you've been working on one for a while, however, you will begin to notice seconds and even microseconds. If your program takes five seconds to save data or post a transaction, a day will come when you find yourself tapping your feet in exasperation during those five seconds. If you prefer a Windows or a Mac environment, you will sacrifice a little bit of speed, most likely more with Windows than with the Mac. You won't really get a feel for a program's speed, however, until you start filling the program with data and using it.

Navigation   What commands move you through the program? Can you type one letter and go from writing a check to entering a new vendor's name? Can you get back to the check with another keystroke? Some programs have more cumbersome operating styles than others and might require you to back up through several steps to get from one program module to another.

Number crunching   Sooner or later, a few of your clients might want to use your records for some forward-looking business analysis. Financial ratios, such as internal rate of return and debt versus equity, are relatively simple to set up on a spreadsheet, and some accounting programs can easily export that data to spreadsheets. Other programs have these calculations built in so you can deliver them to your clients automatically.

Simplicity   How comprehensive is your own bookkeeping expertise? If you are a beginner, you might want to work in a program that provides extra guidance and accounting support, even if you must sacrifice some high-end features to do it.

Extras   Some programs come with payroll modules and some don't. While you can always buy a freestanding payroll program later when you do payrolls for some of your clients, you might want to buy a program that includes this feature already. Some service clients, such as attorneys and building contractors, often bill by the hour and want a program that tracks their time as well as their money. A popular feature that not all accounting software has is project costing—a module that allows you to break down a client's business activities by project, product, or profit center.

Manufacturing and retail clients require you to find programs with inventory management capabilities. Some programs have data-compatible tax form modules. These modules are all extras that differ from one program to another and should be considered when selecting software.

Technical support   A toll call or 800 number, support fee or free support is less important than the quality of the service. Are the phones answered quickly and conscientiously? Is the technical support staff friendly, patient, and accounting knowledgeable? There's really only one way to find out—call and chat. You can ask others who have used technical support lines how much help they received, and how quickly they received it.

Necessary forms   You can easily end up spending more on preprinted forms, checks, and other similar accounting forms than you spend on your software package, so a quick check of who sells compatible forms and how much they cost is worthwhile. Some programs are starting to include formatted forms within the program, allowing you to print them out on plain paper. The sidebar discusses the forms you might need.

Paper products

In selecting a software package, don't forget that paper products are a part of the equation. Invoices, checks, and statements often require multipart forms preprinted to match your accounting program, and you might find yourself eventually spending more money on preprinted forms than you do on your software.

Several firms have looked at the growth in accounting software sales and found a market niche selling the preformatted invoices, checks, statements, and payroll forms that go with them. Your program might allow you to format your own multipart forms, but you might find you prefer the preprinted and formatted forms for their convenience, appearance, and ease of use.

You can send for catalogues of paper products from the following firms. Some sell forms designed to work only with specific programs.

NEBS Computer Forms & Software
500 Main Street
Groton, MA 01471
(800) 225-9550

M-USA Business Systems, Inc.
PO Box 230
Covington, GA 30209-0230
(800) 777-4257

dataPRINT
PO Box 910
Milton, WA 98353-9906
(800) 346-5316

Peachtree Forms
10150 Alliance Road
Cincinnati, OH 45242
(800) 553-6485

RapidForms
301 Grove Road
Thorofare, NJ 08086-9499
(800) 257-8354

Safeguard Business Systems, Inc.
PO Box 7526
Fort Washington, PA 19034-9798
(800) 962-0923

Deluxe Business Forms & Supplies
1125 Kelley Johnson Boulevard
PO Box 35100
Colorado Springs, CO 80935-9907
(800) 328-0304

Upgradability   You might start a client on an adequate low-end program and then see the client's business grow to multiple locations, profit centers, employees, and accounting needs that surpass the program. Some accounting software publishers will bring you along—their mid-range and high-range programs will accept the data keyed in on their basic programs, and the interface and command system is the same at all levels. Other software companies only give you part of the advantages—they'll import data but you'll have to learn a new system as you move up the complexity ladder.

Setup ease   It can take hours to set up the chart of accounts for a new client. Some programs include preformatted charts of accounts that are business-specific, others might include one to copy, and others don't provide these charts at all.

Cash accounting   Many, even most, small businesses operate on a cash-based accounting system, where transactions are not realized until they actually occur. Several software packages won't allow cash accounting, however, and operate only in accrual mode, where invoices sent out are listed as assets and bills received are liabilities. Particularly if you expect small-business clients, make sure the program you pick is one that allows cash-based accounting.

Aging   Some clients want invoices aged, so they know when to rebill clients and can pay their own bills on a regular (and not too early!) schedule. Some programs are flexible enough to allow aging at any schedule you or your clients devise, others offer standard preselected aging periods.

Open periods   How many years (or periods) of data can you access at once? Some programs require you to close out a month, quarter, or year and then will not allow you to get back in to record late activity. Others allow open access to past records.

Custom invoicing   Terms, notes, item prices, and tax rates change from invoice to invoice and client to client. Will your program allow invoice formatting?

Mailing list   If you are invoicing for your clients, you'll need their customers' names and addresses on file. Will the program let you use that list for other purposes? If your client wants a set of mailing labels for all his customers, can you supply that from your accounting program?

Word processing capabilities   You'll want your reports to look great, so make sure you have a program that allows you to customize the look of the reports you send your clients.

Autosave and backup   Some programs save as you go and don't let you exit until you've saved and backed up your work. Choose for yourself whether you will be vigilant about backing up your work, or whether you want a program that makes you do it.

Automatic and batch processing   When you enter a transaction, most programs automatically post it to the general ledger. This keeps all your totals up to date all the time and saves you from entering it to the ledger as a separate step. Most accounting programs also allow you to select batch processing as well. Batch processing allows you to enter data rapidly and then post it in batches when you are ready. Batch processing saves time between each transaction and allows you to zip through data entry.

How can you find out which programs would be best for you? There are several sources.

Finding information

Ask   If you know any bookkeepers or accountants, ask them which programs they use and which ones they like. If you are comfortable in an online environment, you can use computer bulletin boards to find software users who are happy or unhappy with particular programs.

Go to the library   The major computer magazines analyze and review accounting software around once a year, a necessary schedule because the software changes so fast. Accounting magazines and professional journals also review these software programs regularly.

Hire an expert   Getting someone who knows a lot about accounting software to advise you isn't a horrible idea, but there is a catch: many so-called consultants sell and work with only one or two programs. A fee-only true accounting expert will probably cost you almost as much as one of the accounting programs itself. Go this route only if you already know you will have clients with special needs. CTS, described in the final section, has nationally recognized expertise in the area of accounting software evaluation. *Accounting Today* magazine recently lent its name to a new accounting software guide. *Accounting Today's 1992 Directory of the Top 100 Software Products* is available for $21.95 if you write to the following address:

Accounting Today TOP 100 Directory
c/o Lebhar-Friedman Inc.
425 Park Avenue
New York, NY 10022
(212) 756-5167.

Put it on a spreadsheet   If you already have a computer and spreadsheet, you can order literature on all of the major programs and then compare them in a grid of your own design. Computer Training Services Inc., of Rockville, Maryland, offers a template formatted for Lotus 1-2-3 that helps you apply your own ratings to accounting programs.

Settling into a software routine

Now that I've encouraged you to embark on a major marketing survey to find the best possible accounting package for you and your clients, I have to tell you one other bit of information: you probably won't find one. Your clients will all have different needs, and you'll find that no one program answers all of them. Most working bookkeepers find they use more than one program, but settle on two. Often, the program they use most is a basic accounting program, such as One-Write Plus or ACCPAC Simple Accounting. They then add a higher-level program for their clients with specialized needs.

Your clients' programs

New and potential clients will call and ask you to work with the program they just bought, which might not be a favorite of yours, or even familiar to you. What should you do then? Working (and profitable) bookkeepers seem to take two different approaches to this question, and neither one of them is "Fine, whatever you say is okay with me." The first approach is, "I don't mind it, but I'll have to charge you extra for the extra time I spend learning and using a new program." The second approach is, "No."

Working bookkeepers caution you to be very careful about agreeing to work on a new program that you haven't selected for your own reasons. Working in a new program will cost you time as you spend hours learning your way around a new program, building a chart of accounts from scratch, and the like. It may ultimately cost you clients, too, as you find that after investing those hours in the program that it doesn't answer your client's basic questions or reporting needs.

"The one thing I wouldn't do again, and wouldn't advise anyone else to do is use lots of different software programs," says Terri Conlon, a New Hampshire bookkeeper. "Just stick with the one, two, or three programs you're comfortable with and don't go off on different ones just because someone asks." It's not easy to do, especially if your client list is rather short and you're just building up a clientele. In the long run, however, you'll be happier if you say "That program isn't really the best choice for your business. Let me use the program I've selected for you."

Three of the most popular accounting programs are described in this subsection to give you an idea of the variety available. Choose one that's right for you.

"We sell One-Write Plus Accounting for the goodwill factor," says Wayne Schultz, a Wethersfield, Connecticut certified public accountant who specializes in setting clients up with hightech accounting packages. "It's inexpensive, compares to higher-end software, and is so easy to use that clients can use it themselves. They don't really have to pay us for something they can go into a computer store and buy and set up alone."

Among accounting professionals, One-Write Plus has been known as a low-cost, low-end program that can handle basic business needs but not much more. Now, however, it's getting renewed respect from bookkeepers who appreciate its ease of setup and lack of complexity. "I used to think it was rinky-dink, but I started using it at a client's office, and now I'm going to send for it myself," says Wanda Walter, a bookkeeper from Lanham, Maryland. "It's really fast."

One-Write Plus *is* limited, and not the program for your clients who want to run job cost figures or very specialized customized reports. With 13 preformed charts of accounts (including one for bookkeeping businesses), however, it's an easy program to set up and start running.

The basic program lists at $129.95 but can be bought on sale for less than $80. It includes a master module or general ledger, an accounts payable module, and an accounts receivable module. The program also has a "SuperTrack Module" that allows you to track customized information, including investment portfolios, rental properties, employee sick and vacation times, inventory levels, and escrow accounts.

A more comprehensive package, One-Write Plus Accounting Works, also includes a payroll module; @Accounting, a link-up that allows you to export data to your spreadsheet program; Get Paid Plus, a library of business letters that you can merge with your customer and vendor files; and DataSave, a program that prompts you to save your data to floppy disks every time you exit the program. One-Write Plus Accounting Works lists for $199.95 but can be purchased for $129.

When you go into One-Write Plus, a main menu will be displayed. The menu will give you a choice of five options: Master Module, Accounts Payable,

Accounts Receivable, SuperTrack, and Setup and Utilities. Once you've set up your accounts, you'll spend most of your time in the Master Module, the heart of the program. Figure 8-14 is a schematic of how the Master Module is organized.

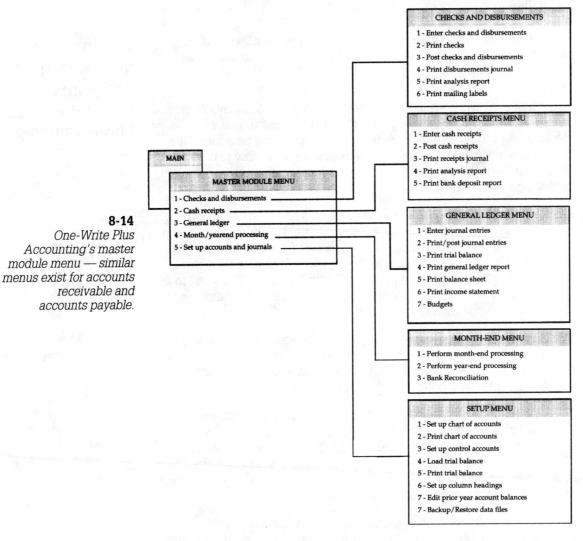

8-14
One-Write Plus Accounting's master module menu — similar menus exist for accounts receivable and accounts payable.

M.Y.O.B. When the editors of *PC/Computing* magazine were asked to select the "Best Values for Accounting," they picked M.Y.O.B. by Teleware. Over at *PC Magazine*, the editors picked M.Y.O.B. out of a series of 16 accounting programs for its "Editors Choice" award. *MacWorld Magazine* has given M.Y.O.B. its "World Class Award" in the category of business accounting software. David "Dr. Mac" Lawrence, a Glenwood, Maryland consultant who spends his time setting up clients' accounting programs, says unequivocally that "M.Y.O.B. is my number one favorite program."

The program's popularity rests on three advantages. It is full-featured enough to satisfy most small businesses. It is very easy to use, even for a person with limited bookkeeping and computing skills. It also has the Macintosh/Windows graphic capabilities that allow users to print user-designed checks, invoices, and reports. "Your invoices can look as good as your brochures or business cards, " says Lawrence.

M.Y.O.B. does not have a payroll module, and it is not the best program for monitoring job costs or profit center activity. It's an ideal small business accounting program for people looking for that "user-friendly" interface. Figure 8-15 shows, for example, the check-writing screen in M.Y.O.B. It really looks like you're writing a check. This is also a good example of the Macintosh or Windows interface.

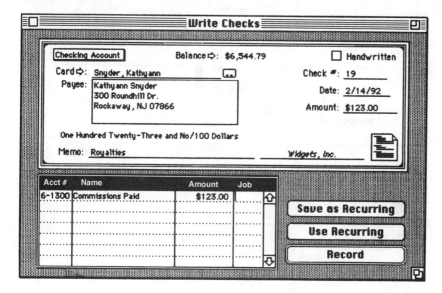

8-15
M.Y.O.B. check-writing screen looks like a paper check and register.
Teleware, Inc.

M.Y.O.B. allows you to format plain-paper forms and comes in Macintosh and Windows versions. It lists for $249, but can be found for less than $150.

Harmony, by Open Systems, is a program that can help run your practice in addition to providing accounting records. This software package is integrated with a spreadsheet, word processor, information manager, and systems manager that allow you to customize reports, print canned letters, manipulate data, and do mass mailings without ever leaving the program. Its utilities allow you to back up data automatically, spell check your work, and print labels. Figure 8-16 shows how Harmony is organized.

Harmony

As an example of the different extras Harmony has, the program includes a sample dunning letter in its word processing file that interfaces with the accounts receivable data. You can create a letter like the one shown in FIG. 8-17 by pushing just a few keys. You don't have to reenter the financial

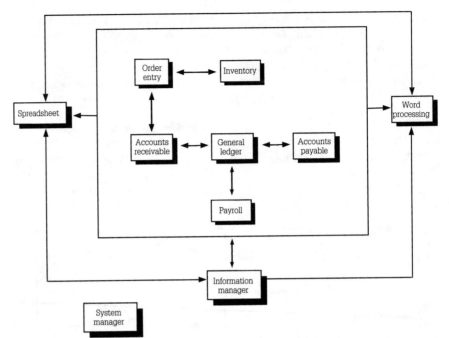

8-16

The Harmony program schematic: word processing, spreadsheet, and other utilities built into the data flow. Open Systems, Inc.

8-17

This dunning report file is preformatted in Harmony but users can customize it to fit their stationery, clients, and individual needs. Open Systems, Inc.

ACE BUILDERS

1588 SE 31st Street
Paducah, KY 42001

December 1, 1992

Dear Customer,

The purpose of this letter is to remind you that your outstanding balance of $10645.20 is now 30 days past due. Prompt payment of this amount would be appreciated.

Thank you for your attention to this matter.

Sincerely,

Earl Chapman

Earl Chapman
Credit Manager

information that's already in the ledger to create letters like this on behalf of your clients.

If you like the idea of spending your whole day in one program, Harmony might be worth the investment. It's word processing and spreadsheet programs are full-featured enough so that separate integrated programs are unnecessary for most bookkeeping and accounting offices.

CTS: Accounting software expertise

Sheldon Needle, president of CTS in Rockville, Maryland, knows more than you'd ever want to about the accounting programs of the world, and he's willing to share his expertise for a price. A corporate finance officer and systems analyst, Needle started CTS in 1983 for the purpose of evaluating accounting software. His belief—that all accounting programs have subtle and not so subtle differences that can make a difference to you and your clients—means you should be careful in choosing programs. For larger companies, this selection process alone can take months, he asserts.

The CTS software guides rate accounting programs on hundreds of features and lists their advantages and disadvantages. Several of the guides, including the *Guide to Small Business Accounting Software Priced Under $500*, are available with Lotus 1-2-3 templates so you can perform a needs analysis on your computer to see which programs would fit you better.

While the guides are not cheap—the Small Business guide sells for $75 without the template and $95 with it, and a guide to high-end accounting software sells for $495—these guides can be a good investment if you are frequently called upon to recommend software systems for clients. They can also save you the time and money involved in experimenting with programs that are ultimately disappointing.

Figure 8-18 is one page of a 22-page requirements analyst worksheet that CTS distributes with its Lotus evaluation spreadsheet. It shows the detail and variety of features in even the simplest accounting software packages. Users can read through the elements and their definitions, rating the ones that they really care about and the ones they don't and then key their requirements into the spreadsheet. The formatted spreadsheet gives the programs numerical ratings that correspond to grades, with the highest-graded program being the one most likely to fulfill your needs. See the sidebar for guidelines CTS has available as well as CTS's address.

The following guides are available from CTS at 11708 Ibsen Drive, Rockville, Maryland, 20852, (301) 468-4800.

CTS guides

❑ Guide to Accounting Software for Microcomputers
❑ Guide to Client Write-Up Software for Microcomputers
❑ Guide to Accounting Software for the Construction Industry
❑ Guide to Accounting Software for Property Management

❏ Guide to Profitable Microcomputer Consulting
❏ Guide to Small Business Accounting Software
❏ Guide to PC-Based Software for the Manufacturing Industry
❏ Guide to Time and Billing Software for Lawyers
❏ Guide to Medical Practice Management Software
❏ CTS Annual Software Survey

CTS The Requirements Analyst   **General Ledger Worksheet**   **Small Business Systems**

ELEMENTS	MUST HAVE	LIKE	DEFINITION
Budget Preparation:			The following items allow you to prepare a budget within G/L.
Annual budget over 12 months			
Last yr. budget moved to this yr.			
Last yr. actuals moved to this yr.			
Last yr. actuals incr. by %			
Current year actual by period			Some systems may require that you print a report to get this data.
PROCESSING FEATURES:			
All cash transac can be entered to GL			Both cash receipts and cash disbursements may be entered through G/L.
Check printing from G/L			You can print a vendor check directly from G/L.
Able to change account balances			Assuming password access, the account balance field can be changed.
One-sided journal entries possible			Some users want to be able to enter an unbalanced journal entry. Some systems allow through a setup option, others simply don't allow it.
Closing by module			Preclude further entries for the current period by application.
Compress transactions function			Summary entries by account to save disk space.
Accounting tutorial			On-line tutorial to help inexperienced bookkeepers.
Void transactions (after posting)			The system will reverse the entry for you and bring the books back to their original state before the entry was made.
Passes subsystem detail to G/L			Detail of entries to AR, AP will go over to G/L.
Option to pass detail to G/L			
Detail maintained full 12 months			The detail transactions are retained for the full fiscal year.

8-18 *This CTS requirements worksheet is 1 of 22 pages the company circulates with its Lotus 1-2-3 program evaluation templates.* CTS, Rockville, MD

9 Developing company identity & image

This is the 1990s, and it *is* all about image. The right business identity and company image can draw clients to you, keep those you would prefer not to service away, offer calm reassurance to your current clients, and help you wake up happy to start your business day. You can use your image in your marketing plan to sell the very attributes of bookkeeping for which potential clients may be looking. You can use your image to convey:

- Reliability.
- Business professionalism.
- Special expertise.
- Accuracy.
- Seriousness of intent.
- Approachability.
- Speed.

or any other client-winning concepts you'd like to have as part of your service.

You can't avoid image by claiming to stick only to substance and avoiding the trappings of perspective (such as grumbling, "I'm a great bookkeeper. I don't have to worry about image."). As Sylvia Ann Blishak, author of *Improving Your Company Image* (1992, Crisp Publications, Inc.) points out, your company will have an image whether you develop it or not. If you don't plan your attack, you just might end up with a corporate identity that says "low-budget," "disorganized," or "out-of-date" instead of that "great bookkeeping" look you thought you were projecting.

You create your paper image with business cards, stationary, and a logo, and your physical image by your appearance, behavior, and phone presence. First, however, is the central task of company image-making: your company name.

The name game

Think about it. People take nine months, numerous books, and the advice of friends, neighbors, and relatives to name a baby. On the other hand, too many businesses get named in a couple of minutes, on the way to the bank, for example, where the owner intends to open her first business checking account. Naming your business is the first step of many that you'll take to develop a company image that attracts new clients, comforts old clients, and makes you feel good about your company. Take your time.

Calling yourself AAAAAAAA Bookkeeping Service might get you first place on the yellow pages list, but it won't do much else for you. A name that sounds like your profession—serious, streamlined, and reliable—will do much more to draw customers to you. Think about it: when you're browsing through the yellow pages yourself, do you call AAAAAAAA Carpet Cleaning or AAAAAAAA Refrigerator Repair? Probably not. You most likely look for the one that is the best, the closest, or looks (as much as is possible from a yellow pages listing) reputable.

Similarly, forget cute. Cute is okay if you are a haircutter or give children's parties, but businesspeople don't expect cute (or really want it) in a bookkeeping service. People expect you to be fast, efficient, accurate, trustworthy, and reliable as a bookkeeping service. If your name can convey that, you'll have an edge over all the AAAAAAAA services ahead of you.

Don't rush through the decision to name your company. You will live with this name a long time. Sit around with a pad and pencil and brainstorm names for a few hours. Go back to the list days later. Scribble the names across letterhead, fake business cards, and in pretend ads. Try them out on your friends and relatives. Check the Yellow Pages and make sure there isn't already someone out there with the same (or a similar) name. Because you'll be establishing only a local business, you don't need to hire a trademark attorney or a national search for the legal rights to your name. You will only need to make sure it doesn't infringe on some other local business.

Use your own name

You can always use your own name, as in John Powell Bookkeeping. Many clients like the personal touch and are reassured by the fact that you are willing to put your name on your work. But if, in the future, you decide to expand your business by adding other junior (or even senior) bookkeepers, will customers all insist that "John Powell himself" do their work?

What if you have an unusual, hard-to-pronounce, or even unfortunate name, like Nancy Numbercruncher? (Actually if your name really is Nancy Numbercruncher you would *have* to use it. Who could resist?) With other names, it's a judgment call, and the judgment might as well be yours. Some people believe a particularly ethnic or hard-to-spell-and-say name could turn potential customers off. We all know, however, of ethnic and unusual names that have become famous along with their companies. Using your own name, even if it is unusual and hard to pronounce, conveys personality and professionalism, and it is easy. You already own it.

"Saturdays, Too Bookkeeping," "Depend-On-Powell Bookkeeping" and "Speedfast Bookkeeping Service" are all names that convey something extra to potential clients. Someone browsing through the yellow pages for a bookkeeper might be drawn to "Accuracy, Inc., Bookkeeping" or "Comprehensive Bookkeeping Services" or "Bookkeeping OnLine." Pick one special part of the business that you are really good at and highlight it. If you choose to go with a simpler name, or your own name, use a slogan or tag line to put on all of your printed materials along with your name.

Offer a benefit

Customers respond well to superlatives. If you are John Powell, you might consider being "John Powell Elite Bookkeeping" or "Powell's Best Bookkeeping Service." Or even "Superior Bookkeeping and Accounting Services by Powell."

Boast a bit

Stake out a niche   You've already spent time positioning your company. Are you going to establish a special niche by aiming your service at home-based businesses, small retailers, or physicians? Are you going to be the neighborhood bookkeeper for all the small businesses sprouting up in your town? Consider putting that idea in your name, such as "The Doctor's Dependable Bookkeeping Service" or "Allentown Bookkeeping" or even, "Allentown's Best Bookkeeping Service."

Realize, though, that such a name will ultimately be limiting as well. If you aren't getting enough business from all the doctors in Allentown, will you be able to attract plumbers from Philadelphia without changing your name? Probably not. A safer alternative might be to keep your name generic, "Dependable Bookkeeping" and adopt different slogans for your ads or business cards that focus on the niche of your choice.

Particularly in today's market, the emphasis is on being up-to-date. Every small business owner is buying accounting software and trying to figure out what to do with it. You will attract many of them if you can use the word *computer* or some variation in your name, such as CompuBooks. Be aware, however, that some of those inquiries you attract will be businesspeople who want you to go on-site and set them up with the accounting programs they've already bought, so they can run them. Names such as "Next Century

Convey a modern approach

Bookkeeping" always sound modern, even if you (or your children) are around to do business for more than one century.

Avoid a name that will date you. You can probably figure out that you don't want to be "20th Century Bookkeeping" anymore, but think about being overrun by technology as well as time. Maybe a few years ago "Adding Machine Accounting Services" was a good name, but not any more. Ditto with "Sharp Pencil Bookkeeping."

Leave room to grow

As you develop your business, you might find yourself offering more than just bookkeeping to your clients. Maybe you'll do their payroll, or fill out their tax forms, or even help in strategic planning. Does your name convey this broad ability? If you intend to offer these other services from the beginning, use *business services* in your title instead of *bookkeeping*. You can also call your company "Bookkeeping and More" to publicize the breadth of your services. If you don't intend to offer broader services immediately, don't worry about leaving room to grow. You can always call yourself "John Powell Best Bookkeeping" today and "John Powell Best Business Services" tomorrow without losing clientele or momentum. See the sidebars for how to ensure your name is a good one and some examples of names already being used.

What's in a name

Once you've developed your company name, check and see if it meets these objectives:

❑ Is it easy to remember?
❑ Does it convey a benefit?
❑ Does it make you happy?
❑ Will it stand the test of time and technology?
❑ Will it avoid limiting you geographically?
❑ Does it define your expertise?
❑ Does it sound smart?
❑ Is it different from any other business names in your community right now?

Real bookkeeping names

The following are names successful bookkeepers are using now:

Mary's Bookkeeping Service in Arlington, Virginia—Mary Greiner has been a no-nonsense bookkeeper for 40 years and takes a personal approach to meeting and servicing clients. Her name conveys all that.

Falcon Accounting Services in Boston, Massachusetts—"Falcon is in my family crest, and I thought it was distinctive," says Karen Wetmore. "I want to go beyond bookkeeping and work as a management consultant, business planner, and budgeting expert. My name has proved to be a benefit in getting business."

Lionel Martinez of Tampa, Florida—He has developed a solid reputation for quality bookkeeping in the greater Tampa area. His business is now a family matter, too. His wife runs the office, his daughter does tax work, his son is a CPA. Lionel capitalizes on his good reputation, however, by operating his business under his own name.

The Company Clerk in Lanham, Maryland—Most businesses view bookkeepers as administrative extensions of their staffs, Wanda Walter believes, and she likes to take a modest, reassuring approach of a dependable (and not overly expensive) staff member. "Clients don't want to see their (bookkeeping) money spent in a big flashy way," she says. The Company Clerk exudes modest dependability.

Facts & Figures in Conway, New Hampshire—Terri Conlon focused on the core of bookkeeping: the information and numbers that are the end-product for her clients. "The bookkeeping function of any business deserves a lot of credit and respect," she says. When clients come to Terri, they are looking for hard information.

A logo

You can run a business for a lifetime and become quite successful without ever bothering to use a logo, but a design that visualizes what you are trying to say about your business can give your paper presentations punch. Beth Roll, who runs a very successful bookkeeping business in Los Angeles, loves her logo so much she won't talk about it. "My logo is an excellent marketing tool, and it is very effective. I know that if you put it in your book, everyone would want to copy it," the otherwise effusive Beth told me when I asked about her marketing strategy. She is so happy with her logo and marketing strategy, as a matter of fact, that she is carefully protecting it now in consideration of the day when she licenses it nationally.

Roll thought up her design idea herself and then paid a commercial artist to clean it up and offer suggestions for improving it. She uses it on her business cards, corporate brochure, and gift items that she distributes. "It's gotten to the point in the community where when I go to a trade show, people come up to me and say they've seen my cards and remember my company."

A logo can be your company name in an artistically designed lettering arrangement, or it can be a picture symbol. To develop a logo on a budget, mess around with ideas yourself, using your initials, your company name, and different graphics that represent what you want your business to say. Then, consider hiring a graphic artist to finish the job for you. You can also hire a lower-priced art student who might be happy to have the work for his portfolio. No logo at all, however, is far better than the off-the-shelf little pictures of computers, calculators, and adding machines that most print shops can offer you. Don't even think about it; they look tacky.

In deciding on a logo design, make sure it works in black and white, even if you are laying out money for a two-or-more color print job. You'll want it to photocopy and fax.

"I love my logo," says Ingrid Landskron, a bookkeeper from Mahwah, New Jersey. "To me it says "professional, competitive, and serious but with personality." Ingrid had a professional artist design her logo, her letterhead and her business card, but he did it for free. The artist was a business contact in Ingrid's networking group and spent some time with her in front of the computer, playing around with designs. He then sent her home with some to review. Once she'd decided which design to go with, it cost her $500 to get her stationery, business cards, and envelopes printed. Her business card is shown in FIG. 9-1, and her stationery is in FIG. 9-2. You can't see the colors but they are shades of green on a quality ivory paper.

9-1
Ingrid Landskron's business card, designed for free by a business network buddy.

This design is a departure for Ingrid, who initially used a staid, plain business card and letterhead. It only took her a few months to switch. "I wanted to convey the image of a business that's not flat." The All-In-1 name also brings in clients who know they can also turn to Ingrid for basic ledger work, payrolls, and tax preparation. "I like to do everything, and I want them to know it."

A slogan

You don't want to mess up your printed material with too many words or too much noise. Any artist will talk about the benefits of white space. Most business cards and stationery designs, however, do have room for a business saying or slogan. A slogan can accomplish a lot. A simple benefit-selling slogan, such as "Top dollar bookkeeping at rock bottom rates" or "Specialists in computerized accounting" can position your company and attract clients. A philosophical slogan, such as, "Do it once, do it right" or even "We Love Ledgers" can give your printed material more personality, which can also attract clients. Be careful not to let your personality intrude too much, though, or it can turn other potential clients off.

All-In-1
Bookkeeping
Service

P.O. Box 539
32 Brookwood Drive
Mahwah, N.J. 07430
Tel/Fax 201-529-5242

9-2
*Ingrid Landskron's
stationery, which matches
her business card.*

Business cards

Business cards are a very important aspect of your company's personality, and besides, you can hand them out wherever you go.

My two cards

Here's one of my best business secrets, about to be a secret no more: I have two business cards. One, which I send to women's magazine editors and other generalists, has a cute picture of a pencil underlining my name. The card says, "Linda Stern, writer and editor." I used that one for about a year, but felt uncomfortable with it at certain financial meetings. A significant number of my writing assignments are financial, which brings me into contact with serious Wall Street types and the publishers who cover them. I thought the pencil card too cutesy for these assignments, so I did another one. My second card is straightforward on ivory paper and says only, "Linda Stern, Financial Journalism."

When I go to financial meetings, such as conferences of mutual fund executives, I bring the "financial journalist" card with me. When I go to meetings where I'll mostly meet other writers or editors, or editors of "cutesy" magazines (which shall remain nameless, as I'm probably getting in enough trouble already), I bring my "writer and editor" pencil card. If I am to meet both types of people, I keep both sets of cards with me.

My apologies here for using my own "writer" cards as an example in a book about bookkeepers. Principles exist here, however, that you can apply to your bookkeeping business. Suppose you've decided you have special expertise in one or two areas of bookkeeping, such as restaurants and building contractors. Both require specialized accounting procedures, and the owners of those businesses get nervous hiring a general bookkeeper who has never serviced their type of company before.

For about $50, you can get a bunch of nice looking cards printed up that look like FIG. 9-3. For $50 more, you can get another stack of business cards that say what is shown in FIG. 9-4. Throw in another $50 for your basic business card, shown in FIG. 9-5.

Imagine taking the first card to a meeting of local restaurateurs, or even spending a day hand-delivering it to all the restaurant owners in your community. Imagine sending the second one to all the building contractors listed in your yellow pages with a cover letter explaining your knowledge of their bookkeeping needs. Those cards will pay for themselves in a hurry! (See the sidebar for pointers in designing your business card.)

9-3
Niche-building business card.

Jane Williams

Restaurant Industry Accounting

1234 Main Street
Baltimore, MD 21201

Phone: 410-634-5789
Fax: 410-555-9876

```
┌──────────────────────────────────┐
│                                  │
│          Jane Williams           │
│     A Builder's Best Bookkeeper  │
│                                  │
│                                  │
│   1234 Main Street    Phone: 410-634-5789  │
│   Baltimore, MD 21201  Fax: 410-555-9876   │
│                                  │
└──────────────────────────────────┘
```

9-4
Another niche, another business card.

```
┌──────────────────────────────────┐
│                                  │
│                                  │
│          Jane Williams           │
│  Fast, Accurate Computerized Bookkeeping  │
│                                  │
│                                  │
│   1234 Main Street    Phone: 410-634-5789  │
│   Baltimore, MD 21201  Fax: 410-555-9876   │
│                                  │
└──────────────────────────────────┘
```

9-5
All-purpose business card.

In planning your business card, consider the following:

- ❑ Keep it clean. Don't muddy it up with different pictures, sayings, or details.
- ❑ Pay for a heavy stock paper. Skimpy cards bend, fold, mutilate, and look junky.
- ❑ Pick a paper color and stick with it—for your cards, envelopes, stationery, and anything else you get printed.
- ❑ Don't create a foldover or nonstandard sized business card. These don't fit in business card holders and are often thrown away.
- ❑ If you have any special credentials, such as a Bachelor's degree in accounting, membership in the American Institute of Professional Bookkeepers, or 20 years in the business, put that at the bottom of the card.
- ❑ Avoid cute.

Business card design

Your letterhead and envelopes should look like your business cards. The letter paper should be serious, with only one typeface or typestyle on it, and should include your logo, if you have one. You can create letterhead on your computer, and then just print it out on your laser printer as you need it.

Stationery

You can save a lot of money, and get a look that suits you best, by designing your paper image on your computer. If you have a graphic design program, or even a word processing program with a good choice of fonts, you can spend time playing around on the computer and printing out sample business cards, stationery, envelopes, and the like.

If you are not a graphic artist and have no experience in letterhead design, you'll do okay if you follow one maxim: keep it simple. Don't use more than one font (typeface) on your letterhead, and keep your envelopes, business cards, and stationery all looking basically the same. Once you've come up with a design you like, you have two options. You can take the computer file on disk to a typesetting company, which will set the camera-ready art for you. (Typesetting will result in a sharper image than you could get on your laser printer.) Then, you can take the camera-ready art to a printer and have the printer print your cards, stationery, and other paper supplies from the typeset art.

There is an even cheaper alternative for your letter paper and envelopes. You can simply set up a letterhead and blank envelope design in your computer. Then, when you need to write a letter, simply type it into the blank letter form and print out the letterhead and the letter together. Similarly, your envelope file should include your return address; simply type in the address of the person to whom you are writing. If you use this inexpensive system, your letters will not be quite as sharp as professionally typeset letters and envelopes would be. They will be far, far cheaper, however, and will look quite good if you have a good quality printer and a quality font.

If you've hired an artist to design a logo for you, ask her to scan the image into a computer and give you a copy of it on disk. Then, using a graphics program, or the graphics portion of your integrated program, you can manipulate your logo to fit your envelope, letter paper, and business cards.

Laser-printed paper doesn't come out quite as sharp looking as real typeset stationery, but it is probably as good as you need at a far more affordable price. Black ink on white, gray, or ivory paper is perfectly acceptable, and you might not think it worthwhile to use any other colors, as they can greatly raise the cost of your printing job.

Other custom-printed papers

If you can afford it, consider getting report covers custom printed with your company name and logo. Get large envelope address labels printed at the same time. Then, when you send off your monthly reports, you can do so in distinctive style. When you pay for all this extra printing, of course, your rates will need to be higher than if you took a lower-budget approach to your mailings. You'll look professional enough, however, to charge more and attract a better-paying group of clients. You might also find it worthwhile to get memo pads or bookmarks printed to match the rest of your "paper identity."

Jackie Denalli, an Orlando, Florida, business consultant, urges her clients to use their fax cover sheets as yet another marketing opportunity. If you can, include your logo and your name, address, phone, and fax numbers in the same typeface as you use on your stationery (though the arrangement and size can differ). Use the fax cover sheet to list upcoming events (such as tax-filing deadlines) or to display a comprehensive list of the services you provide.

Your fax cover sheet

There isn't much leeway when it comes to keeping a business image on your home phone. Clients who pull your number off a yellow pages listing or newspaper ad will try you once. If they don't get an answer, or they get a busy signal, it's unlikely they will ever call back. Always answer the phone in a clear and professional manner. If your business line is the same line as your home phone, you may not want to answer it, "Reliable Bookkeeping." You can, however, answer it, "Mary Smith," or "Good Morning, this is Mary Smith." You will not be able to share a line if you have children who are teenagers. Instead of buying them their own phone, get yourself your own phone and make them share.

Answering the phone

Use an answering machine, voice mail, or answering service to make sure your phone always gets answered. If you are going to operate with one line, use call waiting or the voice mail system sponsored by your local phone company so that the line is picked up even if you are currently on it. What conclusions do you draw about a business when its line is busy?

Finally, don't leave a message that says, "Welcome to my voice mail system," if your callers only hear one message, can leave only one message, and get no buttons to push. You may know it's a voice mail system and not an answering machine, but it sounds pretentious.

Many home-based entrepreneurs completely avoid meeting clients at home because they are too self-conscious about the personal look of their house, or too busy to keep the home "client-ready neat" all the time. They always visit clients at the client's place of business or arrange to meet in restaurants or other public places. Then there are people who have the luxury of totally professional at-home meeting places. Maybe they have a second room they use as a conference room, or even a separate entrance to their office area. They encourage clients to come to them and see they mean business.

Your house

What about the rest of us, who are somewhere in the middle? You can make your home support your company image without turning it into a cold, uninhabited place. Do the following:

❏ Keep your yard and outside entrance well maintained.
❏ Keep the inside entrance and walkways to your office neat and clear of toys, athletic equipment, shoes, and other personal effects families leave around.

- Keep your house and office really clean, even if you must hire professional help to do it. Note that if you do hire a cleaning service or individual, you can deduct from your business taxes the prorated portion of their pay that goes to cleaning your office.
- Offer coffee, tea, water, or soft drinks to your visitors. (Unless you are poring over their tax returns and don't want to be *pouring* over their returns. Sorry.)
- Put your pet away. Don't force a client who is uncomfortable with dogs to pet your puppy. Don't put your clients in the position of wondering whether your cats wrestle in your office when you aren't there. A goldfish is okay.
- If your office is cramped, show it to your client, but hold your meeting at the dining room table or in the living room. Holding your meeting here will add a nice touch of intimacy to the meeting without seeming as laid back as the kitchen table.
- Don't forget to keep the guest bathroom in tiptop shape.
- Dress nicer than you would if you were home alone, but not as nice as you would for a meeting out in the business world. A nice shirt and pair of slacks will do, or you can mirror your clients if you know what they will wear.
- Look at your house with a critical eye and ensure that it conveys a mood of organization, care, and warmth.
- You don't have to hide all your personal touches. A client who walks past your vacation photo collection to get to your office might just find another common point of interest in the photo.

You

Finally, the ultimate image maker is you. Whole books have been written about how people win businesses by looking, moving, acting, and talking right, but most of it is common sense.

Home-based workers do need to work a little harder to maintain image, so make sure you are professionally dressed when you leave your home office to go on client calls. Do what it takes to feel good about the way you look, whether that means regular expensive haircuts, a gym-based workout program, a couple of pricey suits, a good raincoat, or all of the above. Avoid too much makeup, extreme styles, or too much jewelry. Speak clearly, and try to keep your voice at a moderate level. If you have to err, err on the loud side rather than the soft. And, finally, make lots of eye contact.

10 Marketing your business

Marketing is where you really put your entrepreneurial proactivity to the test. It's been proven time and again that the people who are the best bookkeepers don't necessarily run the most successful bookkeeping businesses. This statement holds true for all service businesses. You must have selling skills as well as small-talk skills. You need to be persistent, too, and willing to spend time and the energy to let potential clients know you exist. You can be the best bookkeeper ever, but if people don't know your business exists, they won't call.

You can do a great deal at minimal expense to highlight and distinguish your bookkeeping business. In the most general of terms, marketing includes everything you do or say that presents your business to the world. We've already covered much of the image aspects of marketing in chapter 9. In this chapter, we'll explore specific ways that bookkeepers like yourself drum up business and win new clients.

Marketing begins with research. Before you put pen to paper or phone to ear, you need to analyze your market. Do companies in your area buy bookkeeping services? Why? How much do they pay?

After research comes identification. Who are your potential clients? Where are they? What do they need? What do they want? Are they in particular sectors?

The next phase of marketing is targeting. Which clients will be the best, and who do you most want to reach? Where can you find them? What are your chances of reaching the best potential clients? Pick the markets you most want to reach.

Then you must plan. Your marketing plan is your specific approach to the markets you've targeted. Will you spend money on ads? Where will you place them? How about a direct-mail campaign? Or public relations? How about cold calls, trade show exhibits and newsletters?

The rest of the marketing dance is easy. It just takes money, time, or both. Implement your plan by placing the ads and making the calls. Follow up by recontacting potential clients who seemed like good prospects. Finally, do it again. And again. And again. Anyone who watches television probably knows the basic rule of advertising and marketing: repetition works. Use FIG. 10-1 as a guidepost as you step through the phases of marketing, discussed in more detail in the following subsections.

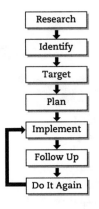

10-1
Even the simplest of marketing efforts follows these stages.

Marketing research

"Just do some seat-of-the-pants research," suggests Ken Norkin, president of KN Creative, a marketing communications firm in Takoma Park, Maryland. "You don't have to hire a market research firm, just make some phone calls." Call some companies who you think are potential bookkeeping clients and explain that you're not soliciting business, just looking for information. Ask them if they use outside bookkeeping and why or why not, how much they pay for the service, and what they would want in a bookkeeping service and why. For example, ask them, "Would pickup and delivery services be important to you? Would you only hire someone who would work on your computer system?"

If you are calling small businesses, you might speak to the business owner directly, and he just might express an immediate interest in hiring you. Be prepared to discuss your services. If you're not ready yet, ask him to tell you about his needs and make an appointment to call him back with your ideas for how to improve his financial information.

Attend business meetings in your community; go to Chamber of Commerce or Rotary Club luncheons and ask about how members get their accounting work done.

Questioning the competition isn't as easy. If the market is tight, you will know because other bookkeepers might be unwilling to share any information with you at all. If, however, there is a big demand for bookkeeping in your community, your competition will be more open about welcoming you in.

In calling the competition, you can take two approaches. You can call and let the competition believe that you are a potential client inquiring about rates. While not entirely honest, this method is used all the time. Or, you can seek out the older, established bookkeepers in your community and hope one will mentor you as you start your business. Often, people who are well-established in their field are generous about bringing new people in and secure enough to be unbothered by the potential competition.

Market identification

Once you have a good feeling for how your market shapes up, start finding the people who will really be your clients. Some of this identification is objective. What types of businesses can use your services? Small retail establishments, building contractors, churches, taxi companies, cleaning services, medical offices, restaurants, dry cleaners, copy shops, and pet shops are all examples of the types of businesses that frequently use outside bookkeepers. Accountants, attorneys, and financial planners also frequently refer bookkeepers to their clients.

Some of the identification phase is also subjective. What types of businesses do you feel most comfortable working for? Restaurants, medical offices, and churches in particular have specialized accounting needs. If your personal background brought you into frequent contact with these types of establishments (maybe your father was a doctor or ran a deli) you might want to focus in that direction. Maybe you just like florists and don't want to deal with home-improvement contractors (or the other way around). Even in your subjective mode, avoid being overly picky and limiting.

Targeting the market

Targeting is when you really decide whether you'd rather spend time or money. If you've more of the former than the latter, start compiling your own list of potential customers. "That's what the phone books are for," says Norkin.

Create lists of potential clients from the business listings in the Yellow Pages, and create lists of potential referral targets (attorneys, CPAs, and such). You can organize this list on your computer and mail to those on your list automatically. Once the list is compiled, call each business and ask for the name of the business owner. Don't be shy about asking about the spelling of a person's name.

If you would rather spend money than time, you can buy a list. Professional mailing list brokers (they'll probably be in your Yellow Pages, too, under advertising or direct-mail services) can sell you almost any list of people you want. If you need a basic list of businesses in your geographic area, it can cost you about $30 per 1,000 companies, and many brokers require that you buy at least 3,000 company names. Low-priced lists won't have the names of the business owners, however. You still need to make those calls or expect to pay $60 to $100 per 1,000 for a more detailed list, according to Norkin. Usually, when you buy a mailing list, you are buying only a single use of the names on it—making follow-up calls twice as expensive.

You can target your market in other ways as well. Find out where your potential clients hang out and what they read. Is there a business paper in your city? Are there centrally located business supply stores, copy shops, or software stores where you can reach your prospective customers? Is there a local chapter of the American Institute of CPAs, where you could find lots of referrals at the same lunch table?

Make a habit of scanning the help wanted pages for companies hiring full- or part-time accountants and bookkeepers. Sometimes you can talk them into hiring a freelancer instead.

Planning

The planning phase is when you make the most difficult decisions about how to spend your precious marketing minutes and dollars. It helps if you actually write down a marketing plan of attack. What will you do, and in what order? Make a list of tasks for yourself and develop a marketing schedule. The following are many budget-conscious ideas that have worked for other bookkeepers around the country.

The yellow pages

"The yellow pages really work. Unfortunately, they cost more than they should," says Wanda Walter of The Company Clerk in Lanham, Maryland. "Don't let them talk you into a big ad." Walter has found that her small ads work as well or better than the large display ads she has placed in the past. Why? She has a theory: "My philosophy on bookkeeping and accounting services is that we are like administration people. We are overhead, not money producers. People don't want to spend their money on big, giant ads for overhead services, and they don't want to see you doing it, either."

Having a yellow pages presence is important, but Walter is right: a small ad will do just as nicely.

The General Ledger newsletter relates the following[1]: Imagine pulling 15 inquiries a month from a half-inch box ad in your local yellow pages at $47 per month. That's what Chris Bihler of Bookkeeping Backup in Phoenix, Arizona, gets. She's been doing basic bookkeeping for one- to two-person companies for nearly six years at a minimum of $60 a month, at $25 per hour.

At least one caller a month brings some work, and 2 percent of all callers become clients, totaling 15 to 20 jobs a year. "It's absolutely paid for itself," she says. Her five-line ad (she also has a one-line white pages listing that brings in business) reads as follows:

> Bookkeeping Backup
> For small businesses and individuals.
> + Word processing and office support.
> Free pickup and delivery.
> (Address and phone number)

"Free pickup and delivery" is what does it, she says. Only one call a month is for word processing.

After callers say what they think they need, Bihler asks questions to get details: Do you need checkwriting? Do you need your checkbook balanced? Do you need help with payroll? Do you need sales tax reports done? How many employees do you have? How long have you been in business? The average call lasts 5 minutes. Some take as many as 30 minutes, but these longer calls usually result in business. Sometimes she must use an answering machine, but has received jobs from messages left on it.

When people call, remember to be friendly to establish a rapport promptly. If they are not comfortable on the phone with you, they won't come to see you. The best sales tool is helping a caller right on the phone. Use humor to put them at ease and show no pressure exists. Key factors to callers are your rate and proximity—and their own comfort level.

Find a mentor

"I was lucky to find a mentor," says bookkeeper Karen Wetmore. "I started out doing small jobs for her while I took accounting courses. She took me under her wing and strongly suggested that I establish a quality identity for myself. One day someone called her and asked if she could do two hours a month of bookkeeping work. It was too small of a job for my mentor, so she passed it on to me. Since then, all of my clients but one have come through referrals from her and from my existing clients." See the sidebar for how to find a mentor.

• • • • • • • • •

[1]Reprinted by permission from *The General Ledger* newsletter, published by the American Institute of Professional Bookkeepers, Rockville, MD. All Rights Reserved.

How to find a mentor

In the best relationships, you find each other. But there might be more experienced and established bookkeepers who are willing to give newcomers a helping hand. Maybe an established bookkeeper in your town is willing to pass small jobs your way. If you are still in training to be a bookkeeper, offer to do an internship with such an established business. Look also to your accounting professors and teachers for business advice as well as referrals.

Network like crazy

Networking is not as easy to describe and plan as many other marketing methods, but it remains the number one way in which most bookkeepers get business. "I started networking before I set up my business," says Ingrid Landskron of Mahwah, New Jersey. "It was the first thing I did before I left my job. I set up a home-based business network on the computer called CompuNet. Soon, I got a lead from a lawyer who lived about 30 miles away and had a lot of backlogged work that needed to be done." Through the group, she's received client referrals and met the artist who designed her letterhead and business cards for free.

Go to business meetings and tell everyone you meet and know that you're now in business for yourself. Use other nonbusiness group affiliations—the PTA, the soccer team moms, the chess club, the charity group—to spread the word. One California bookkeeper says he switched dentists about four times in the first couple years of his business. He kept changing until he found one that would sign on with *him*. Now dentists constitute a significant portion of his client list.

Because most bookkeeping clients arrive by word of mouth, it is crucial that you do dependable, quality work for the first few clients who come through the door. After that, they'll start telling their friends about you, who will start telling their friends. "When I started in business, I went out on the street, knocked on doors, talked to friends, spread the word, and advertised in the Yellow Pages. I think in 22 years, maybe we've gotten two or three clients out of the Yellow Pages," says Lionel Martinez. "The majority of our business is word of mouth."

Advertise

"I got some of my best clients by advertising in the newspaper," says Mary Olcott Greiner of Arlington, Virginia. "I put a simple little classified ad in the *Washington Post* under Positions Wanted and got a wonderful response. People were calling me to do their bookkeeping; lawyers were calling to refer clients."

Advertising can be a more expensive way to find clients than direct mail and it can help you create a recognizable upscale image. See the sidebar for suggestions about where to place your ads.

Church directories, PTA newsletters, high school play programs. These are all relatively inexpensive ads and hit a lot of people who never buy bookkeeping services. They also hit some that do. And, because they appear in special-interest publications, these ads can create a feeling of goodwill among potential clients, who like the idea of doing business with someone who supports their kids' school, for example.

Your local business paper. Chances are, however, this paper gets well read and doesn't come cheap. If you intend to advertise in your local business paper, you need to do so on a regular basis. One-shot ads just don't draw the clients.

The computer consulting section of the weekly business pages. This is the section that runs in your daily newspaper.

The classifieds. It worked for Mary Greiner!

When you decide to place an ad, think carefully about what message you want the ad to convey. Go back to the last chapter, when you isolated the advantages you had to offer and came up with a slogan. Review the inquiries you first made and think about what businesspeople really want in a bookkeeper. See the sidebar on ideas for ads.

Convenience:
❏ "We'll pick up and deliver."
❏ "Available for evening and Saturday consultations."

Speed:
❏ "Results while they're still useful!"
❏ "Two-day turnaround service."

Comfort:
❏ "Don't worry about a thing. Mom's Best Bookkeeping can clean up the mess in no time."

High-tech:
❏ "The best, most comprehensive financial reports in town. You'll want to frame them."

One of the best ways to advertise is to use a targeted ad. To do this, you focus your ad on one aspect of the business that you want potential clients to think about. For example, the hottest issue among bookkeeping clients today is automation. Many of them are faced with the challenge of putting their books on computer for the first time, and they are overwhelmed. These people are being told that they can buy any over-the-counter software program and make it work for them, even if they have no accounting

Outlets for ads

Ad ideas

background and even if they are already too busy to take on this added task. They are being sold programs in the under-$200 range that might or might not do what they need, but that are guaranteed to be time-consuming to the accounting neophyte. Most businesspeople really don't have the time to deal with automation, though they feel they should.

The ad in FIG. 10-2 capitalizes on that anxiety and confusion. It is targeted to the clients that might eventually call you in to help them with their accounting troubles. Where you place this type of ad could increase its impact. If the ad ran in a newspaper's weekly business section, amidst all the computer and software ads, it would catch eyes that are browsing for solutions. Even if potential clients ignored the ad in their quest for the perfect accounting program, they'd be likely to remember it once they bought the

10-2

Go after a bookkeeper's biggest market with this ad: small business owners who want to automate their books, but aren't there yet.

STOP!
Don't Buy That Accounting Software.

...Before you celebrate the bargain you are getting with that $125 accounting program, think about how much time and money you'll spend learning to use it, feeding it data, and throwing it away when you discover it doesn't give you the kinds of reports you need.

Call us first. At **CompuBooks**, we already own all the accounting software you'd ever want, and we have the know-how to use it. Our low monthly fees will save you time, energy and the headaches of hiring and training bookkeeping personnel. We'll pick the software that serves your business best and deliver the crisp, clean, timely reports you need to run your business better.

Compubooks...*We already have all the software.*
1221 Spring Street, Harrisburg, PA 17110
(717) 555-1212

© KN Creative

program and then found themselves just as bogged down in accounting questions and work as before. An ad such as the one shown should be run regularly in the same spot, so those browsers could come back to it. It's direct, eye-catching, and different.

If you've become adept enough at desktop publishing, you can typeset your ads yourself, but most newspapers will do it for you for free or a nominal fee. Keep the ads clear and sparse. Busy ads are a turnoff.

Direct mail

Direct mail is labor-intensive and expensive, but direct mail is one of the best ways to reach your target market. Today's computers and software make it easy, even for a neophyte, to run a direct-mail campaign. You can use your computer to perform a mail merge.

Mail merge is a concept with which every home-based businessperson should become familiar. You probably already are—on the receiving end. When you get a letter from a magazine you've never subscribed to that says, "Hello there, **Linda Stern!** How are things on **Hickory Avenue?**" you have received a mail-merged letter. Not a very good one, either!

Mail merge occurs when you combine a letter (or envelope, or other word processing document) with a list, such as a database of the names and addresses of possible contacts. You can combine a "Dear CPA" letter with a list of accountants in your community, for example. Or, a new-client letter with your list of clients or, an introductory letter to a list of businesses in your community that might purchase your services.

Now that technology has improved, the merged additions are seamless, unlike the preceding example. No more will you see names in different typefaces that don't line up with the rest of the type. Even a simple word processing program with mail merge capabilities (most word processing packages have them) or a contact management program allows you to easily do mail merges on your computer. In one day you can send hundreds of letters to potential clients and client referrals in your community, each printed out individually with the name of the addressee on the letter and the envelope.

Keep records of who you've mailed to and when. Many contact management programs can automatically record that information for you. Set your letter up to print on your stationery, as Ingrid Landskron did with the letter shown in FIG. 10-3. (Imagine it on the stationery pictured in the previous chapter.) Her letter is formatted for mail merge. When it prints out, instead of {FNAME} {LNAME}, for example, the letter contains the first and last names of the person to whom it is addressed.

To conduct a proper direct-mail campaign, pick a target market and send a letter (mail merged or not) to those in your target market explaining your

September 28, 1992

{FNAME} {LNAME}
{ADDRESS}
{CITY} {STATE} {ZIP}

Dear {SALUT}:

Do you know your present outstanding receivables? Are your clients being billed on a regular basis? Do you enjoy performing your bookkeeping tasks?

If the answers to any of the above questions is "NO", you need the efficiency of a reliable bookkeeping service. Many small business owners and sole practitioners start out with the idea that "one person CAN do it ALL" -- the accounts payable, accounts receivable, payroll, etc., but soon find out that it is more efficient, not to mention cost effective, to hire a bookkeeping service. They know that they can leave the bookkeeping to a trustworthy steward, freeing themselves to concentrate on their own business enterprise .

All-in-1 can perform those bookkeeping services for you! We offer efficient, reliable service in your office or ours, manual or computer, at a low monthly cost. We invite you to call today, to set up a free consultation to find out how All-in-1 can help you say "YES" to the above questions!

We look forward to hearing from you!

Sincerely,

Ingrid R. Landskron
President

10-3

Ingrid Landskron's mail merge letter, which lines up perfectly with her stationery.

services. Expect about a 1-percent response rate. "You can bump up that response rate a bit by including a self-addressed postcard for people to return," says Ken Norkin. "Let them put the postage on it themselves. They will if they are interested, and you'll save money."

You can write different letters for each target market (one to contractors, one to CPAs, and one to dry cleaners, for example) and set your computer to send the right letter to the right target list. You can also opt to send attractive postcards instead of letters. You can print about 1,500 of one design for $500. Print a bold headline on one side, such as "Your Accounting Worries are Over." On the other side, write a brief message about your services. Make sure to leave room for the address and stamp.

If you know a printer that can easily run envelopes, it's better to print the addresses directly on the envelopes rather than printing labels. It looks more personal and is more likely to get opened.

Consider giving a free talk to the businesspeople in your community about "Small Business Recordkeeping: What to Keep and What to Toss" or "Payroll Rules You Need to Know" or "How are You Doing? The Numbers Will Tell." You can offer these services through a local trade or business group.

Offer seminars

Consider also contacting the local computer and software stores. They might sponsor you to speak at a local computer fair or on a Saturday in their store about computerized accounting systems.

Besides putting your name out and possibly bringing in clients, these activities will give you great public speaking experience. You never know when you'll need it!

You should have a brochure about your company that explains what you do and how you do it. You can use the brochure in several ways: hand it out to businesspeople you're visiting, send it to callers who request more information, and display it in places where businesspeople congregate.

Write a brochure

If you aren't experienced at writing or page layout, pay someone who is (or barter your services for theirs). A simple two-sided brochure with two colors and no photos can be written and laid out for between $200 and $600; you will then spend $600 to $1,000 printing 1,000 of them.

Your brochure can be your most important marketing tool. I know someone (a writer, no less) who spent all the above dollars creating and printing a brochure and then discovered it had both a typo and grammatical error in it. Get other detail-oriented people to carefully proofread it for you.

In your brochure you can list your services (but not your fees), talk about your special expertise and some of your bigger clients (after you've checked with them, of course). You can get testimonials from clients for the back cover. You can also make the back cover a self-mailer, with space for a stamp and address.

While a second generic brochure about bookkeeping that you can also send out. "10 Questions Your Bookkeeper Should be Able to Answer" or "What You Really Need to Know About Accounting Software but Were Too Confused To Ask," for example, might indirectly draw clients to you.

When you think about it, the bank is a logical place to go for new business. It always has small-business owners lining up loans for their fledgling firms. Take time to meet the business bankers near you. Write them a note, leave

Go to the bank

them your business card, and let them know that you are available for quality bookkeeping for their clients.

Target CPAs "If I could find a reliable bookkeeper, that would make me so happy," says Douglas Perreault, a Tampa, Florida, CPA. "Lionel Martinez (he's mentioned elsewhere in this book) is so busy, and there isn't anyone else in Tampa. Either they try to take my accounts over, or they have a real lack of professionalism and knowledge. My clients are desperate for good bookkeeping, and I end up doing it." No good bookkeepers in Tampa? Doubtful. No good bookkeepers who have found Doug Perreault? Probably.

Competition can exist between CPAs and bookkeepers, but they are really very dependent on each other. A practicing CPA generally doesn't want to take the time (and most clients don't want to pay his fee) to do basic ledgers and other bookkeeping tasks. Yet CPAs are constantly asked to refer bookkeepers. Write another targeted letter and send it to all the CPAs in the local phone book.

Get a lawyer Attorneys help clients incorporate and pay business taxes. If the attorneys know you and trust you, they can include your name and address as a standard part of their new-business setup package. Lawyers are good bookkeeping customers, too. Many run independent offices, bill at rates too high to justify their taking time to run their own accounting software, and don't have accounting problems big enough to justify full-time bookkeepers.

Wear out your shoeleather Post signs or business cards at copy shops and business supply stores. If you live in a small town with a business district, go to every store, introduce yourself as a neighbor of the business, and present your services. "The difference between somebody who makes it in this business and someone who doesn't," says Stephen Sahlein, copresident of the American Institute of Professional Bookkeepers, "is personal drive. The people who really push get ahead."

Publish a newsletter A newsletter is no easy "spare-time" activity, but it can bring new clients, service existing clients, and maybe even make you money on the side. Consider starting with a one-page "alert service" flyer for your clients that you type and print on your computer. Tell your clients when payroll taxes are due, what new rules the IRS just concocted for them, and business management tips (such as best office supplies for organizing your financial records). Send your flyer out once a month to existing and potential clients. Once you set up a newsletter and continue writing it, you'll find it easier and easier to put out every month.

Public relations Good public relations, or "PR," is really very tricky. It's the skill of getting favorably mentioned in articles that will draw clients to you, or at least make your name familiar to them when you come calling for work. At its best, PR is better free publicity than you could generate with all the advertising dollars in Ross Perot's budget. But it's very hard to do.

Get to know the business reporters in your town. Reporters tend to be suspicious of people foisting stories on them, so don't be a pest. Write a letter or press release, with a story idea (one per press release) that relates to bookkeeping topically. Don't write a press release about yourself. Write it about "recordkeeping tasks to do before the end of the year" or "painless ways to automate your office." Quote yourself in the story as a source. Write a cover letter telling the reporter that you are available as a source on financial or tax or accounting stories.

An exception to writing about yourself: You should write press releases about yourself *as a company* rather than as an individual for distribution to local business papers. For example, when you first open your doors, write a release that says, "CompuBooks, a new full-service automated bookkeeping company, opened for business on Tuesday, October 11" and include your address and phone number in the short story. If you land a particularly big client, send an announcement to the business column of your local paper that says, "McDonald's Corp. has selected Barbara's Bookkeeping for its $120-million accounting contract," for example.

If any of your releases do get picked up or you are quoted in a story, make sure that you clip it and make plenty of copies to send to your current clients and include in direct-mail packages to your prospective clients.

Cold (bleah) calls

The worst way to get business, from both the caller's perspective and the callee's, is making cold calls on the phone. It works though. Whole books have been written on tricks of the trade by people who sell lightbulbs, magazines, aluminum siding, and shares of gold mines. They all do it because cold calling can weed out potential clients from people with no potential faster and cheaper than anything else.

If you want to try this approach, you can cover a lot of ground in a hurry. Make yourself spend an hour every day making calls, or 100 calls a week, or a similar goal. Call during business hours, identify yourself politely, and ask who handles the company's bookkeeping and accounting needs. If it sounds like they have potential as a client, offer to send them more information.

Gimmicks

Little calendars and keychains with your name on them do keep you visible, and there are mail-order companies that will print your name on anything. How about inexpensive pocket calculators for the targets (such as CPAs or lawyers) who you think might send you really good referrals? Send out holiday greetings, occasional notes to your current clients, and hot prospects mailing lists. Give away accordion files (for saving receipts) to hot prospects, or offer "One Accounting Question Answered Free" booths at business conferences. Marketing can be fun, if you give yourself the time to be creative.

Follow-up

What do you think happens if you do a direct-mail campaign and get a 1.5 percent response, and then send the same letter to the same list all over again? You get another 1.5 percent response! Repetition works (that's why I keep repeating it) and some people who were interested the first time but lost your letter will call this time. Other people who weren't even interested will also call. People who were out of their offices and never saw your first letter will answer the second time.

Follow-up can involve resending the same package to the same list (if you know you'll be doing it twice, you can often get a discount price from the list broker), or it can involve a new approach. Often, direct mail letters followed by warm calls (as opposed to cold calls) will achieve the same response.

Once you've contacted a potential client, don't wait for them to get back to you. Give them a couple of weeks and then get back in touch with them. Either they'll turn into a client, they'll tell you "No" in ways so uncertain you can strike them off your list, or they be wishy-washy and you'll stop pursuing them as you devote more and more time to paying clients and hotter prospects.

Do it again

Once in a while, start completely over with your marketing. Rethink your plan, if not your market research, and try a marketing attack you hadn't considered before. Keep marketing, even after you are busy with paying clients. Every business has turnover, and you'll want to bring in new clients to replace ones you are bound to lose (don't take those personally, either).

Marketing to existing clients

Your best prospects are your existing clients, as the business cliché goes. Above all, keep the customers who are already in your corner satisfied. First, do it with top-notch service. Then, remember their needs. It doesn't take a lot to keep a client happy if you are doing good work. Do the following as well:

- ❏ Remember to thank them for their business.
- ❏ Call them once in a while, even when they don't have any work for you, to remind them of a tax filing or rule change or just to say hello.
- ❏ Send them little clips about their field that they might not see. Don't bother clipping from a local paper for a local business, but, if you get an accounting magazine that has an article on hiring your children, for example, you can photocopy it and send it to your family-owned business clients.
- ❏ ALWAYS take and return phone calls. Even if you are too busy to really engage in conversation or answer a complicated question, take or return the call. Say, "I'm working on a deadline now, can I call you this afternoon?" Your clients will like that you take the time to call them, and they will respect that you don't interrupt another client's important work at the ring of a telephone.
- ❏ Say yes to your clients as much as possible—Even if you have to hang up the phone and find someone else to do the work or answer their question for you.

Remember the following points as you conduct your marketing:

Set goals   How many letters will you send per month? How much money will you set aside to advertise in 1994? Who are you determined to reach? These goals will help keep you on course and make you feel like you've accomplished something when you can tick them off. You can also set rejection-based goals to make you feel better, such as, "Every time a meeting doesn't pan out, I'll send ten more letters."

It's a numbers game   If you always have lots of letters in the mail, phone messages on spindles, ads in the papers, and brochures on desks, you will end up with a busy practice.

Keep marketing even when you are busy   Otherwise you'll find your business cycles too severe—the busy times when you don't market will be followed by slow periods in which you do nothing but market.

Repetition works   Don't be shy about mailing the same letter to the same company more than once. It will often work the second time. Or even the third. Think about how many times you get direct-mail packages from the same companies.

Quality counts   You don't need to spend top dollar on four-color glossy brochures, but you do need to have materials that look classy. If you are going to pay $500 every time you get a brochure printed, you might as well pay somebody $300 up front to get it written and designed right.

Consistency works, too   If you advertise in the local business paper, you'll draw more business by running the same ad—or a similar one—than by changing your look every week or month. Figure out what your message is. (Are you the fastest? The best for retailers? The one who offers pickup and delivery convenience?) Keep that message in every ad, brochure, and presentation. People will start to think of you as the bookkeeper to call for your niche.

Patience is a virtue   Marketing doesn't always pay off right away. Sometimes you go after a client, make a good impression, and then he decides to let his sister-in-law do his business books anyway. Make a good impression and he'll be back after she messes up. Or, he'll pass your name to a colleague who happens to mention that she's looking for someone to do her books.

Marketing is an investment that pays off   Marketing is usually not free. Its costs money and time. When finances and hours are tight, it's easy to convince yourself that it's a waste of both, but if you stick with it, you will be rewarded.

Marketing gets your foot in the door You still have to sell yourself and your services to the potential client who calls. And you still have to be good.

Marketing makes you feel good Not much is more depressing, when you are in business for yourself, than sitting in your office all day and waiting for the phone to ring. When you resolve to actively market your business, you can feel good about what you're doing, even when you're in a slump. Call 20 people and you're likely to reach one who is interested or who knows someone else who is interested in your business. Write a good letter and, at the end of a nothing day, you'll know you've done something. You've been proactive, the number one indicator of a successful businessperson!

Using "The Whole Package"[2]

The key to success in freelancing is using the whole package of methods to get your name recognized, says American Institute of Professional Bookkeepers member Patty Marx Miller, of My Bookie in Newhall, California. She now has 20 regular clients averaging $250 a month each. Her package has three parts:

Join every local group you can The day Miller started freelancing, she joined the following:

- Chamber of Commerce—"I go to business mixers, join committees, attend meetings, and participate."
- Leads Club, which is a chapter of Leads International (a women's networking group)—"I got my first six clients here. They've referred other clients," she says.
- Pro-Net—a networking club that's since dissolved.
- Soroptimist's Club—a charitable service club.

"Belonging (to these organizations) has direct benefits—a strong trust is built over time as people get to know you and see how well you work on committees and projects," she says. "Soon they feel comfortable recommending you to business associates. Some groups let members speak, which gives you a chance to show what you do and hand out brochures."

Advertise in the local papers Miller put an ad the size of a business card in the business section of her local Sunday paper. It cost her $175 a month. Although it was four months before her first call came, it has netted her four steady clients who yield $12,000 in annual income.

The ad is eye-catching. Her logo is a little old lady with a green eyeshade, pencil behind her ear, book in hand, sitting under a lightbulb with a phone but no desk. The copy says, "My Bookie Bookkeeping Services—you can bet on us. Custom bookkeeping services. Customized financial reports. Payroll check writing. Tax return service. We pick up and deliver." The ad includes her address and phone number.

• • • • • • • • •

[2]Reprinted by permission from *The General Ledger* newsletter, published by the American Institute of Professional Bookkeepers, Rockville, MD. All Rights Reserved.

"Because my ad is catchy, whenever I go anywhere, even to a stationery store for the first time, people say, "Oh, I've heard of you," she says.

Introduce yourself to local CPAs   Miller called five when she was starting and stressed that she didn't do income taxes, only payroll and sales taxes. This let them know she was no threat. She says many CPAs do bookkeeping and are trying to get away from it.

"The key is getting to see prospects in person," she says. "I offer a 'free evaluation' estimate to prospects. It's usually much less than they expected. Most firms assume bookkeeping fees are the same as CPA rates." For prospects who want references, she keeps a list of five current clients, updated as needed.

Marketing is not something you do once, or even once a year. It's a continual process. Its many components work together to bolster your image in the business community. Follow your business plan schedule; spread out the letters, calls, ads, and appearances so your name is always going out to people.

Implementation

11 Managing your finances

The day you become a business, you enter a new financial world—one in which you must think like a corporation, even if you are only one person, sitting at a computer in the basement of your house. You must set your fees at rates high enough to assure you a reasonable lifestyle and low enough to assure you a steady stream of clients. You must think of the money coming in and out of your checking account as taxable events in the life of your business.

You need to pay estimated taxes on your estimated earnings, take care of your own overhead, and keep your own records. Your overhead will include fringe benefits such as health insurance and retirement accounts. Your business records (an area in which you admittedly have an edge over other one-person businesses) should be clean enough to satisfy an IRS auditor and detailed enough to give you real answers about how your business is running.

Self-employment finances can be broken down into five areas, all of which is covered in this chapter:

- The financial costs and benefits of self-employment.
- Taxes.
- Recordkeeping.
- Setting fees.
- The psychological aspects of seesaw income.

When are you a business?

The issue of when you are a business is important to the Internal Revenue Service and, therefore, to you. Once you are a legitimate business, you can deduct your business costs, even if they are higher than your earnings, and produce a tax loss.

If the IRS deems your business a hobby, you still can deduct your costs, but only up to the amount that offsets earnings in the activity. Only a business can take a business loss. For that reason, it behooves you to become a business as quickly as possible. How do you do that? Earning money is the easiest way to prove to tax auditors that you are a business. If you can show a profit in three out of five years, you're a business unless the IRS can prove otherwise.

That's the slow way to establish a company, however. What about in the first year, when you are buying your computer system, your stationary, and your supplies, as well as doing mailings? It wouldn't be surprising for someone to show a loss in the first year (or partial year) in which she set up a new bookkeeping company.

The IRS has a list of 13 questions that determine the business-versus-hobby test. And sad to say, one of them is just having too much fun. If the IRS thinks you are deriving too much pleasure from your work and not making money, it can determine that you run a hobby and not a business enterprise. Practically speaking, that applies more to people who set up tourism research businesses or rock and roll bands than it does to bookkeepers. See the sidebar for the quickest way to prove you are a business.

Proving you are

The simplest way to prove you are a business before you show a profit is to act like a business. Set up a separate checking account. Keep businesslike hours. Solicit clients. If you can demonstrate that you spend $400 on a mailing trying to drum up clients, as well as another $250 printing business cards and stationery, that's how you show you are legitimately going after profitability, even if it's escaped you so far.

Financial costs & benefits of being a business

The biggest surprise that hits most self-employed people the first time they pay income taxes is the self-employment tax. This tax pays for Social Security and Medicare, and it hits those of us who are self-employed twice as hard as the rest of the world because we pay twice as much.

Here's why: when you work for a company, you pay 6.2 percent of your income to Social Security (up to an income of $55,500) and 1.45 percent of your income to Medicare (up to an income of $130,200). This amount adds up to 7.65 percent, and it's a figure your employer matches with its own contribution on your behalf. Your employer considers this figure part of your compensation, but because you never see it taken out of your pay, it's invisible to you.

When you work for yourself, this half becomes clearly visible. You pay both halves of the Social Security and Medicare taxes off your business net profit; that's an added 15.3 percent tax on top of your income taxes. If you are in the 28-percent or 33-percent tax bracket and live in a state with an income tax of 5 or 6 percent, you are approaching (or surpassing) a 50-percent tax rate on your business income. Thus, it behooves you to deduct as many expenses as legitimately possible from your taxable business income. You can deduct half of your self-employment tax from your 1040 tax return, a break that saves only a fraction of what it costs you.

What are the other hidden costs of self-employment? Long-term security, which can be seen financially as employee benefits. After you've been in business for a few years (at the longest), you should build a retirement plan into your rate structure. If you were employed at someone else's company, you'd most likely have a retirement plan.

The same is true of health, life, and disability insurance. If you don't have a working spouse whose benefits you can use, don't scrimp on these necessities. A disabled self-employed person can end up even more impoverished than one who had some protective benefits on the job. You do get a little help from the tax man in this instance. Self-employed people can deduct 100 percent of their retirement benefit contributions (up to certain levels) from their taxable income.

Taxes

While your business can take several forms, it is most likely a sole proprietorship, which means that you will report your business income and expenses on a Schedule C, shown in FIG. 11-1. The best way to familiarize yourself with your taxes as you start your business is to carefully review Schedule C for deductible expenses, and similarly, read IRS Publication 535, Business Expenses, for more ideas in deductibility. The following are some of the best, and some of the most overlooked, business deductions.

The home-office deduction Read chapter 4 for a detailed explanation of how to take the home-office deduction. Don't forget to take this deduction. If you are giving up a room in your house that could otherwise be a guest room, family room, or bedroom, you are making a sacrifice to the business. It's legitimate, it's lucrative, and it's legal.

Business equipment Section 179 of the tax code lets small businesses deduct up to $10,000 on business equipment in the year they buy the equipment, instead of taking years to depreciate it. This deduction is a huge tax break and means that you can deduct your entire computer system (as long as it is used solely for your business) from your business income in the first year of operation. This provision includes furnishings as well: your desk, chair, and lamp are all business equipment.

SCHEDULE C
(Form 1040)

Department of the Treasury
Internal Revenue Service (5)

Profit or Loss From Business
(Sole Proprietorship)

▶ Partnerships, joint ventures, etc., must file Form 1065.

▶ Attach to Form 1040 or Form 1041. ▶ See Instructions for Schedule C (Form 1040).

OMB No. 1545-0074

1992

Attachment
Sequence No. **09**

Name of proprietor | Social security number (SSN)

A Principal business or profession, including product or service (see page C-1)

B Enter principal business code (from page 2) ▶

C Business name

D Employer ID number (Not SSN)

E Business address (including suite or room no.) ▶
City, town or post office, state, and ZIP code

F Accounting method: **(1)** ☐ Cash **(2)** ☐ Accrual **(3)** ☐ Other (specify) ▶

G Method(s) used to value closing inventory: **(1)** ☐ Cost **(2)** ☐ Lower of cost or market **(3)** ☐ Other (attach explanation) **(4)** ☐ Does not apply (if checked, skip line H)   Yes | No

H Was there any change in determining quantities, costs, or valuations between opening and closing inventory? If "Yes," attach explanation

I Did you "materially participate" in the operation of this business during 1992? If "No," see page C-2 for limitations on losses

J Was this business in operation at the end of 1992? . . . .

K How many months was this business in operation during 1992? . . . . . . ▶

L If this is the first Schedule C filed for this business, check here . . . . ▶ ☐

Part I Income

1	Gross receipts or sales. **Caution:** *If this income was reported to you on Form W-2 and the "Statutory employee" box on that form was checked, see page C-2 and check here* . . . . ▶ ☐	**1**	
2	Returns and allowances	**2**	
3	Subtract line 2 from line 1	**3**	
4	Cost of goods sold (from line 40 on page 2)	**4**	
5	**Gross profit.** Subtract line 4 from line 3	**5**	
6	Other income, including Federal and state gasoline or fuel tax credit or refund (see page C-2) . . . ▶	**6**	
7	**Gross income.** Add lines 5 and 6	**7**	

Part II Expenses (Caution: *Do not enter expenses for business use of your home on lines 8–27. Instead, see line 30.*)

8	Advertising	**8**		**21**	Repairs and maintenance . .	**21**
9	Bad debts from sales or services (see page C-3) . .	**9**		**22**	Supplies (not included in Part III) .	**22**
10	Car and truck expenses (see page C-3—also attach **Form 4562**)	**10**		**23**	Taxes and licenses . . .	**23**
11	Commissions and fees. . .	**11**		**24**	Travel, meals, and entertainment:	
12	Depletion.	**12**		**a**	Travel	**24a**
13	Depreciation and section 179 expense deduction (not included in Part III) (see page C-3) .	**13**		**b**	Meals and entertainment .	
14	Employee benefit programs (other than on line 19) . . .	**14**		**c**	Enter 20% of line 24b subject to limitations (see page C-4) .	
15	Insurance (other than health) .	**15**		**d**	Subtract line 24c from line 24b	**24d**
16	Interest:			**25**	Utilities	**25**
a	Mortgage (paid to banks, etc.) .	**16a**		**26**	Wages (less jobs credit) . .	**26**
b	Other	**16b**		**27a**	Other expenses (list type and amount):	
17	Legal and professional services .	**17**				
18	Office expense	**18**				
19	Pension and profit-sharing plans .	**19**				
20	Rent or lease (see page C-4):					
a	Vehicles, machinery, and equipment	**20a**				
b	Other business property . .	**20b**		**27b**	Total other expenses . . .	**27b**

28	**Total expenses** before expenses for business use of home. Add lines 8 through 27b in columns ▶	**28**	
29	Tentative profit (loss). Subtract line 28 from line 7	**29**	
30	Expenses for business use of your home. Attach **Form 8829**	**30**	
31	**Net profit or (loss).** Subtract line 30 from line 29. If a profit, enter here and on Form 1040, line 12. Also, enter the net profit on Schedule SE, line 2 (statutory employees, see page C-5). If a loss, you MUST go on to line 32 (fiduciaries, see page C-5)	**31**	
32	If you have a loss, you MUST check the box that describes your investment in this activity (see page C-5). If you checked 32a, enter the loss on Form 1040, line 12, and Schedule SE, line 2 (statutory employees, see page C-5). If you checked 32b, you MUST attach **Form 6198**.	**32a** ☐ All investment is at risk. **32b** ☐ Some investment is not at risk.

For Paperwork Reduction Act Notice, see Form 1040 instructions.   Cat. No. 11334P   Schedule C (Form 1040) 1992

11-1

IRS Schedule C — the form on which sole proprietors report their income.

Publications When you subscribe to tax journals and business magazines to keep up with accounting issues, or to local business papers to keep up with the client population in your community, deduct, deduct, deduct.

Supplies Supplies are probably the most obvious, least overlooked tax deduction, but use it to rationalize a well-stocked desk. There's no excuse for anyone who operates a home-based business to have to share a stapler with his family.

Cleaning   Do you have someone come in and clean your house and office every week or two? Clearly a luxury, but if you can afford it, having your office cleaned is legitimately deductible. It will help you stay organized, too. Prorate the house cleaning just as you prorate the home-office deduction. (You are not, however, permitted to deduct the prorated costs of getting your yard maintained, even if you do so to keep your entrance client-pleasingly clean.)

Phone service   If you have a separate business line, it is totally deductible. If you use your family phone, you aren't permitted to deduct even a portion of the monthly service charge, but you can write off all long-distance business calls and business-related add-on services, such as call waiting.

Telecommunicating   If you use on-line services or bulletin boards for business, such as finding customers or doing research, you can deduct the portion of your connect and subscription charges that is work-related.

Interest   If you buy a couch for your living room and put it on your family's Mastercard, that interest you pay is just not deductible. If you charge your business equipment on a credit card, however, and take a year to pay it off, all the interest is deductible on your Schedule C as a business interest. (A portion of your home mortgage interest is also deductible against your Schedule C if you take a home office deduction. It's worth more on your Schedule C, though, than on your 1040 Schedule A deduction list, because it offsets both the self-employment tax and the income tax.

Gifts   Do you buy your clients a basket of fruit for the holidays? Or send out calendars and keychains throughout the year? All of these gifts are deductible, as long as you don't spend more than $25 per gift.

Entertainment   You can still deduct 80 percent of the business lunch, dinner, or breakfast—just record the names of your dining companions and the nature of your discussion.

Maintenance and repairs   Keep your computer and copier running well; all upkeep costs are deductible.

Business trips   Trips are tricky. If you went to Florida for a week to take the kids to Disney World and to see your mother, but also stopped off on the way to take a client to lunch, you can deduct the lunch, or 80 percent of it, anyway, but not the trip. If you went to Florida for a convention and took your mother to lunch, you can deduct the trip, and 80 percent of your lunch, but not your mother's. There are strict rules about prorating trips when you combine business and pleasure. If you did go to Disney World you might see Jiminy Cricket, anyway, who would tell you to always let your conscience be your guide.

Child care   Just because you work at home does not mean you don't need to pay someone to watch your kids while you work. The child-care credit is more than a deduction, but it doesn't come out of your business income. It's a separate tax credit that you get by filing Form 2441 with your income tax return.

Local transportation   You can deduct the wear and tear on your car in two ways. You can either record every auto expense and prorate it for the amount of its business use, or you can just deduct 28 cents (for 1993) per mile of business use. The first method is more labor intensive for you and can only be used if more than half the mileage you put on your car in a year is business mileage.

Professional fees and services   Did you pay an attorney to help set up your business? Or a courier service to deliver reports to your clients? All professional fees and services are legitimately deductible costs of doing business.

Memberships   If you belong to the American Institute of Professional Bookkeepers, the National Association of Tax Preparers, or any of the other organizations that serve your field, your dues are deductible. So are any dues to local business networking organizations, such as the Chamber of Commerce.

Estimating taxes

If you are in transition from an employed position to the self-employed life, you need to stop thinking that your taxes are automatically deducted from your paycheck, and get into the habit of sending money to the federal and state government four times a year to cover the income tax you expect to owe. You will be expected to make these payments on April 15, June 15, October 15, and January 15, which is also when you catch up with any tax liabilities for the previous year. You will not be reminded. You will, however, be penalized if you fail to pay enough in estimated taxes.

How can you estimate taxes on income if you are starting a business and don't know how much you will make? Just keep a running tally of your income and expenses and pay enough every quarter to cover the income you've made in that quarter. As years go by and you can guesstimate your annual income, you can pay estimated taxes equal to the taxes you paid the previous year and escape penalties.

If your business is slow to get off the ground, or part-time, you can sometimes avoid estimated taxes in the beginning by having more income withheld from your paycheck or from your spouse's paycheck to cover your estimated taxes. When you are doing your estimating, remember to include the effects of the self-employment tax as well as regular income taxes.

Recordkeeping

To take all of these nice deductions, of course, you must document them, something you probably know more about than the average bear. Keep all receipts, canceled checks, and similar proofs of expenses paid. You might find, however, that the records you keep for yourself do not need to be as detailed and sophisticated as those you keep for some of your clients. If you already are using one accounting program that you are totally comfortable with, you can put your own business records in it. If you think that's overkill, keep a straight list of your income and expenses on a spreadsheet.

Set up each column in the spreadsheet (or each expense account in your chart of accounts) to correspond to a line item in the Schedule C. Number each receipt to match the line item of your list, or the transaction number in your accounting program. Use an accordion file for your receipts, with a separate section labeled for each category of expense. Also keep a log in your car, so that you can note beginning and ending mileage, trip mileage, and the business purpose of every trip you intend to deduct.

Setting your fees

This is the part you've been waiting for, I know. What does everyone else charge and how much can I charge? There was a reason for me leaving it for the end of the chapter: you need to get a realistic sense of how much overhead you must build into your fees and *not undercharge*.

Setting fees is a delicate balance; especially if you are new to bookkeeping and you feel the need to low-ball your rates. Rates that are too low will hurt: they will hurt your profession, by driving down rates and expectations on the part of clients and potential clients. They will also hurt you in two ways. If you charge too little, you won't be able to make a decent wage at bookkeeping, and you'll start cutting corners that will show up in lower-quality service to clients. You'll lose potential clients right away who want quality accounting work, not the cheapest.

Tampa bookkeeper Lionel Martinez sums up his philosophy on rates like this; "My advice is to do quality work. We are not the cheapest ones in town, but we are known as responsible, and we set a fair fee. There are people out there who will do work for nothing, but when you need them, they won't be there. And the clients who want you for nothing will jump across the street for $1 less anyway."

Hourly versus fixed

Should you set hourly fees or job fees? What about retainers? When you are first starting, you might want to stick with hourly fees for a few reasons. You aren't established enough to command the monthly minimums of your more well-known competitors, and you can start building a practice with what falls off of their table. Even more practically, you might not know how long and involved various tasks are. You might arrive at flat fees that underestimate the amount of work you need to put into a job. See the sidebar on how to estimate how much a job will cost.

How many hours, and how much per hour?

These are the big questions. The really short answer to this question is this: bill $\frac{1}{1000}$th of what you want to make in a year. If you want to earn $50,000 a year, charge $50 an hour.

There is a formula behind the short answer. The formula for determining how many hours you can actually bill in a year is:

Gross hours per year:	
40 hours/week × 52 weeks/year	2,080 hours
Less days off:	
Vacation (three weeks)	120 hours
Holidays (typically 13 days)	104 hours
Sick leave (1 week)	40 hours
Subtotal, days off	264 hours
Net available workdays	1,816 hours
Less:	
Marketing (about 20 percent of available time)	363 hours
Administrative and reading (½ hour a day)	112 hours
Downtime (no work available, about 15% of time)	273 hours
Wasted time (15 minutes a day, ha ha)	56 hours
Subtotal, subtractions from available time	804 hours
Total billable hours per year	1,008 hours

There's nothing wrong with starting low and slowly raising your rates and minimums as you establish yourself. "I had one client who I charged $500 the first year I had him," says Roger Goodeve, who charges his clients an annual retainer. "It was way too low. But when I went back to him and raised it significantly for the next year, it wasn't a problem." The client was so happy with the service, says Goodeve, that the client's annual fee has gone from $500 to $3000, and he still feels like he's getting good value for the money.

Monthly minimums or flat charges can work best for you and your client. It comforts them, because they know there's a ceiling on what they'll be spending for bookkeeping. It also helps you schedule work flow. And, as you gain efficiency, it helps you build an hourly rate into your fees that might be higher than what your clients would actually pay. "If my clients knew what my hourly rate came out to, they'd drop dead," says one bookkeeper who only charges flat fees.

What does everyone else charge?

The best way to determine rates is to determine what the market will bear. Call potential clients or the competition and see if you can extract rate information from them as part of the marketing research routine described in chapter 10. Bookkeeping is local: what might seem too high in one city is too low in another.

Broadly speaking, the bookkeepers interviewed for this book charged between $25 and $50 an hour, with the people at the lower end having less experience and working in less expensive parts of the country. In big cities on both coasts, $50 an hour seemed a standard, if not always reachable, base. See the sidebar for what other bookkeepers are charging.

Maine   To set people up on their own accounting system, $75 an hour. For bookkeeping, $50 an hour.

New Hampshire $25 an hour for bookkeeping.

New York   "I started out at $25 an hour. A big mistake! Number one, people think you are only as good as the amount you charge. And number two, I couldn't live on it."

Florida   "We de-emphasize how long each job takes and put people on retainer for monthly write-ups. Our minimum is $100 or $150 a month, and we bill hourly after that for end-of-the-year work or special reports."

New Jersey   "I try to get $50 an hour, but I don't always get what I want."

California   "My minimum rates are $45 an hour, and I have monthly minimums, too. Otherwise it just isn't worth my while."

Maryland   "I only charge $30 an hour, but I prefer to get a monthly retainer. I don't think I have anyone now that I bill at less than $300 a month."

New Jersey   "My rate is only $20 an hour. My costs are low and I wouldn't feel comfortable charging much more than that."

Vermont   "I charge my clients $60 an hour for 'donkey work' when their records are messy and I have to decipher all of their receipts. That teaches them to put their records in order fast."

Who charges what

The American Institute of Professional Bookkeepers (AIPB) surveyed its freelancing members at the end of 1992 to see what typical charges were. Here's a summary of their results:

The AIPB survey

- At least 41.5 percent of freelancing members do so full-time and average $27 an hour; 58.5 percent freelance part-time (in addition to a full-time job) and average $22 an hour.
- At least 71 percent of freelancers have solo practices and average $27 an hour; the 28.3 percent who have employees average $32 an hour.
- Almost half of the full-time independent bookkeepers in the survey have different fee structures depending on their clients, 40.7 percent always charge by the hour, and only 8.3 percent always charge by the job.

- Average rates in the New England, Mid-Atlantic, and Pacific regions average $27 an hour; in the East-North Central, South Atlantic, and West-South Central areas, the average was $32 an hour.
- More-experienced bookkeepers charge higher rates than newcomers. (Is this because they have more experience to offer or because they've learned not to undercharge?)
- *Bookkeepers who ran their businesses on computers averaged $27 an hour; those who performed the work manually averaged $22 an hour.*

People make mistakes, and there isn't a self-employed person who hasn't lost money on some jobs by underbidding them. With experience, you'll get a better feel for the true cost of a job. You'll also learn that you'll lose surprisingly few clients when you do decide it's time to raise your rates. See the sidebar for average hourly rates.

AIPB survey of average hourly rates

This survey includes bookkeepers who are moonlighting. Note that they typically charge less than full-time freelancers.

Hourly Rate	Percentage Charging this Rate
$10–$14	16.9
$15–$19	20.6
$20–$24	16.0
$25–$29	17.8
$30–$34	8.6
$35–$39	4.3
$40–$44	3.2
$45–$49	1.4
$50–$54	1.1
$55–$60	1.1
over $60	2.0

Life on a seesaw income

For many people, the hardest part of running a home-based business is keeping their equilibrium while their income bounces up and down. You might find that you collect a lot more money in some months than others. During tax season, you'll most likely be busy boosting your cash flow. The summer months might be slow.

There are financial and psychological ramifications of a seesaw income. The financial ramifications are obvious: you need to conserve your money when you are flush so that you'll have it to spend during lean times. Psychologically, the financial seesaw can be even more difficult. You need to adopt a certain serenity in the face of family finances that might be decidedly non-serene. The following are some ideas for handling the financial ups and downs of self-employment.

Try to vary your clients Avoid becoming overly dependent on one client, and avoid building a practice of clients who all want their books done once a year during January. If you have some monthlies, some quarterlies, and some companies operating on non-calendar fiscal years, your cash will flow a little smoother.

Use credit You can use your credit cards a little more freely than you otherwise would. Sometimes during startup, you might need to use your checking account's overdraft features or your credit cards to smooth your payments (or delay them until that next check comes in).

Live beneath your means When you are building a business, the best advice is to live as cheaply as you can and defer major luxury expenses while you put money back into the business. Don't spend the last penny every month.

Work out a budget Your budget should give you a rough but realistic idea of how much money you need every month. When you make more than that amount in a month, put the extra money into a savings account—for when you make less.

Take a regular draw Come up with a bare-bones salary that your business can afford to pay you every month. Then draw that amount, on a regular basis, from your business checking account.

Turn down low-paying work You are better off, in the long run, having some really lean times and using them to market yourself to quality clients rather than filling up your schedule with low-paying, slow-paying clients who keep you too poor and too busy to grow.

Picture a worst-case scenario This image is just to get it out of your system. Imagine other ways you could make money if you had to. Think about what would happen if your business failed outright. Life *would* go on.

Think about the people you most admire in life Chances are, these people you most admire are not the wealthiest that you know. Learn to value the intangible assets of your lifestyle.

Preparing for retirement

Establishing a retirement account and contributing to it on a regular basis is one of the best things you can do for yourself as a self-employed person. The money you contribute is exempt from taxes, a break that in itself can save you almost 40 percent of the amount contributed after federal, state, and local income taxes. Even better, the money builds tax-free until you are ready to tap into it after you are age 59½.

As a self-employed individual, you can establish a simplified employee pension individual retirement account (SEP-IRA) or Keogh account. A Keogh account is more like an official corporate plan—it gives you more tax breaks in declaring the money when you take it out, and you can shelter more money in some Keogh plans than you can in SEP-IRAs. Keoghs must be established before the end of the calendar year, if your business is on a calendar year, but you can contribute up through April 15 of the following year and still count it against the previous year's taxes. A SEP-IRA is simpler to set up, and you can establish it as late as April 15 (if you are on a calendar year and that's your filing deadline).

You can shelter 15 percent of your business income per year in either of these accounts, and certain types of Keoghs allow you put away 10 percent more. Both of those percentages are based on your net business income minus your retirement contribution, plus half of your self-employment tax. This is a complicated circular rule that leads to a more complicated calculation, which ultimately becomes simple and lets you set aside as much as 13.0434 percent of your business net in an IRA or 20 percent in a Keogh.

A bank, a brokerage, or a mutual fund company can help you set up one of these accounts. If you have employees, consult an attorney or accountant who specializes in benefits, because the different types of plans have different implications for covering workers.

Do it anyway. Think of retirement plans this way: if you only put $2,000 a year into a tax-deferred retirement plan, and it's invested in a *conservative* stock mutual fund, you'll have $169,000 in 25 years.

12 Why a modem?

A modem is a little box that allows your computer to talk to other computers through telephone lines. You'll never need to know the following little fact, but *modem* stands for modulator/demodulator. Modems inspire great fear among the uninitiated—there are people all over this country who have modems but are too intimidated to try them, or don't have the first idea about what to do with them. If you are one of those people, consider the following story.

Rosemary Peavler is a business professor at Morehead State University in Morehead, Kentucky, who runs a bookkeeping business on the side. Her business is conducted almost entirely by remote control with her computer, modem, and telephone line.

She finds her clients on-line. She participates in special-interest groups on CompuServe, an international on-line information and bulletin-board service, where she can discuss financial planning and tax and bookkeeping issues. Other participants sometimes respond by expressing an interest in hiring her. She mails them her resume through CompuServe's electronic mail.

She services her clients on-line. With PC Anywhere, which is remote-control software, she can actually dial into a client's computer from her home office. "If we both have the same software, I can dial up and actually be on their computer. I see on my screen what they are seeing on their screen. We can both be looking at the same reports and talking about the numbers."

She researches on-line. Sometimes she's faced with a question she can't answer, so she'll post it on one of the computer bulletin boards. Another user—who might be in Denver or Cincinnati or Anchorage—pops up with the answer. A slew of libraries, including specialized tax and accounting sources, are also available on-line.

She communicates with employees on-line. When Rosemary hires a student or helper to do basic bookkeeping for her, she can send the information from her computer directly to the helper's computer.

She could (but doesn't, yet) use her modem to send information back to her computer from a laptop when she's working in the field. She could also file tax returns electronically with her modem, another use to which the modem could easily (and profitably) be put.

Still afraid of that little box? To anyone who bills hourly, time is money. And there's little that saves as much time as computers talking to each other without people getting in the middle to translate or retype information. Just relax, and let your PC do the talking.

You might already have a modem

Many of today's computer systems (and virtually all laptops) come with an internal modem. It's built into the computer. If it isn't, you can buy a good-quality modem for $100. You'll need a communications program as well to translate the computer information to signals that can travel on a phone line and then translate incoming signals back. Once you install the software and read enough of the manual to learn how to use your modem, you're ready to let your computer do the talking.

Five ways to use your modem

1. The next best thing to being there   You can go to your client's office, work on his accounting software, and send the data back to your computer for final formatting and reporting. Or, you can go to his office, enter data into your laptop, and then send it from your laptop to your computer. If you are working with a staff accountant or office manager, they can send reports and data directly from their computer to yours; you can massage the data reports and send them back. You can also use a remote-control program to work in your clients' program from the comforts of your own office.

2. Research and technical support   Many accounting and tax journals, publications, and index files are available through the on-line services listed in the following section. If you encounter a tricky situation, and you aren't sure how to enter it, you can go on-line and find citations and even full texts of articles on the subject. There are too many on-line information sources to name here, but among the ones you'll find in the services listed are the *Journal of Accountancy*, the *Accounting & Tax Index*, the *Small Business Administration*, the *Electronic Yellow Pages*, and many, many more.

Most major computer programs (including accounting software programs) also offer on-line technical support and meeting places. If you are using One-Write Plus and are having a problem, for example, you can dial up the Meca forum in CompuServe, post your question, and check back a few hours later for an answer. Chances are you'll have feedback not only from the company but from other One-Write Plus users who have faced similar situations.

3. Network   The major on-line services also offer bulletin boards, where people of similar interests can congregate. That's where Rosemary Peavler gets all her clients. Even more valuable than new clients, sometimes, is a place to meet (electronically) other bookkeepers who don't mind sharing their secrets with you because you're in different parts of the country. Participants in on-line conferences and message boards can trade stories about favorite programs, sticky client problems, and even rates. And, of course, expertise. If you are about to go after your first nonprofit client, for example, you can place a notice asking for advice on nonprofit bookkeeping.

Ingrid Landskron credits her participation in CompuServe's "Work From Home Forum" with much of the successful start of her business. Through contacts she made there, she started a home-based business network for those in New Jersey. That's where she found her first clients, too. At the same time, she's kept in touch with other bookkeeping and tax professionals active on the CompuServe forum; experts there have supplied prompt, accurate questions for every tax or accounting question she's had to post.

She's also kept up a running dialog with Terri Conlon, a New Hampshire-based bookkeeper. The two have shared tips and marketing strategies that have paid off for both of them.

4. Free software   Many people develop software for fun or for the experience of it and upload those programs to bulletin boards. You can find bulletin boards in the on-line services that specialize in whatever type of computer you might have; there will be libraries of computer art and all kinds of software: calendars, backup programs, financial calculators, and even communications programs for dialing up the services in which you find them. In these computer-oriented bulletin boards you'll also find more networking opportunities and people who might have experience in software areas where you don't.

5. Filing electronic tax returns   You don't have to be someone special to become an "electronic filing service," reminds the Internal Revenue Service. You only have to have a computer, a modem, a communications program, and the ability to set them all up to dial into the IRS. The IRS will send you the right specifications, set you up with a practice run, and make sure you're in.

Online resources

The following services provide a variety of non-bookkeeping-related services, as well as the previously mentioned business advantages. You might find yourself using them, for example, for their weather reports, travel reservation systems, or stock market reports. Before selecting a service, call and find out exactly what programs they offer and what their price structure is. You can always try out a few—most only charge for usage, and you can always quit when you want. Most also offer free trial months when you buy the setup packages. Some are included free in new computer packages.

Dow Jones/News Retrieval

Dow Jones & Co., Inc
PO Box 300
Princeton, NJ 08450
(800) 257-5114

Dow Jones offers full text articles from the *Wall Street Journal* and other economic and investment oriented statistics and data libraries.

CCH ACCESS Online

Commerce Clearing House, Inc.
4025 West Peterson Avenue
Chicago, IL 60646
(800) 248-3248

The entire Library of Commerce Clearing House tax reports, including newsletters on tax issues, full text of the Internal Revenue Code, and libraries of state tax and tax court information is available here on a pay-only-for-what-you-use basis.

DIALOG

3460 Hillview Avenue
Palo Alto, CA 94304
(800) 334-2564

The grandfather of all on-line information services, Dialog now houses more than 400 specialty databases, including the aforementioned Accounting and Tax Index. It's expensive—depending on the database you're searching, an on-line research project can run more than $100 an hour, and it's not consumer-oriented like the following four services. DIALOG also offers Knowledge Index, a less-expensive alternative aimed at home-based users who can call in during nonbusiness hours.

CompuServe

500 Arlington Centre Boulevard
PO Box 20212

Columbus, OH 43220
(800) 848-8990

CompuServe offers special-interest bulletin boards called forums, including a Work-At-Home Forum and an Investors Forum. The biggest, most comprehensive, and also costliest of the consumer-oriented online services, CompuServe also houses more than 800 full text and abstracting databases through its IQuest collection. Owned by H&R Block, CompuServe also has an on-line tax-help service, though it's aimed more at consumers than tax professionals.

GEnie

401 North Washington Street
Rockville, Maryland 20850
(800) 638-9636

GEnie offers more than 300 services, including bulletin boards for home office workers, investors, and other business professionals, as well as programs to download and information databases.

America Online

8619 Westwood Center Drive
Vienna, Virginia 22182
(800) 827-6364

America Online offers an on-line small-business network, programs to download, and on-line databases.

Prodigy

445 Hamilton Avenue
White Plains, NY 10601
(800) PRODIGY

The populist service Prodigy is aimed at families and charges a flat monthly fee rather than the time-based connect charges of the other services. It includes an investor bulletin board, market statistics, and news reports, but it doesn't have the on-line databases of the more full-featured services.

Strictly Business!

933 Varsity Blvd.
Columbus, OH 43221
(614) 538-9250 (data line)

Strictly Business, a national bulletin board for business-minded people, offers on-line software libraries and peer advice on issues facing small business owners. You'll incur long-distance charges, but the participation fee is a negligible $25 a year, and you'll be able to network nationally on issues like how to start and manage a business, how to raise financing, business resources, franchising, and the like. You might even find some clients!

13 Tips, tactics, & troubleshooting

You've already printed your business card, hung your shingle, pulled in your first client, and delivered your first set of monthly statements. *Now* the questions really start. How do you get paid? What happens when you don't? What do you do when a client asks you to be dishonest? How do other bookkeepers handle these situations? How will you find out when payroll rules change? (They always do, don't they?)

Think of this chapter as a reference book within a reference book. It's a compendium of advice from fellow bookkeepers around the country about the situations you'll face as your business grows.

How to get paid

The first rule of getting paid in any business is this: you have to ask for it. "I used to just let my fees be due anytime," says Lenore Kondrat, a tax preparer from Mahwah, New Jersey. "But some people stiffed me altogether, and others kept stringing me along. Now, everyone has to pay me COD (cash on delivery). I've lost a few clients over it, but they were the ones that always wanted to string me along, anyway." For ongoing bookkeeping clients, cash on delivery might be unnecessarily stiff terms, but the principle of asking for your money remains unchanged.

The best way to ask for money, of course, is to send an invoice. If your invoice clearly states how much you are expected to be paid and when, it will do more to bring your money in than anything else. Most of the software programs you will use for your clients can prepare invoices. Note that those invoices that get paid the quickest usually say *invoice* on them. (Some businesses have even balked at paying *statements*.)

Include your terms on your invoice—30 days net is typical. Some independent businesspeople have had luck levying interest, or a monthly rebilling charge, on late payments that must be reinvoiced.

Prequalify clients

Prequalify your clients up front, even if this step is simply a conversation in which you clearly explain your rates and terms. Let your clients know you are a small business and depend on regular cash flow to keep operating.

You can also receive merchant status for American Express and a major bank credit card such as Mastercard or Visa. Then, if your clients complain of cash flow problems, you can tell them that you will put their charge on their credit card. (Some clients might even let you charge your fees directly and adjust their accounts automatically. It isn't sound business practice to allow the person in charge of the books to pay herself, however, so don't be offended if they won't go that far. You might find yourself doing everything except signing your own check.)

What to do when you aren't paid

Of course, there are those clients who will string you along on a regular basis. Most of these just want to hold off paying until the last possible second; a few really will skip out without paying. The good news is that this doesn't happen often in the bookkeeping business. Many of your clients are sharing their financial secrets with you and looking for regular monthly or quarterly service; they aren't likely to take one balance sheet and run. They are also people who, by definition, value clean finances, or they wouldn't be hiring a bookkeeper.

When it does happen, however, be assertive. If your terms are 30 days net and the check doesn't show up by day 35, give your client a call. If he is a good client and admits to having cash flow problems or claims to have lost your bill, you might permit leniency. If, on the other hand, you have bad feelings about the clients, tell them they have 60 days or you will suspend service. Don't do any more work for them, either, until they bring their account with you up to date. See sidebar for how to get ornery clients to pay.

Getting them to pay

A trick for getting the orneriest clients to pay up: once you've decided that a client isn't going to pay without going to court, take him there. Or *almost* there. Fill out all the forms to file suit in small claims court. Before you file the papers, send the (ex, by now) client a copy, along with a letter that says, "Unless payment is received by October 21, these papers will be filed."

I hope you never have to use it! But this system does work.

There are problem clients, and there are problem clients. The following are some examples of what I mean.

Personally, you like these people. But, they bring in grocery bags full of hard-to-read receipts, forget to record checks when they write them, and lose their bank statements. These problem clients are one of the easiest problems to deal with! Do the following:

The nice, but labor-intensive client

- Give them a nice notebook system for recording everything and attempt to train them into being organized; or
- Tell them you'll do it all for them but must charge them plenty for your time.

Usually, once you've billed this client at your hourly rate for two days of sorting through receipts and calling the bank for duplicate statements, your client will see the light and get organized. If not, you can earn a tidy living keeping him organized—bill him at your top rate and hire a less-experienced helper to do what one bookkeeper calls "the donkey work."

The not-nice, labor-intensive client

The best thing about working for yourself is this: you don't have to take abuse. When a client is really unpleasant, you can fire him. The bookkeepers interviewed for this book agreed that their profile of the worst client was the one who never took their phone calls or read their reports, but then called in anger after bouncing a check or running into a cash-flow problem. You are a professional, and if you have a client whose account is difficult to manage and who is abusive, just tell him to go elsewhere.

You don't have to really like everyone you service, or get rid of every client who is not perfect. Clients with easy books and difficult personalities can be handled professionally and briefly. And, if every client you have is difficult and abusive, be honest and ask yourself if *you're* the one with the problem.

The unresponsive client

What do you do with a client who says he wants complete bookkeeping services, but never gets you his statements on time, isn't around to take your phone calls, and generally doesn't keep up his part of the bargain? Sometimes, this situation is just temporary as a client goes through an extremely busy period, but sometimes it's a person's basic mode of behavior. You can offer to pick up and deliver statements and reports if that will get you the contact and information you need. You can also explain, in a polite letter accompanying an incomplete monthly statement, that you can't do the work without the input.

Typically, these situations get resolved one way or another. Either the client starts delivering the materials you need, or it becomes clear that he really doesn't want complete bookkeeping service and will drop off your client list. "Now I can tell when a person is really serious," says one bookkeeper who has been running her own business for more than 10 years. I used to take on clients even when I could tell they weren't very serious. The more particular I got, the more they backed off; now I can spot it ahead of time."

The forest-fire client

This client always calls in a hurry. You're in the middle of working on someone else's books and he wants you to pull his file immediately and tell him how much he spent two years ago on freight charges. Or call his bank "Right now!" and find out where his bank statement is. If you are a parent, you already have an edge with this kind of client, because you can explain to him, as you do your children, that you only have two hands . . .

No, just kidding. You need to be a little more professional than that. Do learn, however, to say no to immediate requests if they are part of a pattern. Just say, "I can't interrupt what I'm doing now, but I'll be happy to call you back at 2:00." Explain that you take all of your clients' work very seriously and find it isn't good practice to interrupt bookkeeping work.

Alternatively, protect yourself from the phone when you really don't want to be disturbed by letting your answering machine or answering service take the call.

The "dumb" client

This client can become your favorite! He (or she) understands so little about the finances of his own business that he makes silly mistakes. Overpays taxes every year, pays extra money for costly accounting software he doesn't need, forgets to file estimated taxes. This client is good to have because you not only keep his books, you teach him how to save money and time. He'll be so grateful—you'll end up with a client for life.

The last word

The last word on problem clients: Trust your intuition. If it feels squishy from the beginning, it will probably turn to mush.

When you are asked to cheat

Unfortunately, this situation happens. If a client walks in the door and point-blank asks you to prepare two sets of books, "a real ledger and a ledger to show the IRS boys," it's an easy decision for you. He is asking you to do something clearly unethical and illegal. But what if it's a more subtle problem? Something just isn't right about his books, and you know it.

Here's how one bookkeeper handles it: "I have, on occasion, seen books that didn't look good, and I consider it my duty to warn my client. The people at the IRS aren't stupid. When a guy consistently has expenses of $5,000 a month and only makes $12,000 on his business, he's not going to get away with it, anyway. On the other hand, sometimes I have a suspicion that everything isn't kosher, but it's not concrete and there's nothing I can prove. The retailer who puts $20 in his pocket here or there is a good example—I only have a suspicion, and I'm not required by law or ethics to act on a suspicion."

Another bookkeeper tells of a client who asked to have his books manipulated so he would never pay income taxes. "He came in with this big rap about how he didn't believe in paying taxes, and I said, 'Uh oh, I think you need to find another accountant.'"

Draw your own line in the dust, but do so before you are presented with a situation you must resolve. Draw it well on this side of the law, too: you don't need a client putting you out of business. It just isn't true that "everybody does it."

The self-employed bookkeeper can be lonelier than the Maytag repairman. If you work at home, send messengers for files you need, and spend your days in front of your computer, you can find yourself wallowing in solitude. You need human interaction, but you can get that from family, friends, and neighbors who have nothing to do with your business. However, you also need the professional contacts and the information that comes with that human interaction.

Getting information & support

The best advice is to join a professional association where you can meet fellow bookkeepers and trade stories, either personally or through association publications. See the next two subsections for two professional groups that might meet your needs.

Most states also have statewide accountancy organizations with varying requirements: in many cases, preparing tax returns is enough to get you in. You can also join local home-based business networks and more general business organizations. They'll supply tips on how to manage your business, good potential client contacts, and practice. "I wasn't very good at networking," concedes Joan, an East Coast bookkeeper. "So I trained myself to be better at it. I joined the National Association of Women Business Owners and the Chamber of Commerce, and went out and met everyone. I've gotten much better at dealing with people," she said.

If you don't find a home-based business network in your community, consider starting one—entrepreneurs love to get together to talk about their common problems, such as what phone systems they like and how they found trustworthy employees. You can start by putting an ad in the community newspaper or by just spreading the word to everyone you know.

It's also important that you keep the information flowing into your home office. Look at the list of tax and accounting publishers in chapter 15 and send for their catalogues. Pick a newsletter or two to keep you up to date on changing accounting rules or tax requirements.

The American Institute of Professional Bookkeepers (AIPB) is the only membership organization in the country dedicated to the businesses at the

The AIPB

heart of this book. Despite its monopoly status, however, it does a quality job of bringing information to its 33,000 members.

The AIPB also offers members a technical hotline that operates during business hours. If you're stuck on an accounting question, you can call this number and learn how to handle the specifics of your situation. The organization also offers home study courses (see chapter 2) and state and federal tax forms.

The institute publishes two regular publications. *The Journal of Professional Bookkeeping and Management* is a technical journal with original articles and reprints from other accounting and management publications on issues of concern to professional bookkeepers. *The General Ledger* is a monthly newsletter that includes legislative and regulatory updates on bookkeeping and tax preparation, practical business management tips, bookkeeping lessons and quizzes, and membership surveys.

The AIPB serves self-employed and corporate bookkeepers. Annual dues are $39; there is an additional charge for the *Journal of Professional Bookkeeping and Management*. Write to the AIPB, Suite 207, 6001 Montrose Road, Rockville, MD 20852, or call (800) 622-0121.

The NSPA

The National Society of Public Accountants (NSPA) is not by name or focus a bookkeepers organization, but it does offer many of the services useful to bookkeepers, especially those who prepare tax returns or delve into higher levels of accounting than the basic ledger.

The Society offers an accreditation program through the Accreditation Council for Accountancy and Taxation, and offers almost 100 courses, seminars, and self-guided textbook and computer programs on all aspects of accounting and tax preparation. In addition, members can order inexpensive resource guides, including:

- Model Letters, Contracts, and Agreements for Accounting Practices
- Income and Fees of Accountants in Public Practice
- Marketing Professional Services
- Generally Accepted Tax Accounting Principles
- Synopsis of State Laws Regulating the Public Practice of Accountancy
- Practical Survival in the 1990s

The Society publishes public information brochures on such topics as "Choosing Your Professional Accountant and Tax Practitioner" and "Tax Return Preparation, Facts and Figures" that members can buy in sets of 100 and distribute to their clients. Members also receive discounts from financial publishers and receive several publications, including the *National Public Accountant*, a monthly professional journal, and the *Washington Reporter*, a biweekly newsletter that updates NSPA activities as well as regulatory developments. At accounting and tax seminars, members have the opportunity to meet others in their field, and you can also find other members through the NSPA directory. To qualify for full-voting active membership in the NSPA, you must meet one of four criteria:

- Enrollment before the IRS (explained in chapter 15).
- A state license to practice accountancy.
- An associate degree or baccalaureate degree with 24 semester hours in accounting.
- Accreditation by the Accreditation Council for Accountancy and Taxation.

Even without these qualifications, a practicing bookkeeper or tax preparer can qualify for associate membership status. Associate members receive all of the benefits of active membership, except they cannot vote in society elections and referendum.

Fees for active membership are $120 per year; for associate membership it is $84 per year. Write to the NSPA, 1010 North Fairfax Street, Alexandria, VA 22314-1574, or call (703) 549-6400.

How to hire help

"You can really make a lot of money in this business hiring people if they do a good job," concedes Mary Olcott Greiner, an Arlington, Virginia, bookkeeper. "But, if their heart isn't in it, you can lose a lot of clients." You can also find yourself training your own competition. Most bookkeepers, however, who have become employers say it is worth the effort.

Start by following this maxim: only hire (and pay for) the help you really need. A first step might be hiring another company to do certain tasks for you—this can be an answering service to pick up your phone, or a messenger service to collect client files and deliver your finished reports. A second step might be hiring people for specific closed-end jobs—you can use high school students or find a local handicapped workshop to do a mass mailing, for example.

Finally, you might want to bring in other bookkeepers to enter data and process records. You can hire these bookkeepers two different ways. Hire them as subcontractors to prepare reports and key in information, and pay them by the hour or the task. You can also hire part-time and full-time employees who will be in the office with you to answer the phone, run errands, and meet clients as you wish.

There are advantages to either approach, but the biggest advantage goes to the first: you aren't paying someone for time you can't use, and you aren't getting into a situation where you have to pay benefits and withhold payroll taxes. Be careful hiring an independent contractor, though. The IRS has cracked down on companies using "independent-contractor" arrangements to mask true employment situations. If the person you hired works only for you and works regular hours, you could have trouble proving that he is an independent contractor and not really your employee.

To find good employees, contact your local junior college or university and ask about accounting students; advertise in student newspapers and community newspapers. Network in your usual haunts—you might find someone in your bowling league who has some expertise or who wants to be trained. See the sidebar for information about hiring your own children.

How to hire your kids

One of the main advantages of self-employment is being able to hire your children. When children are old enough to be responsible, you can pay them to do simple business tasks. As they get older, their responsibilities (and salaries) can grow.

There are tax advantages to this as well as educational benefits. Your children's earned income most likely is taxed at a lower rate than yours—it's a good way to shelter some of your income while feeding their college fund.

Children like being brought into the business. You can let them start when they are about eight—they can put address labels on mass mailings, empty your office wastepaper basket, recycle your office paper. As they get older, you can train them in your field and pay them a respectable salary for the work they do. You can even—if you can find a bank or broker to help you—help them set up an Individual Retirement Account with their earnings. Sure, they'll have to keep the money locked up for about 50 or 60 years, but when they're ready for it, they'll probably have a million dollars!

As you staff up, you might want to have your employees specialize. In Beth Roll's California garage-turned-bookkeeping office, for example, one employee answers the phones and performs all the bank reconciliations and accounts receivable. A second employee works on accounts payable and general ledger reports. The computers are linked, so anyone working on a client's account can access any part of the account from their own computer.

How to manage stress

You may already know that bookkeeping can be a high-stress job. You are driven by deadlines, and it's likely that everyone's deadlines come at the same time. In tight times, you're the first victim of blame-the-messenger syndrome. Even when your client doesn't blame you, it's no fun to deliver bad news. The bad news often has an extra kick for you: when you are preparing books for financially troubled businesses, you can sometimes see your clients leaving before they actually do.

The "know better" syndrome affects bookkeepers, too. Sometimes, you can look at a company's books and know better than your client how to run her company, but she doesn't want to hear that, she just wants the statements, thank you.

No bookkeeper-specific magic solutions exist for working off the stress. It helps to be organized and keep a good calendar. If client personalities stress you, you can minimize difficult contacts by hiring an assistant to deliver reports and answer the phone. You can protect your schedule by setting aside specific times for client contact.

And, of course, you can eat right, exercise, hug your loved ones, and smell the roses daily to minimize that stress. Remind yourself that not many jobs allow flower sniffing between the hours of 9 and 5.

For the most part, this book has taken a cheerleader approach to building a bookkeeping business. You can do it! There's lots of work out there! It's easy! All true, but the other part of the story is this: in the current economic climate, it's a very competitive world. The key to making it in the bookkeeping/accounting services business is *service*. And the key to getting new clients is keeping the ones you have happy enough to start passing your name around. People hire you because they think you can save them time and hassles. Make sure you save them both. If you can even save them some money in the bargain, so much the better. Here are 10 tips for keeping your customers satisfied:

How to keep clients (happy)

1. Don't make mistakes. Review your work and review it again, until it's clean, clean, clean.
2. Bring them business. If you have a client who is a commercial artist and another who runs an ad agency, put them together. Referrals mean as much to them as they do to you.
3. Think about them even when you're not being paid to—send them a memo if tax laws that affect them change, for example. Once a year send an inexpensive holiday gift. If you aren't big on joining the holiday rush, time the gift for their birthday or the anniversary of the day they first hired you.
4. ALWAYS return their phone calls.
5. ALWAYS answer their questions. If you don't know the answer, don't shrug your shoulders and say "Beats me!" Say instead, "I think I know the answer, but I'm not certain. Let me check it out and call you back." They'll be impressed that you admit you need to check it out, and that you know where to look. This response inspires confidence in your abilities.
6. Save them money. Often, you can look over their data and find money-saving opportunities. "You don't need to keep paying this much in estimated taxes," you can point out, for example. Or, "Did you know that you were buying four subscriptions to the same publication?" Follow this strategy and you'll be worth your fee and more.
7. Thank them for the work. Every month, each time you deliver reports.
8. Explain what you're doing. True, they are hiring you so they don't have to learn bookkeeping. But they'll appreciate a quick lesson on how it all goes together, and how you do what you do.
9. Visit them. Even if they deliver their work to you, stop by occasionally to see their companies. Let them show off.

10. Be a sponge. Absorb everything they want to tell you about their businesses. You never know when you're going to need it. Just demonstrating that knowledge in conversations with your clients will keep them from going to other bookkeepers.

When clients ask for advice you can't give

This one's easy! Just as you are trying to get yourself on the referral list of attorneys and accountants, find a couple of them you trust to put on *your* referral list. If your client asks, "Should I buy this car or lease it?" and you don't feel comfortable answering yourself, direct him to a professional you know can.

When you lose a client

Even if you follow all 10 of those suggestions, you will lose a client someday. What's important then is to avoid beating yourself up about it. Clients leave for the following reasons:

- They are tired of paying for bookkeeping.
- Their brother-in-law likes computing and will do it for free.
- They think they paid too much in taxes last year.
- They want to try it themselves.
- They found someone they want to work with instead of you.
- It's Tuesday.

Do all that you can to ensure the parting is amiable. Tell your client you are sorry to see him go and offer to provide his next bookkeeper with the records in whatever format is easiest. (Someday maybe somebody will do the same for you.) If the parting is amiable enough, do an "exit interview." Ask the client why he's leaving and if there are any suggestions he would make about your business. Remember not to burn any bridges. Clients come back all the time, too, after that brother-in-law screws up the books or their families object to their spending all day Saturday in front of their accounting program.

Set performance goals for yourself. Go back to your marketing plan and pick one or two activities to do "in case of losing a client." Do a direct-mail letter, place an ad, or make some cold calls. It's more therapeutic than worrying about your lost client. And you'll have that lost client replaced in no time!

How to organize yourself

Organize any way you can! Many bookkeepers use the DayTimer calendar service, which gives them a little book to carry around in which they can write their daily schedules, appointments, and To Do lists. Others use computer calendars and schedulers. Some use differently colored file folders for different clients or for different types of files, and keep records for different clients on separate (color-coded) floppy disks.

Getting your office organized is a trial-and-error process that consumes time and energy, and keeps consuming them as your business and organizational needs grow and change. Just recognize that organization needs to remain a priority.

These tips are the absolute best tips for running your home-based bookkeeping business.

1. *Never* drink coffee (or any other liquid) near your keyboard or over your paperwork. If you ignore all the other suggestions in this book, stick with this one!

2. Remember that people are funny about money. Give them extra reassurance that you'll be careful and discrete.

3. Keep a to-be-copied file handy. Put everything you need to get copies of in it. You can then go to the copy shop once a day or once a week and always have necessary papers handy.

4. Think of yourself as the best, and act it. You don't have to spend the most for every service and piece of equipment, but avoid acting or appearing cheap. Don't complain about parking or long-distance charges, or skip the good answering machine for the bargain brand, or use skimpy business cards. The clientele you want to cultivate appreciate spending money for a job well done—show them you understand.

5. While getting your letterhead and envelopes printed, get memo pads printed at the same time. You can use these all the time to send notes to your clients and other business contacts.

6. Offer quick-pay incentives. You can collect your fees faster if you give your clients 5 percent off their bill when they pay within 10 days.

7. Offer to pick up and deliver work, even if you have to pay a messenger service to do it. The bookkeepers interviewed for this book said over and over that pickup and delivery was the one service that won them a client over their competitors.

8. Expand your list of potential clients by going on-line on different computer bulletin boards and getting comfortable with remote-control software.

9. Stay current by reading. There's no lack of accounting and tax preparation books, journals, and newsletters. Subscribe to a few of them and stay up to date. You'll feel better about yourself, and someday, someway, that extra knowledge will save you time, save you money, help your existing clients, or win you a new one.

10. Use the technical support. All the accounting software companies have good technical support operators who know computers *and* accounting. Take advantage of it, especially when learning a new program and starting your business.

11. Go to the top. If you are having trouble getting paid by a client, or if you want to sell your services, if you just need information about a new product, start by calling the president of the company. You may not get through to her, but her secretary will know more about how to get your question answered than anybody else. And a referral from the president's office gets your message a higher priority than a referral from the receptionist at the front desk.

12. Make most of your outgoing calls on your personal line even though you have a business telephone line. Your business line will stay free for clients calling you.

13. Specialize, even if you adopt more than one specialty. The future of bookkeeping and everything else is niche marketing.
14. Minimize the number of accounting programs you use. Have your clients adapt to the programs you use, not vice versa.
15. Try to spread out your clients so they don't all have report needs on the same day or week. Get monthly clients and quarterly clients. Also try to get business clients whose tax years end in different months. (Easier said than done, I know. But I said try.)
16. Go to a professional seminar at least once a year. Join at least one professional association. You can learn what's new and have the chance to share stories with other bookkeepers, accountants, and tax preparers.
17. Build tax preparation into your business. It's another level of expense and responsibility, but it will bring in another level of revenue and clients.
18. Have a dedicated line for your fax machine.
19. Be vigilant about backing up data—back up your hard disk on floppies and your floppies onto other floppies. If you are responsible for keeping client data, keep a backup set of disks off-site, such as in a safety deposit box at your bank.
20. Buy a second hard disk to back up your primary hard disk. When (okay, if) your disk crashes, you'll have peace of mind and not lose any workdays worrying about trying to reclaim data. If you can afford it, a whole second computer is a good idea, too. It keeps your business computer "family-free" and 100-percent deductible. It gives you a backup for emergencies (or temporary helpers).
21. Design financial recording forms for your disorganized clients. They'll be more likely to keep track of the information you need, and it will be in a form you can easily use. Hand out accordion files—prelabeled by account categories as well as your name and phone number—as holiday gifts.
22. Be down to earth and avoid jargon. One bookkeeper told me she thinks she gets more clients because she is a woman, and her male clients are less embarrassed to admit to her that they don't know the first thing about finances than they would be to another man. Develop a good method to explain your reports and accounting concepts, so that a client who knew nothing about accounting could understand them but wouldn't be insulted by your presentations.
23. Don't rush into a partnership. If you choose to work with a partner, select him or her very carefully. You can each run your own business in the beginning and refer clients back and forth if you think you might want to work together and might not.
24. While building your business, expect to spend 25 percent of your time marketing.
25. Don't agree to answer phones, do filing, or other secretarial work while you are working on-site at a client's company.
26. Find a good, 24-hour computer service and rental company *before* you need it.

27. Enjoy! Remember that you are choosing self-employment partly because of the freedom it gives you to come and go. So don't forget to occasionally work in your slippers, go to an afternoon movie, or hang the "Gone Fishing" sign from your door. And pat yourself on the back for having such a nice lifestyle.

14 Preparing payrolls

This chapter is where I stick my neck out and make a couple of predictions. You can even call me a year after you set up your business and tell me if I was right. Prediction 1: payrolls will NOT be the most enjoyable part of your job. As a matter of fact, they might become your *least*-favorite, lowest-profit activity as an independent bookkeeper. Prediction 2: Payrolls will, however, bring many of your clients in the door and then keep them there.

Many business owners look for an outside bookkeeper when they hire employees and become responsible for regular paychecks, tax withholding, insurance payments, and such. Payroll is labor intensive, requires compliance with several federal and state laws and regulations, and must be done on a regular schedule. Missed payroll deadlines can bring down a business. Business owners are only too happy to pay you to take care of it for them.

They won't be all too happy to pay you much, though. Competition from the nation's two biggest payroll services—Paychex and ADP—keep rates low in the payroll business. So low, in fact, that some people just don't find it cost-effective to compete with them. "I was shocked to find out how cheap it is to go to a payroll service for your payroll," said David Lawrence, a Macintosh consultant who specializes in accounting programs. "Both ADP and Paychex were willing to take on my business for just $11 per pay period (Lawrence typically only has a few employees), and they didn't want any money at all for the first three months."

Many bookkeepers find that they don't make money doing payrolls. They do attract clients and keep them that way, though. Wanda Walter of the Company Clerk, for example, does payrolls only for those clients who keep her on a monthly retainer for other accounting work as well.

"We used to have quite a few payroll clients, but it's really not cost-effective, and it's too time-consuming," she explains. "I told everyone we weren't going to be doing it any longer, and, to tell you the truth, I didn't care if I lost the clients or not. It just wasn't profitable, and you have to do it at a certain time, so checks can be handed out on payday. You can't do it at your convenience."

Payroll basics

Payrolls can be inconvenient, labor intensive, and unprofitable, but they aren't hard to understand. When you are responsible for a payroll, you have to ensure all the paychecks go out on time and withhold the correct amount of federal and state income taxes, Social Security, and Medicare taxes (FICA), and unemployment insurance taxes (FUTA) employee benefit payment. You need to ensure that payroll taxes are paid on time—stiff penalties are charged for companies who dip into their payroll tax escrow accounts or fail to make their tax payments when they should.

You have to calculate the correct amounts for profit sharing and company retirement plans. You have to keep payroll records on each employee as well as company totals so your clients can assess how much they are spending on labor and where the money is going (such as health insurance). You might also be required to keep past salary records for employees.

Typical payroll tasks

The checklist shown in FIG. 14-1 is from Peachtree Accounting and shows the typical steps you take when preparing a regular payroll with this software. Note that the company prompts you to back up your work after the steps marked with a "B."

The traditional manual payroll system consists of three forms: the payroll ledger, which accumulates all of a company's pay information; the employee cards, which tally the wage history of each employee; and the checks, which, of course, are the part the employees want. A typical manual system is set up with carbon or carbonless multiple-part forms so you can write through all three at once. Typically, the payment amount appears on the check. The detailed breakout of payments to other accounts, such as tax escrow and retirement accounts, appears to the right of the form, on both the employee cards and the ledger.

Software

The good news is that payroll software can take much of the pain out of payrolls. Enter tax rates (most payroll programs now come with federal and state tax tables built in, and you can order updates as tax rates change), and the withholding amount can be calculated automatically. Set up a completed paycheck and a typical pay period, and the program can prompt you to print out the same check in one week, two weeks, 15 days, or a month. Most

Pay Period Tasks

	Update Employee Information and Verify the Changes	B
	Run Update from Job Cost, if you use Job Cost	
	Enter Time Card Hours	
	Print Paymaster Worksheets	
	Enter Payroll Exceptions	B
	Verify Payroll Exceptions	
	Calculate Pay (this is required)	B

	Verify Your Payroll
	    Print the Pre-Check Payroll Register
	    Print the Hours/Earnings Report
	    Print the Hours/Earnings Report
		B

	Print Paychecks (this is required)	B
	Print the Final Payroll Register (this is required)	B
	Post the Pay Period (this is required)	B

Quarterly Tasks

	Complete all Pay Period Tasks (this is required)	
	Print 941 Reports	
	Print California or NewJersey Reports, if applicable	
	Print the Payroll Summary	
	Close the Quarter (this is required)	B

14-1

Typical tasks regularly required in preparing payrolls. Peachtree Complete Accounting

Yearly Tasks

	Complete all Pay Period Tasks (this is required)	
	Complete all Quarterly Tasks (this is required)	
	Print W-2's	
	Create the Magnetic Media W-2 File	
	Re-Activate Inactive Employees Who Should Remain On Payroll	B
	Close the year (this is required)	B
	Change the Status of Re-activated Employees	B

Special Activities

	Enter Manually Written Checks	B
	Enter a Special Check Run	B
	Change Tax Codes	B
	Take FICA on Group Term Life Over $50,000	B

payroll programs are user-friendly. The employee-card screen from One-Write Plus Payroll software in FIG. 14-2, for example, closely approximates a manual employee payroll card. At the end of the year, the programs can calculate W-2 forms for employees' personal tax filing or 1099 forms for any independent contractors on salary.

14-2
Employee payroll card screen from One-Write Plus resembles paper cards of manual systems.

```
One-Write Plus Payroll ||        THE KITE STORE       ||      12/29/92
                ADD OR CHANGE EMPLOYEE CARD - SECTION 1

   EMPLOYEE ID  [____]   TYPE ____  SUSPEND __   HOURLY / SALARY    _____
   NAME         _____          SINGLE / MARRIED  _____
   ADDRESS      _____          EXEMPTIONS FED:  __  ST: __
                _____          EXTRA W/H
   PHONE        _____  OFFICE ____        DATE HIRED         _____
   DEPARTMENT   _____                           DATE TERMINATED    _____
   SOCIAL SEC # _____                        DATE OF BIRTH      _____
   SALARY ACCT  _____                        REGULAR PAY RATE   _____
   COMMENTS     _____                OVERTIME PAY RATE  _____

   DEDUCTIONS      G/L ACCOUNT      CYCLE TYPE BASIS   LIMIT    AMOUNT

   OTHER PAY
   STATE TAX
   LOCAL TAX
   DEDUCTION 1
   DEDUCTION 2
   DEDUCTION 3

        Enter the employee ID.  F6 = Employee list.  Esc = Menu.
 F1 Help F2 Edit F3       F4     F5 Acct F6 Emp  F7 Prev F8 Next F9 Date F10 Save
 Shift ↑  Ytd    Del            Card
```

Add or Change Employee Card - Section 1 Screen

Almost every program listed in Chapter 8 has either a payroll function built in or a separate module that can be purchased separately to interface with the program. One stand-alone payroll program, MoneyCounts Payroll by Parsons Technology, in Hiawatha, Iowa, sells for $49, prepares most payroll tasks, and can be a useful program if your payroll tasks are separate from your other accounting assignments. Data from this program can be exported to other accounting programs, but this software is best used as a separate program for clients who use you for payrolls only. Figure 14-3 shows the main menu screen of MoneyCounts Payroll; the program is simple enough to be almost self-explanatory.

At a minimum, a payroll program should keep employee records, adjust for shift differentials; post taxes; and calculate cafeteria plan fringe benefits, 401(k) retirement plans, health insurance, and miscellaneous deductions that employees opt to have taken from their paychecks.

An efficient and speedy program will enable you to keep your customers satisfied without taking too much time away from the rest of your business. While selecting a payroll program, find out how often and how quickly the software company ships tax table updates and how much they charge for those updates.

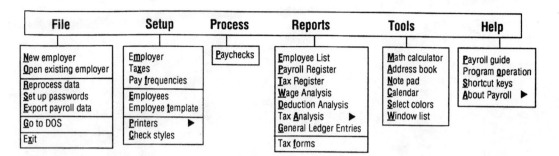

File	Setup	Process	Reports	Tools	Help
New employer	Employer	Paychecks	Employee List	Math calculator	Payroll guide
Open existing employer	Taxes		Payroll Register	Address book	Program operation
	Pay frequencies		Tax Register	Note pad	Shortcut keys
Reprocess data			Wage Analysis	Calendar	About Payroll ▶
Set up passwords	Employees		Deduction Analysis	Select colors	
Export payroll data	Employee template		Tax Analysis ▶	Window list	
Go to DOS			General Ledger Entries		
	Printers ▶				
Exit	Check styles		Tax forms		

14-3 *MoneyCounts Payroll menu shows how the program works.*

Once you're committed to preparing payrolls, you are committed to keeping abreast of developments in one of the more active areas of tax regulation: payroll taxes. The heavy penalties levied on companies that don't deposit their payroll taxes on time are made even less palatable by the complicated and ever-shifting schedule of due dates.

Be aware that 1993 is a year of change for payroll deposit rules. Previously, companies had to file quarterly, monthly, eighth monthly (yes, eight times a month), or daily, depending on the tax liability of the firm. Those deadlines shifted back and forth, too, as often as the size of the firm's payroll tax liability went above or below certain levels.

A new schedule is being phased in starting in 1993 that will require small businesses to file monthly, and larger employees to make payroll tax payments semiweekly. The payments might be more frequent, but they are a lot easier to understand. And, the new schedule might have your clients coming to you *more* often for payroll work.

To keep abreast of payroll tax due dates, either subscribe to one of the tax service newsletters discussed in chapter 15 or order IRS Publications and instructions, including Publication 937, Business Reporting; W-2 Instructions; and Form 940 and instructions for employees' unemployment tax withholding. Remember to contact your state tax authority for comparable state information.

Finding information

15 Preparing tax returns

Expanding your business to include tax return preparation is a big, natural, and potentially lucrative next step. If you have the ability and desire to push yourself, you can make more money in three months preparing tax returns than you can performing bookkeeping the entire year.

"I do upwards of 100 to 120 returns a year," notes one New Jersey bookkeeper, who credits his tax preparation business with keeping his bookkeeping business afloat (and supplying it with a steady stream of clients). Other full-time tax preparers report doing upwards of 500 returns a year.

Some tax preparers earn well over $100,000 processing returns every year, and it's a growing business. Steven O'Rourke, director of professional tax services for the National Association of Tax Practitioners, notes that more and more Americans are using private tax preparers as they enter more complicated investments and find they don't know what to do with the tax forms they receive at the end of the year.

In the past five years, a sea of change has occurred in how tax preparation businesses are run. In the old days, companies known as "service bureaus" completed the forms for professional tax preparers. The preparer interviewed his client, collected key tax data on worksheets, and amassed the appropriate attachments. Then he'd send the whole package to the service bureau, which completed the forms and sent it back to the tax preparer so he could present it to his clients for signature. Of course, the preparer paid his service bureau for every form it completed.

Today, personal tax software has run the service bureaus out of business (although they are reappearing as tax-preparation software companies). The typical preparer now does his own forms on his own computer with his own software, cutting out the extra layer of administration but becoming much more independently responsible for the quality of the forms he generates. In an area where mistakes can be crucial, the loss of the service bureaus removes one extra layer of checking. While the software makes up for less checking by making it harder to make mistakes, some tax preparers use a backup system where they hire someone to key in the returns and then double check the returns. Or, they'll ask a partner to check the returns they prepare.

Tax preparation is an "after-hours" business. Most of your clients will want to meet with you on evenings or weekends. You can, of course, process their forms on your own schedule. Instead of "after hours," however, think "all hours" during February, March, and April, when 80 percent or more of your tax preparation work will be done. As Mary Greiner, who does bookkeeping and tax preparation in the suburbs of Washington, D.C., said ruefully, "I usually miss the crocus and the daffodils altogether, and come out sometime between the tulips and the azaleas."

A taxing schedule

If you intend to offer tax preparation services, perhaps the best advice to consider is this: get as organized as you possibly can before the end of the year. Prepare client worksheets that you can use to interview your clients for their key tax numbers. Consider sending a set of worksheets to each client in December so they can begin filling them out (or at least getting used to them) early in the new year.

Many tax practitioners find it easiest to visit their clients at home in the evening where they can and go through the worksheets together. That way you know you have all the materials needed to complete the tax forms.

Once the worksheets are complete, the rest is easy. Most of today's tax programs don't even require you to know the form structure; you can type the client's data in worksheet form into the program, and the program posts the right numbers to the right forms and fills in the calculations.

Expect to spend extra time answering "where's my refund?" questions for your clients. Expect some hassles, too—unfortunately, many clients assess how good a tax practitioner you are by how large a return you can get them.

Getting started

Practically speaking, all you need to do to get started as a tax preparer is prepare tax returns. There are no federal tests or certifications, although some states have their own requirements. There are no formal training programs, either, though training opportunities exist everywhere.

One of the most popular methods of training is to spend a couple of years preparing tax returns for one of the large national chains, such as H&R Block. That's what Phil Weber, of Tigard, Oregon, did. "In Oregon, you have to work as an apprentice for a couple of years before you can be a self-employed tax consultant. I took the H&R Block basic course; there was only a nominal fee, and it was an 80-hour course with a final exam. Then, I worked in one of their satellite offices for two years." Those were two years well spent, Weber notes. "I saw many varied returns, with rental properties, farm incomes, and investment gains and losses. I'm not sure I would have seen all that if I just started out on my own."

Many of the tax software companies listed in the sidebar also offer training courses, as do trade groups like the National Association of Tax Practitioners. Don't forget on-the-job training—if you have a feel for filling out taxes and have already done your own forms, you can start slowly by doing returns for your bookkeeping clients only, and building to a bigger tax preparation business later. Ingrid Landskron, the Mahwah, New Jersey bookkeeper, got her feet wet processing returns for Lenore Kondrat, of the Mahwah Tax Service. This year she's invested in her own software to prepare tax returns directly for her own clients.

These are the major tax preparation programs used by professional practitioners. Most offer inexpensive or free demonstration packages as well as comprehensive brochures describing their products. Look at a few before you commit to your favorite.

Tax preparation software list

A-Plus Tax
Arthur Anderson & Co.
2803 Fruitville Road
Sarasota, FL 34237
(800) USA-1040

CLR Fast-Tax GoSystem
Computer Language Research, Inc.
2395 Midway Road
Carrollton, TX 75006
(800) FAST-TAX

CPAid Master Tax
CPAid Software, Inc.
1061 Fraternity Circle
Kent, Ohio 44240
(800) 227-2437

Digitax
Digitax, Inc.
3001 South State Street, Suite 201
Ann Arbor, MI 48108
(800) DIGITAX

Lacerte
Lacerte Software Corp.
4835 LBJ Freeway, 10th Floor
Dallas, TX 75244
(800) 765-7777

LMS/Tax
SCS/Compute, Inc.
12444 Powerscourt Drive, Suite 400
St. Louis, MO 63131
(800) 488-0779

ProSystem FX
CCH Computax, Inc.
Worldwide Postal Center
PO Box 92938
Los Angeles, CA 90009
(800) 457-7639

Quick Tax
SCS/Compute, Inc.
2444 Powerscourt Drive, #400
St. Louis, MO 63131
(800) 488-0779

TAASCforce
Tax & Accounting Software Corp.
6914 South Yorktown Ave.,
Tulsa, OK 74136
(800) 998-9990

Tax Advantage
Prentice Hall Professional Software
2400 Lake Park Drive
Smyrna, GA 30080
(800) 241-3306

Tax Commissioner
Taxbyte, Inc.
1801 Sixth Avenue
Moline, IL 61265
(800) 245-8299

Tax Machine
SCS/Compute, Inc.
12444 Powerscourt Drive, #400
St. Louis, MO 63131
(800) 488-0779

Tax/Pack Professional
Alpine Data, Inc.
737 South Townsend Avenue
Montrose, CO 81401
(800) 525-1040

Tax Partner
Best Programs, Inc.
11413 Isaac Newton Square
Reston, VA 22090
(800) 368-2406

Tax Relief Plus
MicroVision Software, Inc.
368 Veterans Memorial Hwy.
Commack, New York 11725
(800) 829-7354

Tax$imple
Tax$imple, Inc.
431 Route 10
Randolph, NJ 07869
(800) 323-2662

TaxWorks
Laser Systems
7 North Main
PO Box 407
Kaysville, UT 84037
(800) 669-1011

1040 Solutions
1040 Solutions, Inc.
Worldwide Postal Center
PO Box 92938
Los Angeles, CA 90009
(800) 544-9552

Turbo Tax Professional
ChipSoft, Inc.
6256 Greenwich Drive, #100
San Diego, CA 92122
(619) 453-4446

It's a good first step to register with the Internal Revenue Service as a tax
preparer. Request Publication 1045, which lists the various forms and
instructions you'll want access to and also includes Form 3975—Tax

Practitioner Annual Mailing List Application and Order Blank. Filling out that form puts you on the IRS list as a tax practitioner, which means the IRS will send you copies of all tax forms and keep you posted with a practitioner's newsletter. Form 3975 comes with an order form—you can order copies of all IRS forms and publications while registering for the mailing list.

At the same time, order Treasury Department Circular No. 230: *Regulations Governing the Practice of Attorneys, Certified Public Accountants, Enrolled Agents, Enrolled Actuaries, and Appraisers* before the Internal Revenue Service. It will give you tips on what tax preparers are and are not permitted to do.

Penalities

You don't have to meet any federal qualifying standards to become an income tax preparer, but that doesn't mean no one is watching you. Donald Roberts of the Internal Revenue Service explains, "There isn't any certification to become a tax preparer, but once you do prepare returns for a fee, there are certain responsibilities and rules and regulations to which you have to adhere." For example, you must do the following:

- Sign every form you prepare for a fee, and list your tax preparer or Social Security number.
- Furnish a copy of the form to the taxpayer.
- Retain a list of anyone you've hired to assist you in tax preparation.
- Keep copies of the returns you file for your clients.

You must not do the following:

- Endorse refund checks.
- Charge contingency fees (fees based on the size of the tax refund).
- Talk your clients into aggressively claiming tax shelters that you suspect are not legitimate.
- You *especially* must not encourage, abet, or even simply go along with efforts by your client to understate his taxable income.

Penalties ranging from minor to major can be levied against you in any one of these situations. The most serious penalties are reserved for preparers who fraudulently understate income for their clients— this can cost you $10,000 or more in fines, a jail term, and the suspension of your right to practice as a tax preparer.

Becoming an enrolled agent

If you aren't a CPA or attorney and want to attain a higher level of certification, you can become an *enrolled agent*, which means you are licensed to appear before the IRS or in Tax Court on behalf of a client. You don't have to be an enrolled agent to prepare tax returns for a fee, but it does give you a higher level of status and enable you to win more clients in a competitive environment. It also enables you to spend a lot of time studying for a test that even long-time IRS employees say is difficult.

To become an enrolled agent, you must apply to the IRS, send in a $50 exam fee, and take the test at the time specified at your local district office. The IRS offers the Enrolled Agent exam once a year; typically, it is announced in June, conducted in September, and held in only one city per multistate IRS district.

The exam contains four parts that require you to demonstrate a level of competence in individual and corporate tax practice. If you do fail the exam, remember these two points: (1) You can take it again. You have two years to pass it, and only need to retake the parts you missed the previous year; and (2) You are in good company; it's a hard test.

The NATP

Another useful and well-worth-the-investment tool for taxpreparers is membership in the National Association of Tax Practitioners (NATP). At $90 for the first year and $75 per year thereafter, the NATP's biggest benefit is a full-time staff of enrolled agents at its Tax Research Center. Call during business hours with any tax question, and they'll guide you to the right answer (see the final section, which is a quiz on taxes). You will be charged a small fee, in addition to the membership fee, for each question answered.

The association also delivers a monthly newsletter called the *1040 Report*, that updates developments in federal tax law, practical applications, and procedures as well as provides association news. A second newsletter, called *Tax Tips* is available for you to purchase and distribute to your clients. (You can buy this newsletter camera-ready and get an artist to strip in your company's name as a good promotional tool.)

The NATP also sells federal and state tax forms and an array of worksheets, client folders, and the like. It offers numerous tax workshops, one annual national convention, and the chance to network at state and local chapter meetings. Though most of the association's offerings are services for which you'll pay extra, it provides convenient one-stop shopping for many of the tools of the trade.

Setting fees

So, how much can you make preparing taxes? It's a competitive field, but competitive in a weird way, as attorneys and CPAs can charge three or four times the amount a less-credentialed professional charges for filing the same straightforward tax forms.

The fees vary greatly by region. Phil Weber, in Oregon, for example, charges only $50 for a basic 1040, Schedule A and state form during his first tax season , and he expects to be able to process 300 returns—that's $15,000, even if none of his firms have additional schedules or complicating considerations. Lenore Kondrat, a more-experienced practitioner on the East Coast, says her rates start at $120 and go "up and up and up," depending on how complex the returns are. At a rock-bottom minimum, Kondrat brings in $72,000 filing the 600 returns she processes during tax season. Of course, she shares that money with the assistants she hires every year to help her interview clients and key in data. Wanda Walter, of Landover, Maryland, says her average tax preparation fee is $350 per client. "The fees and numbers of returns are all over the place," says O'Rourke. "But of our 14,000 members, I would guess the average practitioner prepares 300 or 400 returns a year."

You can, of course, limit your tax practice to keep you hours sane. O'Rourke cautions that today's responsible tax preparer must make a basic investment in a computer, laser printer, and reliable high-grade software. That's enough of an investment to not make it worthwhile if you aren't processing at least 50 returns a year, he notes. (The economies for those of us who already have computers and laser printers might be figured differently!)

Software

The key to filing taxes, of course, is tax filing software, which is plentiful, better than ever, and not exactly cheap. It's also not exactly universally used yet, either. This year is the first in which H&R Block expects the bulk of its returns to be processed on computer. Many practitioners are still out there using pencils and papers instead of software, though their number shrinks all the time.

Of course, accuracy is a key consideration in selecting tax preparation software, and, while all the major tax programs are considered to be accurate, they don't always deliver the same answers to the same tax questions. When buying a major software package, assume it to be accurate, but take the time to learn how it works, so you understand why it calculates the way it does. If you disagree with how the software handles a specific tax situation, such as depreciation, make sure you can override its automatic calculation.

Don't stop at accuracy. Consider other factors discussed in the following subsections before picking a tax software program. Remember the chapter 8 lesson, too: it's harder to change programs once you've started with one than it is to pick your favorite the first time, even if you have to invest a lot of time and energy in the hunt. Write or phone the software manufacturers listed in the sidebar and request their sales literature. Don't be afraid to call and chat with their technical support staff. Ask other practitioners what they do and don't like about the programs they are using. Factors to consider in selecting tax preparation software are the following:

- Processing
- Speed
- Price
- Release speed
- Worksheets
- State forms
- Professional status
- Electronic filing
- Interface
- Import capabilities

Processing   Some programs allow both batch and interactive processing. These terms are similar to the batch and automatic posting of the general ledger programs discussed in chapter 8. Batch processing goes faster; the program collects all the data entered and does not process it until you give it the command.

Speed   Time *is* money when you have only three months to process as many forms as you can. Pay extra for a program that runs fast.

Price   Knowing how inconvenient it is to switch tax software from year to year, many companies offer low introductory prices to get you in the door and "hooked" on their high-priced updates. Find out about multiple-year pricing.

Be forewarned: Comparing the prices of tax software programs is like comparing apples and tuna fish. Some companies charge more depending on how many returns you file; others charge more if more than one practitioner uses the program, and still others charge on sliding scales based on the number of forms you use.

Expect to pay $2,000 for unlimited use of a good, serious, professional tax preparation package. Some companies offer discounts to preparers who only use the package to file a few returns.

Release speed   Imagine being a major tax software publisher in mid-December. Your programmers are poised at their keyboards waiting for the IRS to drop its final versions of all tax forms in the mail. How long is the turnaround time before a bug-proof program is in the mail to you, the tax preparer?

Worksheets   Some programs give you worksheets that you can print out and bring to your client interviews. They also allow data to be entered in worksheet form, which can speed the process considerably because the program doesn't need to perform the graphical tasks of putting every form up on the screen in what-you-see-is-what-you-get (WYSIWYG) format. Instead, you can fill in the worksheets and let the program post the information to interactive forms while you're focusing on something else.

State forms   Not all programs provide state forms, or even have them available. The programmers who created the state packages might be completely separate from the ones who did the federal package. Make sure the program you select has good software for the state forms you'll be filing most.

Professional status   Of course, you can always buy a personal tax program for under $50 and put all of your clients in that. But you'll lose more than access to all the forms you might need: you'll lose the management features that give you speed. Most professional programs, for example, let you move more quickly from one client file to another, have form letters prepared for your clients, and have printable worksheets for client interviews. Some professional forms even have built-in client billing procedures.

Electronic filing   Filing electronically is a whole separate issue discussed later in the chapter, but know that many of today's tax programs include electronic filing capabilities.

Interface   Some programs feel better than others to you and are more pleasing to use. Interface is an entirely subjective test, but one that you should not ignore.

Import capabilities   Some programs can take data from accounting software and post it to all the right tax forms. Importing can be a major time-saver, especially for those tax returns you file for your bookkeeping clients.

The forms

Even if you use a program that prints all of your tax forms, be aware that you'll still have to buy paper forms. "I like having the form in front of me even when I'm working on a screen," said one Washington, D.C. tax preparer who uses the forms as worksheets when manually entering client information. The IRS distributes one copy of each form (photocopyable) to tax practitioners who request them; you can also buy forms in bulk from the IRS, the National Association of Tax Practitioners, many other tax and accounting publishers. Typically, there is information about purchasing these forms included with your software.

Lacerte tax software

For more than three years, the Lacerte tax packages have been the most popular programs among professional tax preparers. While many other tax programs can efficiently and accurately process tax returns, professionals like Lacerte because of its full-featured support for people who make their living doing tax returns, including client recordkeeping features and complete tax questionnaires for client interviews and on-screen processing.

Many low-volume preparers also prefer Lacerte because it has a unique "remote entry processing" feature that allows preparers to pay as they go if they only process a few returns. The entire Lacerte 1040 package costs $1,795, which is justified if you are doing more than 127 returns. If you are doing far fewer than that, Lacerte lets you buy the software on a "per-use" basis. Low-volume preparers pay a $150 deposit for the Lacerte software and sign up for "remote-entry processing." When preparers complete a tax package, they dial in via modem to a Lacerte central computer to obtain an access code that unlocks each client's tax files for printing. Lacerte then charges the preparer $12.95 for each return filed.

It's worth going through a typical tax filing exercise with Lacerte to see how the system works. There is a big caveat, though. It's not the only software in town, and you can have a happy, successful practice using a competitive brand. I'm using Lacerte as an example because it is the market leader and garnered so many positive comments in my interviews with tax preparers.

In the Lacerte system, tax season starts before tax season, with the $200 program called Proforma. That's preseason software, typically available in November, that generates client-specific tax organizers based on the returns prepared the previous year. The program also includes a preformatted letter, shown in FIG. 15-1, which most Lacerte users send to their clients at the end of December or the beginning of January. The organizer, shown in FIG. 15-2, automatically includes the proper pages and questions for the client, based on the previous year's tax return. Information that stays the same year to year, such as name and address, will already be posted to the organizer, as will multiyear tax data that changes automatically, such as loss carryforwards

15-1

In the Lacerte system, tax season starts before tax season with this letter.

```
                      LACERTE SOFTWARE - DALLAS
                      4835 LBJ FRWY. STE. 1000
                          DALLAS, TX. 75244
                          1-800-765-7777


        ROBERT AND PAMELA COOK
        456 INDIAN SCHOOL RD
        DALLAS, TX 75234


        Dear Bob and Pam,

        The enclosed 1991 Tax Organizer is for your use in assembling
        the information necessary for preparation of your 1991 income
        tax return.

        Information from last year's return is included as a guideline
        for the required information. If any of this information no
        longer applies, please line through it.

        Please include any additional information in the space provided
        or on additional sheets.

        I suggest you review all information requested to ensure you
        provide all information necessary for your particular tax
        situation.

        Your use of this 1991 Tax Organizer will help ensure that your
        tax return is complete and accurate as well help reduce the
        time required and cost of preparation.

        Please bring this organizer as well as other supporting documents
        to your appointment. Your appointment date and time is noted on
        the first page of the organizer.

        If you have any questions, please call.




        Sincerely,




        Donald K. An
```

LACERTE SOFTWARE – DALLAS
4835 LBJ FRWY. STE. 1000
DALLAS, TX. 75244
1-800-765-7777

PAGE 1

1992 TAX ORGANIZER

CLIENT SALES

PREPARER NUMBER [   ]

This tax organizer will assist you in gathering information necessary for the preparation
of your 1992 tax return. Please add, change, or delete information as appropriate.

TAXPAYER INFORMATION	APPOINTMENT DATE AND TIME
	February 12, 1993
	3:00 p.m.

NAME AND ADDRESS

    ROBERT AND PAMELA COOK
    456 INDIAN SCHOOL RD
    DALLAS, TX 75234

COUNTY OF RESIDENCE	TELEPHONE NUMBER (home/work)	STATE RETURN
DALLAS	1-800-765-7777/1-800-933-9999	US

FILING STATUS
JOINT RETURN (2)

	TAXPAYER	SPOUSE
SOCIAL SECURITY NUMBER	123-45-6789	987-65-4321
OCCUPATION	COMPUTER SALES	ATTORNEY
AGE OR DATE OF BIRTH	33150	112559
ENTER "Y" IF BLIND		

DEPENDENT'S NAME (FIRST NAME, MIDDLE INITIAL, LAST NAME)	AGE	SOCIAL SECURITY NO. (REQUIRED IF AGE 1 OR OLDER)	RELATIONSHIP	NUMBER OF MONTHS LIVED IN YOUR HOME	BLANK–CHILD AT HOME 1–CHILD NOT AT HOME 2–OTHER DEPENDENT
ANTHONY R COOK	8	789-45-6123	SON	12	

15-2
The Lacerte client organizer automatically reprints information that carries over from the previous year.

and multiyear depreciation schedules. In addition, the Proforma program shows the clients how much they declared for each questionnaire line item on their previous year's tax return (FIG. 15-3).

While clients are working on their worksheets, Lacerte preparers set up pricing and invoicing data. The program automatically invoices clients when it prints out their final tax package.

Once the preparer has the completed worksheets back, he enters them into the program in one of two ways: batch or interactive. In the batch method

WAGES & PENSIONS

Please enter all pertinent 1992 amounts and attach all W-2 and 1099-R forms.
Las year's amounts are provided for your reference.

WAGES, SALARIES, TIPS, ETC.

		1992 AMOUNT			1991 AMOUNT	
		TAXPAYER	SPOUSE		TAXPAYER	SPOUSE
EMPLOYER NAME		JAY'S COMPUTER				
FEDERAL WITHHOLDING	201		211		2000	
WAGES AND SALARIES	202		212		30000	
SOCIAL SECURITY TAX	203		213		2295	
MEDICARE TAX	204		214			
STATE WITHHOLDING	205		215			
LOCAL WITHHOLDING	85		95			
EMPLOYER NAME						
FEDERAL WITHHOLDING	201		211			
WAGES AND SALARIES	202		212			
SOCIAL SECURITY TAX	203		213			
MEDICARE TAX	204		214			
STATE WITHHOLDING	205		215			
LOCAL WITHHOLDING	85		95			
EMPLOYER NAME						
FEDERAL WITHHOLDING	201		211			
WAGES AND SALARIES	202		212			
SOCIAL SECURITY TAX	203		213			
MEDICARE TAX	204		214			
STATE WITHHOLDING	205		215			
LOCAL WITHHOLDING	85		95			

PENSIONS

PAYOR						
PENSIONS – TOTAL RECEIVED	221		231			
PENSIONS – TAXABLE AMOUNT	222		232			
FEDERAL WITHHOLDING	223		233			
STATE WITHHOLDING	224		234			
PAYOR						
PENSIONS – TOTAL RECEIVED	221		231			
PENSIONS – TAXABLE AMOUNT	222		232			
FEDERAL WITHHOLDING	223		233			
STATE WITHHOLDING	224		234			

IRA DISTRIBUTIONS

PAYOR						
IRA – TOTAL RECEIVED	901		911			
IRA – TAXABLE AMOUNT	902		912			
FEDERAL WITHHOLDING	903		913			
STATE WITHHOLDING	904		914			

15-3
The Lacerte client organizer allows clients to compare their previous-year figures with entries for the current tax year.

(FIG. 15-4), the screen either looks like the worksheets, or just list's, line and code numbers that can be entered rapidly and posted when you choose (FIG. 15-5). The interactive input (FIG. 15-6) lets you move from form to form and enter data directly into the IRS forms (FIG. 15-7).

When all data entry is complete, the forms are printed and the client is invoiced. The letter and invoice print automatically with the final tax package. The final client letter (also preformatted in the Lacerte program) and invoice look like FIGS. 15-8 and 15-9, respectively. The clients' tax forms, of course, look like any other laser printed tax forms.

NET OPERATING LOSS

NOL Carryover	Regular tax	277	
	Alt. minimum tax	459	
1991 NOL Worksheet	Nonbus. income [A]	45	
	Nonbus. ded'ns [A]	46	
1=forego NOL carryback		137	

CAPITAL LOSS (Schedule D)

Capital Loss Carryover	Short-term	41	
	Long-term	42	

SECTION 1231 LOSSES (4797)

Net Section 1231 Losses	1986	191	
	1987	192	
	1988	193	
	1989	197	
	1990	150	

CONTRIBUTIONS (Schedule A)

Contri- bution Carryover	50% limitation	373	
	30% limitation	52	
	20% limitation	53	

INVESTMENT INTEREST (4952)

Disallowed Investment Interest Carryover	Schedule A	189	
	Schedules C & E	188	
	AMT Schedule A	986	
	AMT Sch. C & E	996	
Net Investment Income	Regular tax [A]	249	
	Alt. minimum tax [A]	999	
AMT investment interest exp. [A]		998	

PASSIVE INTEREST (Schedule A)

NOTE: Enter current year amounts on ITP 6.

Prior unallowed passive interest	908	
AMT pr... ...llowed passive int.	956	

G... ...SINESS CREDIT (3800)

NC... ...mounts on ITP 8.		
...	416	

1992 ESTIMATED TAX

NOTE: If no entry is made, date paid will default to the due date.

Overpayment applied from 1990		151	
1st Quarter (due 4/15/91)	Amount paid	152	
	Date (MMDDYY)	236	
2nd Quarter (due 6/17/91)	Amount paid	153	
	Date (MMDDYY)	237	
3rd Quarter (due 9/16/91)	Amount paid	154	
	Date (MMDDYY)	238	
4th Quarter (due 1/15/92)	Amount paid	155	
	Date (MMDDYY)	239	
Paid w/Ext. (not later than 4/15/92)	Amount paid	157	
	Date (MMDDYY)	240	
Former spse. SSN if joint estimates		1010	(11)

1993 ESTIMATED TAX

NOTE: Enter 1 through 7 or actual dollar amount in code 161.

1=apply to 1st quarter, refund excess
2=apply to 1st & 2nd quarters, refund excess
3=apply to 1st, 2nd, & 3rd quarters, refund excess
4=apply consecutively to all quarters, refund excess
5=apply evenly to all quarters, refund excess
6=apply entire refund, estimates if necessary
7=apply entire refund, no estimates

Credit to 1993 (or 1-7 above)	161	
One voucher only: 1=first, 2=second, 3=third, 4=fourth	818	
Rounding: 1=$1, 2=$10, 3=$100, 4=$1000 [O]	966	
1=apply 90%/$500 rules, 2=omit [O]	967	
Increase (decrease)	Income	162	
	SE/other taxes	968	
	Withholding	163	
	1=omit capital gains & lump-sum distribution	771	
	1st quarter [O]	166	
	...nd quarter [O]	167	
	...ter [O]		

15-4
Batch input with Lacerte allows you to transfer data directly from worksheet to computer.

(US)	Client	110B	Terry and Kay Moore		

Line	Code	Amount	Description	Under Review	
1	1601		PHYSICIAN		F1-Help
2	1627	130000			F2-Print
3					F3-Status
4	365				
5					F4-Save
6	1201		DOWNTOWN DEVELOPMENT LTD.		
7	1202		75-654828486		F5-Notes
8					
9					F6-PopCalc
10	1701		1ST RESIDENTIAL		
11	1771		YOUR CITY, STATE		F7-Process
12	1702	20000			
13					F8-Supp Stmt
14					
15					F9-Switch to Interactive

Pgup Pgdn Home End Esc when finished	Alt-D Del Line	Alt-I Ins Line	Code: 276897 Amount: 1585293	F10-Client Information

15-5
Batch input of Lacerte screen allows "heads-down" data entry without using the forms.

The Lacerte user can also use the program to track her own performance. The program generates practice reports like the one shown in FIG. 15-10.

From the Lacerte example, you can see why software aimed at supporting the professional tax preparer is worth more than personal tax software. It's the extras—the worksheets, invoices, preformed letters—that will save time and allow you to prepare more returns during that three-month window.

15-6

Interactive menu of Lacerte allows users to select forms they want.

INCOME	DEDUCTIONS	OTHER
1 Wages & Salaries 2 Interest Income 3 Dividend Income 4 Pensions, IRA Distr. 5 Miscellaneous Income 6 Sch. C, D, E, F, K-1 11 Depreciation	18 Itemized Deductions 19 IRA Deduction 20 Keogh, Alimony, Other 21 Noncash Contr. (8283) 22 Moving Expense (3903) 23 Emp. Bus. Exp. (2106)	31 Invoice,Letter,Appt. 32 Miscellaneous Info. 33 Carryovers 34 Estimates (1040ES) 35 Penalties (2210) 36 Extension(4868,2688) 37 Elec. Filing General 38 Elec. Filing W-2s 39 Sch. D Miscellaneous 40 Amended Ret. (1040X) 41 Control Totals
CREDITS	TAXES	
12 Dep. Care Cr. (2441) 13 Min. Tax Cr. (8801) 14 Gen. Bus. Cr. (3800) 15 Foreign Tax Cr(1116) 16 Fuel Tax Cr. (4136) 17 EIC / Other Credits	24 Alt. Min. Tax (6251) 25 S.S.Tax on Tips(4137) 26 Lump Sum Dist. (4972) 27 Premature Dist.(5329) 28 Child Under 14 (8615) 29 Parent's Elect.(8814) 30 Other Taxes	F1-Help F6-PopCalc F2-Print F7-Process F3-Status F8-Search F4-Save F9-Batch F5-Notes F10-Client

Screen #:   Client 110B-TERRY AND KAY MOORE
———— Under Review ————

15-7

Interactive entry screen of Lacerte allows users to see context of their entries.

ESTIMATED TAX

NOTE: If no entry is made, date paid will default to the due date.

	Overpayment applied from 1990.		
1991	1st Quarter (due 4/15/91)	Amount paid. . . . . Date paid (MMDDYY)	12000
	2nd Quarter (due 6/17/91)	Amount paid. . . . . Date paid (MMDDYY)	12000
	3rd Quarter (due 9/16/91)	Amount paid. . . . . Date paid (MMDDYY)	12000
	4th Quarter (due 1/15/92)	Amount paid. . . . . Date paid (MMDDYY)	12000
	Paid w/Ext. (due 4/15/92)	Amount paid. . . . . Date paid (MMDDYY)	

F1-Help F3-Insert F5-Notes F6-PopCalc F7-Process F8-Code Search F10-Client
———— Under Review ————

Electronic filing

The business of electronically filing tax returns is growing exponentially. In 1986, 25,000 forms were filed electronically. Last year, close to 11 million were. The IRS likes electronic filing because it's less work. Instead of workers sorting paper forms manually and reentering data into the IRS computer, the electronically filed returns go straight to the computer where they can be processed automatically. Some tax attorneys, however, have suggested that the electronic returns are more likely to be audited because they are deposited directly into the system that searches for the anomalies that bcoome audit bait.

```
CLIENT # SALES
                    LACERTE SOFTWARE - NEW YORK
                        120 MINEOLA BLVD. #600
                          MINEOLA, NY 11501
                            516-561-5334

                                              April 28, 1992

    Robert and Pamela Cook
    456 Indian School Rd
    Mineola, NY 11501


    Dear Bob and Pam,

    Enclosed is your 1991 Federal Individual Income Tax Return.
    The original should be signed on the bottom of page two.
    Both spouses should sign.  There is a balance of $4,064
    payable by April 15, 1992.

    Mail your Federal return on or before April 15, 1992 and
    make checks payable to:

                    INTERNAL REVENUE SERVICE
                    HOLTSVILLE, NY 00501

    Your estimated tax payment schedule for 1992 is listed
    below.  Please mail your payments to the address shown on
    your estimated tax payment-vouchers.

                    DUE DATE      PAYMENT
                    4/15/92        4,489
                    6/15/92        4,489
                    9/15/92        4,489
                    1/15/93        4,489
                                  --------
                                  17,956

    The computed maximum deductible contribution to your
    spouse's Keogh retirement plan for 1991 is $15,059.  To
    ensure that your spouse's contribution is deductible,
    $15,059 must be deposited to your spouse's account on or
    before April 15, 1992.

    Please be sure to call if you have any questions.

    Sincerely,
```

15-8
Tax report cover letter of Lacerte automatically tells client balance (or refund) due, and advises them about next year's estimated tax schedule.

Clients like electronic filing, especially those clients who have overpaid their taxes and are anxious for a refund. The refund will come approximately five weeks faster than if the return was filed automatically.

Do preparers like electronic filing? Yes and no. Yes, because preparers can attract a wider variety of clients and can usually charge an extra fee of $20 to do the electronic filing. They can also appear (and really be) on the cutting edge of new technology. No, because some preparers claim it's not worth the money they make on it. Electronic filing can mean double duty—you have to

L'ACERTE SOFTWARE – NEW YORK
120 MINEOLA BLVD. #600
MINEOLA, NY 11501
516–561–5334

ROBERT AND PAMELA COOK
456 INDIAN SCHOOL RD
MINEOLA, NY 11501

April 28, 1993

Form 1040	1991 U.S. Individual Income Tax Return
Schedule A	Itemized Deductions
Schedule B	Interest and Dividend Income
Schedule C	Profit or Loss From Business
Schedule D	Capital Gains and Losses
Schedule E	Supplemental Income and Loss
Schedule E p2	Supplemental Income and Loss
Schedule SE	Social Security Self–Employment Tax
Form 2210	Underpayment of Estimated Tax
Form 2441	Child and Dependent Care Credit
Form 4562	Depreciation and Amortization
Form 4797	Sale of Business Property
Form 4952	Investment Interest Expense Deduction
Form 4972	Tax on Lump–Sum Distributions
Form 6252	Installment Sale Income
Form 8283	Noncash Charitable Contributions
Form 8582	Passive Activity Loss Limitations
Form 8824	Like–Kind Exchanges
Form 8829	Expenses for Business Use of Your Home
1040ES	Estimated Tax Vouchers
Vehicle Exp.	Vehicle Expense Statements

15-9

Lacerte program calculates the invoice as user prepares the tax forms.

Preparation Fee	825.00
COMPUTER CHARGES	50.00
Computer Charge	50.00
Subtotal	925.00
5% discount for payment on delivery	(46.25)
Amount Due	**$ 878.75**

dial up the IRS computer to send in the forms AND print out the forms so your clients can have a copy.

When you file taxes electronically, you use your modem to send the tax data directly into IRS computers, AND you also must file a companion Form 8453 to let the IRS know that you're not filing forms because you sent them via modem. In the early days of electronic filing (about five years ago!), you couldn't file an electronic return for a client who owed taxes. Now, the IRS will accept balance-due returns electronically

1992 PRACTICE REPORT

FIRM NAME	FEDERAL IDENTIFICATION NUMBER	
LACERTE SOFTWARE CORPORATION	75-1111111	
FIRM ADDRESS	TELEPHONE NUMBER	
4835 LBJ FRWY. STE 1000	1-800-765-7777	
DALLAS, TX.	NUMBER OF PREPARERS	CLIENTS IN DBASE
75244	6	1,641

FORMS PROCESSED:

No. Printed		Percentage	No. Printed		Percentage	No. Printed		Percentage
1443	Form 1040	99 %	0	Form 2688	0 %	0	Form 6249	0 %
412	Schedule A	28 %	0	Form 3468	0 %	137	Form 6251	9 %
482	Schedule B	33 %	8	Form 3800	0 %	55	Form 6252	3 %
358	Schedule C	24 %	20	Form 3903	1 %	3	Form 6781	0 %
264	Schedule D	18 %	4	Form 4136	0 %	20	Form 8271	1 %
239	Schedule E	16 %	8	Form 4137	0 %	35	Form 8283	2 %
415	Schedule E p2	28 %	1	Form 4255	0 %	91	Form 8582	6 %
231	Schedule F	15 %	474	Form 4562	32 %	46	Form 8606	3 %
29	Schedule R	2 %	21	Form 4684	1 %	28	Form 8615	1 %
237	Schedule SE (self)	16 %	137	Form 4797	9 %	4	Form 8801	0 %
63	Schedule SE (spouse)	4 %	76	Form 4797 p2	5 %	3	Form 8803	0 %
47	Schedule EIC	3 %	17	Form 4835	1 %	12	Form 8814	0 %
25	Form 1116	1 %	0	Form 4868	0 %	21	Form 8824	1 %
56	Form 2106	3 %	59	Form 4952	4 %	65	Form 8829	4 %
48	Form 2119	3 %	0	Form 4970	0 %	948	Form 1040ES	65 %
828	Form 2210	57 %	14	Form 4972	0 %	10	Form 1040X	0 %
0	Form 2210F	0 %	32	Form 5329	2 %			
0	Form 2439	0 %	5	Form 5884	0 %			
41	Form 2441	2 %	19	Form 6198	1 %			

PROCESSING INFORMATION:

		NO. OF CLIENTS FOR AVERAGE
AVERAGE TOTAL INCOME	87,966	1,445
AVERAGE ADJUSTMENTS	635	1,445
AVERAGE ADJUSTED GROSS INCOME	87,331	1,445
AVERAGE ITEMIZED DEDUCTIONS	8,325	931
AVERAGE TOTAL TAX	33,281	1,445
AVERAGE AMOUNT OWED TO GOVERNMENT	10,952	917
AVERAGE REFUND AMOUNT	3,205	339
AVERAGE AMOUNT BILLED	455	830
TOTAL AMOUNT BILLED	377,744	
TOTAL RECEIVED ON ACCOUNT	1,444	

BREAKDOWN OF RETURN PROCESSING DATES:

January 1 – 7:		February 1 – 7:	3	March 1 – 7:	287	April 1 – 7:	180
January 8 – 14:		February 8 – 14:	4	March 8 – 14:	322	April 8 – 15:	8
January 15 – 21:		February 15 – 21:	3	March 15 21:	306	April 16 – Dec. 31:	
January 22 – 31:		February 22 – 29:	30	March 22 – 31:	222		

15-10
Lacerte allows users to analyze their own tax seasons with a practice summary report.

There are rules governing practitioners who file electronically. The foremost is that they be able to communicate with the IRS via modem. There are other issues as well. "If a preparer who is delinquent on his own taxes applies to be an electronic transmitter, we may not accept them. If they've had problems with their prior-year returns or have received preparer penalties from the IRS, we have the option of not admitting them into the electronic filing system," says Donald Roberts of the IRS.

Assuming your tax history is clean and you can work your modem, however, you can be an electronic tax file preparer. Contact the IRS and request Form 8633, "Application to File Individual Income Tax Returns Automatically." Send the form to the IRS district office that covers the state in which you work. You'll be given an electronic filer identification number and IRS Publication 1345, "The Handbook for Electronic Filers of Individual Income Tax Returns." The identification number qualifies you to prepare tax returns for electronic filing, but there's one more step before you are authorized to be an electronic transmitter. You'll be sent technical IRS publications 1346 "File Specifications and Record Layouts" and 1436 "Test Package" and an electronic transmitter identification number.

The test package can be very complicated—if you intend to use your own communications software—or fairly simple, if you buy one of the many IRS-accepted commercial electronic transmitting programs. (These are available through virtually all of the tax software companies. For your final step to become an electronic filer, you must transmit sample tax returns to the IRS. Once you prove your computer can talk to their computer, you are in business.

The refund anticipation loan

What do you do for the client who is due a $2,000 refund and wants (or needs) that money so badly he'll do anything to get it faster? If you file his taxes electronically, you can offer him a refund anticipation loan that puts the cash in his hands within days (instead of weeks) of his signing the return. But should you?

A refund anticipation loan is a bank loan collateralized by the expected refund. And it's a really bad deal. Typically, banks that do refund anticipation loans charge fees of $35 to $45 to process the loans. They are called fees and not interest because, given the safety of the collateral (the IRS check is sent directly to the lender), and given the short-term nature of the loan (refunds on electronically filed returns typically come in about three weeks, anyway), the fees would probably violate the few usury ceilings left if they were expressed as interest.

Unfortunately, these loans are used by the people at the bottom of the economic chain. These people might not have access to even a credit card, which would actually provide a better loan than the refund anticipation mechanism. (You can borrow $2,000 for a month on a credit card and only pay about $25 for the privilege.)

If you try to convince these clients that they should muddle through until they get their money AND should change their withholding status so they pay $2,000 less in taxes next year, they'll often balk. Your choices are turning them away, which many respected practitioners do, or going along and helping them get the loan. If you choose Plan B, you can probably arrange these loans through a local bank.

Practically speaking, the days of the refund anticipation loan might be numbered. The loans depend on the IRS sending back an electronic signal that means the refund has cleared a preliminary review. Early signs from the IRS are that this early clearance mechanism will be discontinued.

Something new: the 1040 PC

The IRS is already looking beyond electronic filing to another "up-and-coming" tax technology: the 1040 PC program. The 1040 PC program is still paper-driven. Instead of IRS-approved forms (and tax returns that can easily number 20 pages or more), the PC program enables the filer to deliver a couple of pages of numbers to the IRS. The 1040 PC return lists line numbers and amounts, and that's it, except of course, for the name, address, and Social Security number of the client.

What are the advantages? "Paper reduction, big time!" says O'Rourke of the NATP. What about the disadvantages? O'Rourke says, "Is the person who pays me $150 to do his tax return going to be happy with two pages of mumbo jumbo instead of 20 pages of all of the schedules, all printed out and easy to follow? I don't think so."

Many commercial tax preparation programs will begin carrying 1040 PC formats in 1993; you can choose to file a 1040 PC form with the IRS but still print out a full copy of the client's return for him to keep.

Affiliating

You might find that you want the handholding of a national franchise to get you started in tax preparation. As you read in chapter 6, that handholding comes at a price. In the tax arena, however, a national name does help you win clients, and the three biggest franchisors have solid reputations for offering support. Thus, you might find the price worthwhile. The three largest national tax-preparation franchises are:

H & R Block
410 Main Street
Kansas City, MO 64111
(816) 753-6900

Jackson Hewitt
2217 Commerce Parkway
Virginia Beach, VA 23454
(800) 463-8930

Triple Check Income Tax Service, Inc.
727 South Main Street
Burbank, CA 91506
(818) 840-9078

Keeping up with the law

Keeping up with changing laws and regulations is important in the bookkeeping industry; it becomes even more crucial when tax preparation is part of your business. "I subscribe to a lot of periodicals," said Lenore Kondrat. "Accounting is getting to the point where everybody is specializing, like doctors, and you really need to know what's going on."

Luckily, "keeping up" is such big business that there are several successful publishing firms built solely on the task of keeping tax professionals informed. Most of the publishers listed here offer everything from weekly newsletters to online or CD-ROM data to comprehensive texts on very specialized areas of tax law. Call or write for catalogues and then pick and choose those that you need. Remember, in an information-driven society, the person with the most information wins! Scrimp on your office furnishings if you must, but don't try to work in the tax field without enough information.

Warren Gorham Lamont
210 South Street
Boston, MA 02111
(800) 950-1210

Bureau of National Affairs
1231 25th Street, NW
Washington, DC 20037
(800) 372-1033

Matthew Bender
11 Penn Plaza
New York, NY 10001
(800) 223-1940

McGraw-Hill
1221 Avenue of the Americas
New York, NY 10020
(800) 233-1128

Research Institute of America
111 Radio Circle
Mt. Kisco, NY 10549-2697
(800) 431-9025

Prentice Hall
24 Waterbury Road
Waterford, CT 06386
(800) 243-0876

A tax quiz

Question: A client enters your office and tells you that he began an exotic-bird breeding business. He explains that the macaws he will be breeding have a life expectancy of approximately 75 to 100 years. What method of depreciation and class life will you use?

Question: A self-employed painter was helping his father-in-law construct a personal residence. During construction, the home slipped from its foundation and started a rock slide. The rocks rolled down a hill and into a nearby hospital. The hospital sued for damages and won. Is the self-employed painter allowed a business deduction for the damages he was required to pay the hospital?

Question: A professional gambler was considered to be a "valued gaming patron" by the casino. Extensions of credit were given to him at regular intervals, until they amounted to $3 million. The casino then cut him off and filed a suit in court to collect the advances. The court ruled the claims were unenforceable under state law, and the litigation was settled for $500,000. Is the $2.5 million difference considered debt forgiveness income and therefore taxable to the gambler?

Question: Who has to know all this stuff, anyway?

Answers: The modified accelerated-cost recovery system and seven years; no; no; and you do, if you really want to build a successful tax preparation practice in the 1990s.

According to the National Association of Tax Practitioners, who supplied those first three questions, the key to tax preparation success in the future is having a firm grasp on tax theory and the way the tax laws work. "The tax business has changed drastically in the past five years because of computer software," notes Steven O'Rourke, director of professional services for the association. "There's no longer an emphasis on math accuracy, or even on knowing the forms—the software does all that for you. The new emphasis is on tax theory.

"Today's successful planner makes sure all of the issues are addressed; that there isn't any income to report; that all of the W-2s and 1099s match up, that the return is complete," O'Rourke said. "The kitchen counter preparer is gone. He's been replaced by people willing to buy the equipment, keep up with the technology, and really learn the tax system."

Don't panic. That's not to say that you really need to have the tax code in your head, or that you're likely to have wild macaw trainers, avalanche-causing painters, or litigious gamblers among your clients. It is to say that you need to understand how the tax code works, and that you need to know where to find answers for questions like these. One such place is the NATP, which runs a tax answer-line for its members. "Believe it or not, all of those questions came in to us from member calls," said Mary Jo Delfosse, director of administration and finance for the association. "People get into really odd tax situations."

It's more likely, however, that your tax situations will be somewhat less odd. Most clients will have by-the-book returns; you'll get the hardest workout learning the various depreciation systems so you can select the proper one for your client's building and equipment purchases. Even there, you don't need to fill in all the blanks and read all the charts—the software does it for you. Most likely, says O'Rourke, you'll have to key in the price of the equipment, the date it was put in use, and the depreciation method you're electing to use. The software will post it to the proper forms.

16 Boost your bookkeeping income

Everyone needs extra money now and then. The good news is that anyone with good bookkeeping and computing skills can always make money, and sometimes a lot. If you are a working bookkeeper, you have many skills you can use to boost your income beyond preparing balance sheets. Some of these suggestions are strategies that squeeze extra earning power out of your current practice. Others suggest ways to offer new services to different clients. (Those are the types of clients who are do-it-yourself oriented and probably never will come to you (or anyone else) for bookkeeping services.)

It's true that if you get someone hooked on your accounting they'll need you month after month after month. If you set up someone in their own accounting system, they'll only need you until they get it off the ground. There are many companies out there who want to do their own books, however, and just need to get started. You can charge more for computer accounting consulting than you can for bookkeeping. Wayne Schultz, a Wethersfield, Connecticut CPA and accounting system specialist, charges $90 an hour to recommend and set up computer systems. In the same market, bookkeepers charge $15 to $60 per hour for their skills.

Even without a CPA designation, you can get into this market by selling your services in the same way. Terri Conlon, a Conway, New Hampshire bookkeeper who runs her own Facts & Figures Bookkeeping company, charges $25 an hour for at-home bookkeeping services and $30 an hour to set

Set up accounting systems for new businesses

other people up on their own accounting system. "And that's very low, because I'm out here in a country setting," she said. A friend of hers in Portland, Maine, charges $75 per hour for accounting system setups.

Devise a "Get Started" service for small businesses and set a flat fee that covers your going to their office, recommending software, installing it, setting up their chart of accounts, and teaching their staff bookkeeper to run the program. In many cases, you'll find that small businesses have already bought their accounting software and are just looking for someone to show them how to use it.

Teach

As you learned in 2, just about every community college, local adult education program, or business school offers bookkeeping classes. You need to realize that they have to get the teachers somewhere. If you are comfortable with your knowledge of bookkeeping and are people-oriented, you could teach a night or weekend bookkeeping course. If you've been established in business for a while, you might even want to teach a self-employment course to help others do what you've done. Don't worry about competition, either. Sharing what you know is a good feeling, and teaching others brings you up to the expert level, as well as bringing in contacts and client referrals that you wouldn't get anywhere else.

If you are particularly adept at one accounting software package, like Peachtree Complete Accounting, One-Write Plus, or ACCPAC BPI, you can teach people to use that software. Contact the big computer stores in your area, and see if they offer workshops to customers. You can develop your own course and offer it to local computer schools or, if you want to put the time and money into it, offer your own workshop.

Another training opportunity exists in the franchising companies. They often conduct training sessions for all of their new franchisees. If you have any national franchises headquartered near where you live, call and see if they need any bookkeeping/financial recordkeeping trainers for their franchisees.

Teaching works particularly well in a community setting if you are also offering the computer consulting services noted previously. Many small businesspeople might attend your seminars to see how it's done, then decide to hire you to do it for them anyway.

Resell software

Many software companies will license distribution of their products to consultants. If you find yourself setting up many clients with a particular accounting program, call the software company and find out whether they will sell it to you at a wholesale price so you can resell it at the retail level. Be careful, though: pick a product that will sell and a company that doesn't make its money selling software packages to distributors who get stuck with the product. Don't pay an exorbitant licensing fee, either. Don't pay any *fee*, unless you really envision yourself spending a great deal of time selling software and doing computer consulting instead of bookkeeping.

Yecch! Nobody really wants to make collections. If some of your clients are having trouble collecting on the invoices you are processing so nicely, you are in an ideal position to deliver a polite (or not so) phone call or letter demanding payment. Your clients should pay you extra for this service, of course.

Full-time collection agencies are expert at hounding past-due accounts until the accounts are paid. Those people tend to charge half of the money they bring in for their clients. Unless you want to move in that direction and become a full-time collection agent with separate clients for that service, you might want to keep your collection activities limited to the clients you already serve, and charged on a direct fee-for-service basis.

Bookkeeping is one of the easiest businesses to grow, and, if you are good and enjoy the people part of your business, you can hire other people. Your new workers can key in all the transactions while you hunt for new clients and present reports.

Hiring help is an excellent way to provide training to someone who wants to learn computerized bookkeeping. You can pay them $12 to $15 an hour to type data and then mark up their services. That's not an unfair amount either, because you are training them to be computerized bookkeepers. You can also hire bookkeeping part-timers who don't want to aggressively market, to work for you in their homes. Then you could parcel the work out.

You could also hire people of other financial disciplines—tax preparation, collections, organizing, and payroll—and sell your company as a more comprehensive (and higher-billing) business services firm. Then you'll spend almost no time billing, but more time hunting clients to make sure all of your employees are kept busy. You'll also be hunting for office space, because by then you'll surely have outgrown your cozy home computer table.

You are tangential to a lot of areas small businesses need to know about; one of them is small business loans. As a person who prepares financial statements, you know more than the average person about what bankers want to see before lending money to a small firm. Small-business administration loans, in particular, require a highly specialized application process. Become an expert in the business loan package, and you can charge a lot more to prepare a loan package than you can for basic bookkeeping. Preparing loans can be challenging and highly rewarding work.

Another rapidly growing area is pension plans for small businesses, like Keogh and SEP-IRA plans. Many small businesses would set these plans up for their employees if they knew of them, or knew how to fill out the forms.

These are specialized areas and not to be entered into cavalierly. If you invest some time in learning about them, however, you'll be able to sell what you know to clients who may be growing or to other small businesses who need a little information and guidance. Typically, you can charge more per hour for this special expertise than you can for the hours you spend bookkeeping.

Prepare tax returns

Tax returns are one of the major ways that bookkeepers boost their earnings. Some bookkeepers report that they pull in fully one third of their annual pay in the months of March and April preparing returns. It's so big, it earned its own chapter in this book.

Publish a newsletter

If you've read chapter 10 carefully, you might already be publishing a one-to four-page newsletter on tax, bookkeeping, and small business issues to win new clients and keep existing ones happy. The newsletter probably contains information of value to small businesses who are not your clients. The newsletter market (particularly for financial newsletters) is filled right now, so this isn't the easiest way to make money. But it's filled because small businesses have a desperate need for this information. If you are inclined toward the newsletter direction, consider marketing the newsletter to the businesses in your area.

Raise your rates

Remember that your existing clients like you and your work. If you aren't making enough at your current rate structure, perhaps you don't need to work harder, you just need to earn. *Most of your clients will stick with you through a rate increase.* You can replace the ones that don't with a better-paying, more-appreciative level of client.

Prepare payrolls

Unfortunately, the large payroll servicing companies—Paychex and ADP—have become so competitive that it's hard to charge much for doing payrolls, and some bookkeepers report that they only prepare payrolls when they must. There are advantages though: if you know a payroll software program, it can provide steady, regular work and introduce you to a larger universe of potential clients for your other bookkeeping work.

Be a notary public

When you think about it, the people who need documents notarized—accountants, attorneys, realtors, bankers—are often the same people who can recommend or use bookkeeping services. So, even though you'll never get rich notarizing documents at $5 to $10 a pop, you'll expand your client horizons, provide an added service to your existing clients, pick up a few extra bucks, and bolster your "truthful and honest image." People do think notaries are beyond reproach.

Broking services is a whole separate business, but one you could run in addition to your own. Form a network of business consultants who specialize in small business—bookkeepers, advertising specialists, writers, loan counselors, computer experts, and tax preparers. Get to know them and their work well enough to be comfortable selling it. Then, promote the network, as a dependable, stress-reducing way for local small businesses to find the work they need. Take a flat fee for each referral, from the hiring firm or from the person they've hired.

Broker bookkeeping services

Have you noticed the growth in ads by temporary agencies boasting accounting professionals? Temporary agencies have many customers and need people trained in accounting at all levels, and need them desperately enough to take you on your terms. Don Richards Associates, a national accounting temporaries firm with offices in many cities around the country, notes that his firm will pay bookkeepers and accountants from $8.50 to $60 an hour to work temporary jobs, depending on their level of expertise and the tasks they're hired to do. Temping is a good way to fill in your hours during slow periods or while building a practice—you can opt to work one week a month, a couple of days a week, or an irregular schedule while cultivating clients of your own. While it's not entirely ethical to get hired as a temporary and then take the account away from the company that hired you, it's been done. Being out in the temp market can also give you experience with many different kinds of businesses and accounting systems, *and*, once again, expose you to a new circle of contacts who might direct new clients your way.

Do temporary work

A U.S. state boards of accountancy

Contacting your state board of accountancy is a good first step in finding out what rules and regulations will govern your business where you live.

Alabama State Board of Public Accountancy
RSA Plaza
770 Washington Avenue
Montgomery, AL 36130
Attn: Boyd E. Nicholson, Jr.,
  Executive Dir
Tel: (205) 242-5700   Fax: (205) 242-2711

Alaska State Board of Public Accountancy
Department of Commerce and
  Economic Development
Division of Occupational Licensing
  Box 110806
Juneau, AK 99811-0806
Attn: Steven Snyder, Licensing Examiner
Tel: (907) 465-2580   Fax: (907) 465-2974

Arizona State Board of Public Accountancy
3110 North Nineteenth Avenue
Suite 140
Phoenix, AZ 85015-6038
Attn: Ruth R. Lee, Executive Director
Tel: (602) 255-3648   Fax: (602) 255-1283

Arkansas State Board of Public Accountancy
101 East Capitol, Suite 430
Little Rock, AR 72201
Attn: James Ward, Executive Director
Tel: (501) 682-1520   Fax: (501) 682-5538

California State Board of Accountancy
2135 Butano Drive, Suite 112
Sacramento, CA 95825-0451
Attn: Carol B. Sigmann, Executive Officer
Tel: (916) 920-7121   Fax: (916) 920-6547

Colorado State Board of Accountancy
1560 Broadway, Suite 1370
Denver, CO 80202
Attn: Mary Lou Burgess, Administrator
Tel: (303) 894-7800   Fax: (303) 894-7790

Connecticut State Board of Accountancy
Secretary of the State
30 Trinity Street
Hartford, CT 06106
Attn: David Guay, Executive Secretary
Tel: (203) 566-7835   Fax: (203) 566-6192

Delaware State Board of Accountancy
Margaret O'Neill Building
PO Box 1401
Dover, DE 19903
Attn: Sheila Wolfe, Administrative Assistant
Tel: (302) 739-4522   Fax: (302) 739-6148

District of Columbia Board of Accountancy
Department of Consumer and
   Regulator Affairs
614 H Street, NW, Room 923
c/o PO Box 37200
Washington, DC 20013-7200
Attn: Harriette Andrews,
   Board Representative
Tel: (202) 727-7468   Fax: (202) 727-7030

Florida Board of Accountancy
2610 N.W. 43rd Street, Suite 1A
Gainesville, FL 32606
Attn: Martha Willis, Executive Director
Tel: (904) 336-2165   Fax: (904) 336-2164

Georgia State Board of Accountancy
166 Pryor Street, SW
Atlanta, GA 30303
Attn: Barbara Wilkerson, Executive Director
Tel: (404) 656-3941   Fax: (404) 651-9532

Guam Territorial Board of Public Accountancy
c/o KPRM Peat Marwick, Bk. GUAM Bldg
Suite 800, 111 Chalan Santo Papa
Agana, GU 96910
Attn: Judith K. Borja, Chairman
Tel: (671) 472-2910   Fax: (671) 472-2918

Hawaii Board of Public Accountancy
Department of Commerce and
   Consumer Affairs
PO Box 3469
Honolulu, HI 96801-3469
Attn: Verna Tomita, Executive Secretary
Tel: (808) 586-2694   Fax: (808) 586-2689

Idaho State Board of Accountancy
500 South Tenth Street, Suite 104
Statehouse Mail
Boise, ID 83720
Attn: Brenda Blaszkiewicz,
   Executive Secretary
Tel: (208) 334-2490   Fax: (208) 334-2615

Illinois Committee on Accountancy
University of Illinois Urbana-Champaign
10 Administration Bldg.
506 S. Wright Street
Urbana, IL 61801-3260
Attn: Linda Sergent, Secretary
Tel: (217) 333-1565   Fax: (217) 333-3126

Illinois Department of Professional Regulation
Public Accountancy Section
320 W. Washington Street, 3rd Floor
Springfield, IL 627-0001
Attn: Judy Vargas, Manager
Tel: (217) 785-0800   Fax: (217) 782-7645

Indiana State Board of Public Accountancy
Indiana Government Center North
100 North Senate Avenue
Indianapolis, IN 46204-2246
Attn: Sherrill Keesee,
   Administrative Assistant
Tel: (317) 232-3898   Fax: (317) 232-2312

Iowa Accountancy Examining Board
1918 SE Hulsizer Avenue
Ankeny, IA 50021
Attn: William Schroeder, Executive Secretary
Tel: (515) 281-4126   Fax: (515) 281-7372

Kansas Board of Accountancy
Landon State Office Building
900 SW Jackson, Suite 556
Topeka, Kansas 66612-1239
Attn: Glenda Moore, Executive Director
Tel: (913) 296-2162   Fax: (913) 296-6729

Kentucky State Board of Accountancy
332 West Broadway, Suite 310
Louisville, KY 40202-2115
Attn: Susan Stopher, Executive Director
Tel: (502) 588-3037   Fax: (502) 588-4281

State Board of CPAs of Louisiana
1515 World Trade Center
2 Canal Street
New Orleans, LA 70130
Attn: Mildred McGaha, Executive Director
Tel: (504) 566-1244   Fax: (504) 566-1254

Maine State Board of Accountancy
Department of Professional and Financial
Regulation
Division of Licensing and Enforcement
State House Station 35
Augusta, Maine 04433
Attn: Sandy Leach, Board Clerk
Tel: (207) 582-8723   Fax: (207) 582-5415

Maryland State Board of Public Accountancy
501 St. Paul Place, 9th Floor
Baltimore, MD 21202-2222
Attn: Sue Mays, Executive Director
Tel: (410) 333-6322   Fax: (410) 333-1229

Massachusetts Board of Public Accountancy
Saltonstall Building, Room 1609
100 Cambridge Street
Boston, MA 02202-0001
Tel: (617) 727-1753   Fax: (617) 727-7378

Michigan Board of Accountancy
Department of Commerce-BOPR
PO Box 30018
Lansing, MI 48909-7518
Attn: Suzanne Jolicoeur, Licensing
Administrator
Tel: (517) 373-0682   Fax: (517) 373-2795

Minnesota State Board of Accountancy
133 East 7th Street
St. Paul, MN 55101
Attn: Pamela Smith, Executive Secretary
Tel: (612) 296-7937

Mississippi State Board of
  Public Accountancy
961 Highway 80 East, Suite A
Clinton, MS 39056-5246
Attn: Roy Horton, Executive Director
Tel: (601) 924-8457

Missouri State Board of Accountancy
PO Box 613
Jefferson City, MO 65102-0613
Attn: Beverley Shackelford,
  Executive Director
Tel: (314) 751-0012   Fax: (314) 751-0890

Montana State Board of Public Accountants
Arcade Building, Lower Level
111 North Jackson
Helena, MT 59620-0407
Attn: Brenda St. Clair, Administrator
Tel: (406) 444-3739   Fax: (406) 444-1667

Nebraska State Board of Public Accountancy
PO Box 94725
Lincoln, NE 68509-4725
Attn: Marshall Whitlock, Executive Director
Tel: (402) 471-3595   Fax: (402) 471-4484

Nevada State Board of Accountancy
1 East Liberty Street, Suite 311
Reno, NV 89501-2110
Attn: William Zideck, Executive Director
Tel: (702) 786-0231   Fax: (702) 786-0234

New Hampshire Board of Accountancy
57 Regional Drive
Concord, NH 03301
Attn: Louise MacMillan,
  Assistant to the Board
Tel: (603) 271-3286

New Jersey State Board of Accountancy
PO Box 45000
Newark, NJ 07101
Attn: John J. Meade, Executive Director
Tel: (201) 504-6380   Fax: (201) 648-3536

New Mexico State Board of
  Public Accountancy
1650 University NE, Suite 400A
Albuquerque, NM 87102
Attn: Trudy Beverley, Executive Director
Tel: (505) 841-9109   Fax: (505) 766-9049

New York State Board for Public Accountancy
State Education Department
Cultural Education Center, Rm 9A47
Albany, NY 12230-0001
Attn: Douglas Martin, Executive Secretary
Tel: (518) 474-3836   Fax: (518) 473-0578

North Carolina State Board of CPA Examiners
1101 Oberlin Road, Suite 104
PO Box 12827
Raleigh, NC 27605-2827
Attn: Robert Brooks, Executive Director
Tel: (919) 733-4222   Fax: (919) 733-4209

North Dakota State Board of Accountancy
Box 8104, University Station
Grand Forks, ND 58202
Attn: Jim Abbott, Executive Director
Tel: (701) 777-3869   Fax: (701) 777-3894

Accountancy Board of Ohio
77 South High Street, 18th Floor
Columbus, OH 43266-0301
Attn: Timothy Haas, Executive Director
Tel: (614) 466-4135   Fax: (614) 644-8112

Oklahoma Accountancy Board
4545 Lincoln Blvd., Suite 165
Oklahoma City, OK 73105-3413
Attn: Diana Collingsworth, Executive Director
Tel: (405) 521-2397   Fax: (405) 521-3118

Oregon State Board of Accountancy
158 12th Street, NE
Salem, OR 97310-0001
Attn: Karen DeLorenzo, Administrator
Tel: (503) 378-4181   Fax: (503) 378-3575

Pennsylvania State Board of Accountancy
613 Transportation & Safety Building
PO Box 2649
Harrisburg, PA 17105-2649
Attn: J. Robert Kline,
  Administrative Assistant
Tel: (717) 783-1404   Fax: (717) 787-7769

Puerto Rico Board of Accountancy
Old San Juan Street
Box 3271
San Juan, PR 00904-3271
Attn: Luis Issac Sanchez, Director
Tel: (809) 722-2122   Fax: (809) 725-7302

Rhode Island Board of Accountancy
Department of Business Regulation
233 Richmond Street, Suite 236
Providence, RI 02903-4236
Attn: Norma MacLeod, Executive Secretary
Tel: (401) 277-3185

South Carolina Board of Accountancy
Dutch Plaza, Suite 260
800 Dutch Square Blvd.
Columbia, SC 29210
Attn: Fred Stuart, Director
Tel: (803) 731-1677   Fax: (803) 731-1680

South Dakota Board of Accountancy
301 East 14th Street, Suite 200
Sioux Falls, SD 57104
Attn: Lynn Bethke, Executive Director
Tel: (605) 339-6746

Tennessee State Board of Accountancy
500 James Robertson Parkway
2nd Floor
Nashville, TN 37219
Attn: Don Hummel,
  Director of Administration
Tel: (615) 741-2550   Fax: (615) 741-7670

Texas State Board of Public Accountancy
1033 La Posada, Suite 340
Austin, TX 78752-3892
Attn: William Treacy, Executive Director
Tel: (512) 451-0241   Fax: (512) 450-7075

Utah Board of Accountancy
160 East 300 South
PO Box 48502
Salt Lake City, UT 84145-0802
Attn: David Fairhurst, Adminstrator
Tel: (801) 530-6628   Fax: (801) 530-6511

Vermont Board of Public Accountancy
Pavilion Office Bldg.
Montpelier, VT 05602
Attn: Loris Rollins, Staff Assistant
Tel: (802) 828-2837   Fax: (802) 828-2496

Virginia Board for Accountancy
3600 West Broad Street
Richmond, VA 23230-4917
Attn: Roberta Banning, Assistant Director
Tel: (804) 367-8505   Fax: (804) 367-2475

Virgin Islands Board of Public Accountancy
1B King Street
Christiansted
St Croix, VI 00820-4933
Attn: Alan Bronstein, Secretary
Tel: (809) 773-0096   Fax: (809) 778-8640

Washington State Board of Accountancy
210 East Union, Suite H
PO Box 9131
Olympia, WA 98507-9191
Attn: Carey Rader, Executive Director
Tel: (206) 753-2585   Fax: (206) 664-9190

West Virginia Board of Accountancy
201 L & S Building
812 Quarrier Street
Charleston, WV 25301-2617
Attn: JoAnn Walker, Executive Secretary
Tel: (304) 558-3557

Wisconsin Accounting Examining Board
1400 E. Washington Ave.
PO Box 8935
Madison, WI 53708-8935
Attn: Peter Eggert, Bureau Director
Tel: (608) 266-3423   Fax: (608) 267-0644

Wyoming Board of Certified
  Public Accountants
Barrett Building, 2nd Floor
Room 217-218
Cheyenne, WY 82002
Attn: Peggy Morgando, Executive Director
Tel: (307) 777-7551   Fax: (307) 777-6005

B Charts of accounts

The sample charts of accounts in this appendix are part of the One-Write Plus Program. Most other programs have similar examples. Programs that have many charts of accounts built in offer the advantage of quick start up: you can customize an existing chart of accounts faster than you can set up your own.

These accounts offer a good guide to the types of accounts you would want to set up for your own business or the businesses of your clients, should you be using a different program.

Current Assets
Checking account
Savings account
Payroll account
Petty cash
Cash transfers
Accounts receivable—billed
Accounts receivable—unbilled
Allowance for bad debts

Refundable Taxes

Prepaid Expenses
Prepaid expenses
Prepaid insurance

Accounting or bookkeeping business chart of accounts

Prepaid taxes

Other Current Assets
Loans and exchanges

Property and Equipment
Land
Buildings
Accumulated depreciation—building
Building improvements
Accumulated depreciation—building improvements
Leasehold improvements
Accumulated depreciation—lease improvements
Equipment
Accumulated depreciation—equipment
Furniture and fixtures
Accumulated depreciation—furniture and fixtures
Vehicles
Accumulated depreciation—vehicles
Other fixed assets
Accumulated depreciation—other

Other Assets
Partners' loan receivable
Utility deposit
Other assets
Goodwill
Accumulated amortization—goodwill
Organization costs
Accumulated depreciation—organization costs

Current Liabilities
Accounts payable
Credit card—Visa
Credit card—Mastercard
Credit card—American Express
Notes payable—short-term
Employee health insurance payable
Sales taxes payable

Payroll Taxes Payable
Federal withholding tax payable
FICA withholding taxes payable
State withholding taxes payable
Local withholding taxes payable
Accrued FUTA
Accrued SUTA

Current portion long-term debt
Long-term notes—current portion

Notes Payable

Accrued Taxes
Accrued corporate taxes

Other Accrued Expenses
Accrued interest
Accrued other expenses

Non-Current Liabilities

Long-Term Debt Net of Current Portion
Long-term notes—net of current

Notes payable—partner
Notes payable—partner

Equity
Common stock
Additional paid-in capital
Retained earnings
Initial cash balance offset
Partner's capital #1
Partner's capital #2
Partner's drawing #1
Partner's drawing #2
Capital
Drawing

Income
Fees—billed
Fees—unbilled
(less) Fees absorbed

Client-related expenses
Postage
Supplies
Telephone
Travel
Other client-related expenses
(less) Expenses recovered

Expenses
Associates' salaries

Steno and office salaries
Auto expense
Bank service charge
Contributions
Depreciation expense
Dues and subscriptions
Equipment rental
Utilities
Insurance—employee group
Insurance—general
Insurance—partner's life
Interest expense
Legal and accounting
Miscellaneous expense
Office expense
Outside services
Postage expense
Rent expense
Repairs and maintenance
Supplies expense
Taxes—real estate
Taxes—payroll
Taxes—other
Telephone
Travel and entertainment

Other (Income) and Expenses
Fines and penalties
Interest income
Finance charge income
Other income

Income Taxes
Federal income tax
State income tax

Other (Income) and Expenses
Temporary distribution

Contractor or builder chart of accounts

Current Assets
Checking account
Savings account
Payroll account
Cash—trustee account
Petty cash

Cash transfers
Accounts receivable
Mortgages receivable
Notes receivable
Allowance for bad debts
Inventory—land
Inventory—buildings
Construction in progress
Contracts receivable

Refundable Taxes

Prepaid Expenses
Prepaid expenses
Prepaid insurance
Prepaid taxes

Other Current Assets
Loans and exchanges

Property and Equipment
Land
Buildings
Accumulated depreciation—building
Building improvements
Accumulated depreciation—building improvements
Leasehold improvements
Accumulated depreciation—lease improvements
Equipment
Accumulated depreciation—equipment
Furniture and fixtures
Accumulated depreciation—furniture and fixtures
Vehicles
Accumulated depreciation—vehicles
Other fixed assets
Accumulated depreciation—other

Other Assets
Officers' loan receivable
Utility deposits
Other assets
Goodwill
Accumulated amortization—goodwill
Organization costs
Accumulated amortization—organization costs

Escrow deposits
Municipal tax liens and deposits

Current Liabilities
Accounts payable
Credit card—VISA
Credit card—Mastercard
Credit card—American Express
Notes payable—short-term
Employee health insurance payable
Commissions payable
Customer deposits
Sales taxes payable

Payroll Taxes Payable
Federal withholding tax payable
FICA withholding tax payable
State withholding taxes payable
Local withholding taxes payable
Accrued FUTA
Accrued SUTA

Current Portion Long-Term Debt
Long-term notes—current portion

Notes Payable

Accrued Taxes
Accrued corporate taxes

Other Accrued Expenses
Accrued interest
Accrued other expenses

Non-Current Liabilities

Long-Term Debt Net of Current Portion
Long-term notes—net of current

Notes Payable—Officer
Notes payable—officer

Equity
Common stock
Additional paid-in capital
Retained earnings
Initial cash balance offset

Partner's capital #1
Partner's capital #2
Partner's drawing #1
Partner's drawing #2
Capital
Drawing

Sales
Sales
Sales discounts
Sales returns & allowances
Income—installment sales
Rental income
Commissions earned

Cost of Sales
Cost of construction sold

Land and Development
Roads and curbs
Water mains
Engineering
Surveys
Legal and municipal costs
Fill

Direct Costs
Salary—foreman
Wages—construction
Masonry
Carpentry
Plumbing
Heating & air
Sheet metal
Electrical
Appliances
Other subcontractors
Depreciation
Misc. expenses—sales
Payroll taxes—sales

Indirect Costs
Real estate taxes
Heat, light, power
Permits
Landscaping

Depreciation
Occupancy
Cleaning

General and Administrative
Salaries and wages
Officer's salaries
Auto expense
Bank service charge
Contributions
Depreciation expense
Dues and subscriptions
Equipment rental
Utilities
Insurance—employee group
Insurance—general
Insurance—officers' life
Interest expense
Legal and accounting
Miscellaneous expense
Occupancy
Office expense
Outside services
Postage expense
Rent expense
Repairs and maintenance
Supplies expense
Taxes—real estate
Taxes—payroll
Taxes—other
Telephone
Travel and entertainment

Other (Income) and Expenses
Fines and penalties
Interest income
Finance charge income
Other income

Income Taxes
Federal income tax
State income tax

Other (Income) and Expenses
Temporary distributions

Current Assets
Checking account
Savings account
Payroll account
Petty cash
Cash transfers
Accounts receivable
Allowances for bad debts
Inventory—raw materials
Inventory—finished goods
Inventory—work in progress

Refundable Taxes

Prepaid Expenses
Prepaid expenses
Prepaid insurance
Prepaid taxes

Other Current Assets
Loans and exchanges

Property and equipment
Land
Buildings
Accumulated depreciation—building
Building improvements
Accumulated depreciation—building improvements
Leasehold improvements
Accumulated depreciation—lease improvements
Equipment
Accumulated depreciation—equipment
Furniture and fixtures
Accumulated depreciation   furniture and fixtures
Vehicles
Accumulated depreciation—vehicles
Other fixed assets
Accumulated depreciation—other

Other Assets
Officers' loan receivable
Utility deposits
Other assets
Goodwill
Accumulated amortization—goodwill

Organization costs
Accumulated amortization—organization costs

Current Liabilities
Accounts payable
Credit card—VISA
Credit card—Mastercard
Credit card—American Express
Notes payable—short-term
Employee health insurance payable
Sales tax payable

Payroll Taxes Payable
Federal withholding tax payable
FICA withholding tax payable
State withholding taxes payable
Local withholding taxes payable
Accrued FUTA
Accrued SUTA

Current Portion of Long-Term Debt
Long-term notes—current portion

Notes Payable

Accrued Taxes
Accrued corporation taxes

Other Accrued Expenses
Accrued interest
Accrued other expenses

Non-Current Liabilities

Long-Term Debt Net of Current Liabilities
Long-term notes—net of current

Notes Payable—Officer
Notes payable—officer

Equity
Common stock
Additional paid-in capital
Retained earnings
Initial cash balance offset
Partner's capital #1

Partner's capital #2
Partner's drawing #1
Partner's drawing #2
Capital
Drawing

Sales
Sales
Sales discounts
Sales returns and allowances

Direct Materials

Direct Labor

Subcontractors

Factory Overhead
Salaries and wages
Depreciation expenses
Equipment rental
Insurance—employee group
Insurance—general
Miscellaneous expense
Office expense
Outside services
Rent expense
Repairs and maintenance
Supplies expenses
Taxes—payroll
Taxes—real estate
Taxes—other

Inventory Increase/Decrease
Increase/decrease—finished goods
Increase/decrease—work in progress

Other Production Expenses

Selling Expenses
Salaries—sales
Commissions
Advertising
Travel
Miscellaneous expense—sales
Payroll taxes—sales

General and Administrative

Salaries and wages
Officers' salaries
Auto expense
Bank service charge
Contributions
Depreciation expense
Dues and subscriptions
Equipment rental
Utilities
Insurance—employee group
Insurance—general
Insurance—officers' life
Interest expense
Legal and accounting
Miscellaneous expense
Office expense
Outside services
Postage expense
Rent expense
Repairs and maintenance
Supplies expense
Taxes—real estate
Taxes—payroll
Taxes—other
Telephone
Travel
Travel and entertainment

Other (Income) and Expenses

Fines and penalties
Interest income
Finance charge income
Other income

Income Taxes

Federal income tax
State income tax

Other (Income) and Expenses

Temporary distributions

Nonprofit chart of accounts

Unrestricted Fund

Cash in bank
Savings account
Payroll account

Petty cash fund
Cash transfers
Pledges received
Allowance for bad debts
Inventories

Prepaid Expenses
Prepaid expenses
Prepaid insurance
Prepaid taxes

Restricted Fund
Cash—restricted fund
Investments
Grants receivable

Building Fund
Cash—building fund
Investments
Pledges receivable
Allowance for bad debts
Land
Building
Mortgage payable
Accumulated depreciation—building
Building improvements
Accumulated depreciation—building improvements
Leasehold improvements
Accumulated depreciation—lease improvements
Equipment
Accumulated depreciation—equipment
Furniture and fixtures
Accumulated depreciation—furniture and fixtures
Vehicles
Accumulated depreciation—vehicles
Other fixed assets
Accumulated depreciation—other

Endowment Funds
Cash—endowment fund
Investments

Unrestricted Fund Liabilities
Accounts payable—unrestricted
Research grants
Designated future periods

Restricted and Liabilities
Accounts payable—restricted

Building Fund Liabilities
Accounts payable—building
Notes payable

Endowment Funds Liabilities
Accounts payable—endowment

Fund Balances
Fund balance (central)
Unrestricted—not designated
Unrestricted—designated
Initial cash balance offset
Restricted fund balance
Building fund balance
Endowment fund balance

Support and Rev—Unrestricted Fund
Contributions—unrestricted
Special events
Legacies and bequests
Campaigns
Membership dues
Investment income
Realized gain on investment
Miscellaneous
Transfers from other funds

Support and Rev—Restricted Fund
Contribution—restricted
Investment income
Transfers from other funds

Support and Rev—Building Fund
Contributions—building
Investment income
Realized gain sale asset
Transfer from other funds

Support and Rev—Endowment Fund
Contribution—endowment
Legacies and bequests
Realized gain investments

Program A
Program A—unrestricted
Salaries and wages
Fringe benefits
Travel
Advertising
Other

Program B
Program B—unrestricted

Program C
Program C—unrestricted

Program D
Program D—unrestricted

Program E
Program E—unrestricted

Program F
Program F—unrestricted

Program G
Program G—unrestricted

Program H
Program H—unrestricted

Program I
Program I—unrestricted

Transfers to Other Funds
Transfers to other funds

Program A
Program A—restricted

Program B
Program B—restricted

Program C
Program C—restricted

Program D
Program D—restricted

Program E

Program E—restricted

Program F

Program F—restricted

Program G

Program G—restricted

Program H

Program H—restricted

Program I

Program I—restricted

Transfers to Other Funds

Transfers to other funds

C Sample reports

Even the simplest accounting programs allow you to massage data in a number of ways, and the high-end programs offer endless customizing options. The reports in this appendix are samples of some of the common forms and reports that you will be preparing for your clients.

```
Date 03/19/92                    Your Company Name                         Page 1
Time 16:05                        Checks Journal

=========================================================================================
Tran. Check  Check      Payee Name        Invoice Description      Amount   Discount      Net
Num.  Date   Number                        Number                           Taken        Paid
=========================================================================================
Account Num.  102A01   Checking Account
0001 03/19/92 001001   Maintenance Expense  510    Maintenance Expense   150.00    0.00     150.00
                                                                                    ------------
                                                   Total Check                               150.00

0002 03/19/92 001002   Contract Labor       528    Contract Labor      1,050.00    0.00    1,050.00
                                            599    Materials             250.00    0.00      250.00
                                                                                    ------------
                                                   Total Check                             1,300.00

0003 03/19/92 001003   Office Equipment     122    Office Equipment      580.00    0.00      580.00
                                            121    Furniture & Fixtures  645.25    0.00      645.25
                                                                                    ------------
                                                   Total Check                             1,225.25

                                                   Total Account 102A01                    2,675.25

                       Grand Total Journal                                                 2,675.25

Checks Printed  3
```

C-1

Sample check journal from Pacioli 2000.

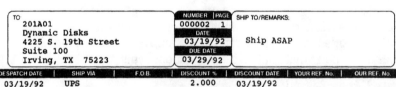

Purchase Order

	NUMBER	PAGE	SHIP TO/REMARKS:
TO: 201A01 Dynamic Disks 4225 S. 19th Street Suite 100 Irving, TX 75223	000002	1	Ship ASAP
	DATE 03/19/92		
	DUE DATE 03/29/92		

DESPATCH DATE	SHIP VIA	F.O.B.	DISCOUNT %	DISCOUNT DATE	YOUR REF. No.	OUR REF. No.
03/19/92	UPS		2.000	03/19/92		

ITEM No.	DESCRIPTION	QUANTITY	UNIT	UNIT PRICE	EXTENDED PRICE	TAX RATE	TAX	TOTAL AMOUNT
DISKS	5-1/4" Disks	25	BOX	10.000				250.00
DISKS-B	3-1/2" Disks	25	Box	15.000				375.00

Net Due   625.00

C-2

Pacioli 2000 purchase order.

Account Number	Account Name	Balance as of 31/01/92	Budget as of 31/01/92	Variance £	Variance %
1	REVENUES	68,577.92	63,030.00	5,547.92	8.8
101	Sales	56,423.23	56,230.00	193.23	0.3
110	Fees	5,623.23	6,000.00	-376.77	-6.3
120	Delivery & Handling	798.35	500.00	298.35	59.7
121	Insurance	562.34	300.00	262.34	87.4
122	Packaging	0.00	0.00	0.00	
123	Surcharge	4,523.65	0.00	4,523.65	
129	Other Trade Revenues	356.78	0.00	356.78	
141	Interest Earned	0.00	0.00	0.00	
142	Other Financial Earnings	214.69	0.00	214.69	
143	Dividends Earned	0.00	0.00	0.00	
144	Discounts Taken	75.65	0.00	75.65	
151	Recovery Bad Debt	0.00	0.00	0.00	
152	Gain on Asset Sales	0.00	0.00	0.00	
153	Other Revenue	0.00	0.00	0.00	
2	COSTS & EXPENSES	59,331.44	79,800.00	-20,468.56	-25.6
201	Cost of Goods Sold	5,646.65	60,000.00	-54,353.35	-90.6
202	Freight	786.56	800.00	-13.44	-1.7
203	Insurance on Purchases	442.88	0.00	442.88	
204	Other Purchasing Costs	0.00	0.00	0.00	
205	Wages	14,569.25	15,000.00	-430.75	-2.9
206	Payroll Benefits	4,458.69	4,000.00	458.69	11.5
207	Employers NIC	560.32	0.00	560.32	
208	Maintenance Expense	2,456.98	0.00	2,456.98	
209	Depreciation Expense	1,800.98	0.00	1,800.98	
210	Amortization Expense	1,520.36	0.00	1,520.36	
211	Leases	12,000.00	0.00	12,000.00	
212	Insurance	825.96	0.00	825.96	
213	Travel	452.65	0.00	452.65	
214	Subsistence	125.65	0.00	125.65	
215	Entertainment	58.97	0.00	58.97	
216	Shipping	97.86	0.00	97.86	
217	Mail/Postage	561.23	0.00	561.23	
218	Phone	886.57	0.00	886.57	
219	General Services	98.00	0.00	98.00	
220	Legal Fees	0.00	0.00	0.00	
221	Accounting Fees	125.00	0.00	125.00	
222	Other Professional Fees	0.00	0.00	0.00	
223	Printing & Stationery	0.00	0.00	0.00	
224	Donations	0.00	0.00	0.00	
225	Licenses/Permits	75.64	0.00	75.64	
226	Subscriptions	0.00	0.00	0.00	
227	Contract Labor	442.36	0.00	442.36	
228	Bad Debt Reserve	0.00	0.00	0.00	
229	Rent	1,500.00	0.00	1,500.00	
240	Advertising	8,891.00	0.00	8,891.00	
241	Promotions	0.00	0.00	0.00	

C-3

Paciolo 2000 prints out a budget versus actual income report.

```
12/31/92 at 1:20PM              THE KITE STORE                    PAGE 1
                       W-2 WAGE AND TAX STATEMENT INFORMATION

EMPLOYER'S NAME THE KITE STORE          EMPLOYER'S ID 99-99999999
123 MAIN STREET                         STATE ID 99999
ANYTOWN, USA 55555


SOCIAL            EMPLOYEE
SECURITY #        NAME/ADDRESS          EMPLOYEE TAX INFORMATION
------------      --------------------  --------------------------------


111-222-3333      Edward J. Johnson     WAGES/TIPS/OTHER        13,538.36
                  345 Ledgewood Circle  FED INC TAX              1,668.92
                  Anytown, USA 55555    SOC SEC WAGES           13,538.36
                                        SOC SEC TAX                839.30
                                        STATE WAGES             13,538.36
                                        STATE INC TAX              676.94
                                        LOCAL WAGES             13,538.36
                                        LOCAL INC TAX               73.64
                                        MEDICARE WAGES          13,538.36
                                        MEDICARE TAX               196.24

233-32-9302       Leslie M. Miller      WAGES/TIPS/OTHER         1,526.00
                  89 South Street       FED INC TAX                146.65
                  Anytown, USA 55555    SOC SEC WAGES            1,526.00
                                        SOC SEC TAX                 94.61
                                        STATE WAGES              1,526.00
                                        STATE INC TAX               76.30
                                        MEDICARE WAGES           1,526.00
                                        MEDICARE TAX                22.13

333-44-6677       Judy L. Williams      WAGES/TIPS/OTHER         1,776.50
                  943 Longview Blvd.    FED INC TAX                248.42
                  Anytown, USA 55555    SOC SEC WAGES            1,776.50
                                        SOC SEC TAX                110.14
                                        MEDICARE WAGES           1,776.50
                                        MEDICARE TAX                25.76

                  TOTALS FOR FORM W-3   TOTAL WGS/TIPS/OTH      16,849.86
                  TRANSMITTAL OF INCOME TOTAL FIT                2,063.99
                  AND TAX STATEMENTS    TOTAL SS WAGES          16,840.86
                  FORMS ATTACHED 3      TOTAL SS TAX             1,044.05
                                        TOTAL STATE WAGES       15,064.36
                                        TOTAL STATE TAX            753.24
                                        TOTAL LOCAL WAGES       13,538.36
                                        TOTAL LOCAL TAX             73.64
                                        TOTAL MEDICARE WAGES    16,840.86
                                        TOTAL MEDICARE TAX         244.13
```

C-4
One-Write Plus W-2 payroll summary report.

Bellweather Cleaning Services

Balance Sheet
December 31, 1991

ASSETS

Current Assets

Petty Cash	$ 87.00	
Cash for Operations	43,300.37	
Cash in Bank	<5,116.73>	
Accounts Receivable	10,844.70	
Cleaning Supplies Inventory	210.00	
Office Supplies Inventory	45.00	
Employee Advances	250.00	
Total Current Assets		49,620.34

Property and Equipment

Furniture & Fixtures	8,400.00	
F & F Accumulated Depreciation	<2,380.00>	
Vehicles	13,500.00	
Vehicles - Accum. Depreciation	<6,150.00>	
Machinery & Equipment	2,275.00	
Mach. & Equip. -Accum. Deprec	<1,107.00>	
Net Leasehold Improvements	1,040.00	
Total Property and Equipment		15,578.00

Other Assets

Deposits	1,000.00	
Total Other Assets		1,000.00
Total Assets		$ 66,198.34

C-5

Sample balance sheet from Peachtree Accounting for Windows.

LIABILITIES AND CAPITAL

Current Liabilities

Accounts Payable	$ 1,020.10	
Accrued Payroll	800.00	
Group Health Ins. Payable	334.00	
Payroll Taxes Due (Summary)	8,548.49	
Total Current Liablilties		10,702.59

Long-Term Liabilities

Notes Payable - First Nat.	5,933.58	
Total Long-Term Liablilties		5,933.58
Total Liablilties		16,636.17

Capital

Capital - Beginning of Year	13,305.74	
Net Income	36,256.43	
Total Capital		49,562.17
Total Liabilities & Capital		$ 66,198.34

Unaudited - For Management Purposes Only

Bellweather Cleaning Services
Income Statement
For the Period Ending December 31, 1991

	Current Month		Year to Date	
Revenues				
Commercial Services Revenues	$ 346.00	100.00	197,246.00	100.00
Total Revenues	346.00	100.00	197,246.00	100.00
Expenses				
Salary Expenses	0.00	0.00	137,547.00	69.73
Supplies Expense	0.00	0.00	824.50	0.42
Vehicle Expense	0.00	0.00	4,612.50	2.34
General Office Expense	0.00	0.00	507.00	0.26
Interest Expense	0.00	0.00	833.18	0.42
Rent	0.00	0.00	7,975.00	4.04
General Office Expense	0.00	0.00	50.70	0.03
Postage Expense	0.00	0.00	17.50	0.01
Utilities Expense	0.00	0.00	3,693.03	1.87
Miscellaneous Expenses	0.00	0.00	1,200.00	0.61
Furn. & Fixture Deprec. Exp.	0.00	0.00	700.00	0.35
Vehicle Depreciation Expense	0.00	0.00	2,250.00	1.14
Mach. & Equip. Deprec. Exp.	0.00	0.00	379.16	0.19
Leasehold Imp. Deprec. Exp.	0.00	0.00	400.00	0.20
Total Expenses	0.00	0.00	160,989.57	81.62
Net Income	$ 346.00	100.00	36,256.43	18.38

For Management Purposes Only

```
                    THE UNIVERSAL CORPORATION
               Statement of Changes in Financial Position
                     7 Months Ended October 31, 1995


FUNDS PROVIDED BY OPERATIONS:
    Net earnings (loss) for the period              88,486
    Items not requiring use of funds:
        Depreciation and amortization               13,867
                                                   ────────
    Total funds provided by operations             102,353

USES OF FUNDS TO SUPPORT OPERATIONS:
    Decrease (increase) in working capital,
    exclusive of cash and cash equivalents:
        Inventory                                   (12,608)
        Trade accounts receivable                    38,792
        Prepaid expenses                               (660)
        Accounts payable                            106,166
                                                   ────────
    Total funds used by operations                 131,690
                                                   ────────
        Net increase (decrease) in funds from  operations   (29,337)

FUNDS PROVIDED BY INVESTING:
    Proceeds from disposal of property and equipment        0
                                                   ────────
                                                          0

FUNDS PROVIDED BY FINANCIAL ACTIVITIES:
    Proceeds of long-term debt                      40,000
                                                   ────────
                                                   40,000
                                                   ────────
TOTAL FUNDS GENERATED                              10,663


FUNDS USED BY INVESTING:
    Acquisition of property and equipment           6,334

FUNDS USED BY FINANCING:
    Reduction of long-term debt                     18,996
    Dividends paid                                        0
                                                   ────────
                                                   18,996
                                                   ────────
TOTAL FUNDS USED                                   25,330
                                                   ────────

INCREASE/(DECREASE) IN CASH AND CASH EQUIVALENTS   (14,667)

ADD OPENING CASH AND CASH EQUIVALENTS              101,409

CLOSING CASH AND CASH EQUIVALENTS                  86,742
                                                   ========
```

C-7
Changes in financial position report from AccPac. ©Computer Associates International Inc. Reprinted courtesy of Computer Associates International, Inc.

UNIVERSAL CORPORATION
2184 Rockcliffe Road
Any City
U.S.A.
92001

INVOICE

NUMBER	PAGE
5019	1
DATE	
Apr 14 95	

SOLD TO
Break-Away Designs
743 Wark Street
Sacramento, CA

93721

SHIP TO
Break-Away Designs
3rd floor
10090 Park Place
Richmond, VA
Attn: Ann
23519

ORDER NO.	ORDER DATE	CUSTOMER NO.	SALES PERSON	PURCHASE ORDER NO.	SHIP VIA	TERMS
1020	Apr 14 95	580	SP	PO90045001	U.P.S.	10 NET 30

QTY. ORDERED	QTY. SHIPPED	QTY. B/O	ITEM NUMBER	DESCRIPTION	UNIT PRICE	UM	EXTENDED PRICE
2	2	0	C1220B	Krugg 220 Arm Tilter-Brwn	463.50	EA	927.00
1	0	1	C1500B	High Back Arm Tilter	292.00	EA	0.00
1	0	1	D1606B	Executive Desk 72"x36"	1,412.10	EA	0.00
2	2	0	D1610B	Executive "L" 71"x35"	670.65	EA	1,341.30
1	1	0	F1270T	Lateral 36" - 2 drawer cu	420.90	EA	420.90
			TY-90096443021 AF-22134569002				
				Extra labor charge			15.00

The chair and desk will be shipped as soon as they are available.

COMMENTS:
** Our spring catalog is available.

MISC. CHARGES	0.00
SALES TAX	105.61
FREIGHT	74.90
TOTAL ▶	2,884.71

```
11/20/92                          Dome Homes, Inc.                         PAGE:   1
                    AR CUSTOMER CASH FLOW REPORT (WITH DISCOUNTS)

 DUE DATE   REF # DESCRIPTION     11/30/92     12/15/92     12/31/92     BEYOND     TOTAL DUE
 --------   ----- -----------     --------     --------     --------     ------     ---------

 ACE001 Ace Builders
 12/14/92  977   Invoice             0.00     12,956.04        0.00        0.00      12,956.04
 11/18/92  995   Invoice        87,689.16         0.00        0.00        0.00      87,689.16
                                -----------  -----------  -----------  ----------  ------------
                                87,689.16     12,956.04        0.00        0.00     100,645.20
                                -----------  -----------  -----------  ----------  ------------


 DAL001 Dallas-Ft. Worth Dome Homes
 12/02/92  1000  Invoice             0.00     81,741.00        0.00        0.00      81,741.00
 11/30/92  2     Invoice         6,179.96         0.00        0.00        0.00       6,179.96
                                -----------  -----------  -----------  ----------  ------------
                                 6,179.96     81,741.00        0.00        0.00      87,920.96
                                -----------  -----------  -----------  ----------  ------------


 GRE001 Greater New York Domes, Inc.
 01/05/93  234   Invoice             0.00         0.00       99.00        0.00          99.00
 12/29/92  972   Invoice             0.00         0.00    87,662.06        0.00      87,662.06
 11/24/92  996   Invoice        88,083.90         0.00        0.00        0.00      88,083.90
 01/02/93  CONSLT Invoice            0.00       123.75        0.00        0.00         123.75
                                -----------  -----------  -----------  ----------  ------------
                                88,083.90       123.75    87,761.06        0.00     175,968.71
                                -----------  -----------  -----------  ----------  ------------


 KAN001 Kansas City Geodesic Homes
 12/08/92  975   Invoice             0.00      6,723.92        0.00        0.00       6,723.92
 12/08/92  988   Invoice             0.00     77,031.95        0.00        0.00      77,031.95
 12/02/92  CONSLT Invoice            0.00       125.00        0.00        0.00         125.00
                                -----------  -----------  -----------  ----------  ------------
                                    0.00      83,880.87        0.00        0.00      83,880.87
                                -----------  -----------  -----------  ----------  ------------


 LOS001 Los Angeles Construction Co.
 12/16/92  994   Invoice             0.00         0.00    57,239.18        0.00      57,239.18
                                -----------  -----------  -----------  ----------  ------------
                                    0.00         0.00    57,239.18        0.00      57,239.18
                                -----------  -----------  -----------  ----------  ------------


 SUN001 Sunshine Homes, Inc.
 12/07/92  997   Invoice             0.00     25,244.07        0.00        0.00      25,244.07
 12/02/92  CONSLT Invoice            0.00       125.00        0.00        0.00         125.00
                                -----------  -----------  -----------  ----------  ------------
                                    0.00      25,369.07        0.00        0.00      25,369.07
                                -----------  -----------  -----------  ----------  ------------


                                -----------  -----------  -----------  ----------  ------------
                               181,953.02    204,070.73   145,000.24        0.00     531,023.99
                                -----------  -----------  -----------  ----------  ------------
```

C-9

Cash flow report from Harmony. Open Systems, Inc.

D The bookkeeper's get-started checklist

If you're building a business and a new career from scratch, keep an eye on this list to make sure everything's covered.

- ❑ Analyze your ability, affinity, and commitment.
- ❑ Brush up on or learn new bookkeeping skills.
- ❑ Talk to your family about your plans to work at home.
- ❑ Talk to other bookkeepers about their work.
- ❑ Measure your space. Is there enough for what you'll need?
- ❑ Measure your money. Do you have a reserve fund that can carry you through six months of gearing up?
- ❑ Write your state board of accountancy for any regulations you need to know about before you set up shop.
- ❑ Inquire about local zoning and business license laws.
- ❑ Decide on the form your business will take.
- ❑ Write a business plan. How much will you spend? How much will you charge? What do you need to make?
- ❑ Review your insurance. If you are quitting a job, will you need to buy life, health, and disability coverage? What about business liability?
- ❑ Open a business checking account.
- ❑ Set up your own accounting records. Don't lose track of start-up costs.
- ❑ Paint, wire, and carpet your space.
- ❑ Bring in or buy your furniture.
- ❑ Buy a computer system, a fax, and a phone.

- ❏ Call several software companies and request demonstration disks and brochures.
- ❏ Buy your accounting software and any other programs you expect to use early in your business.
- ❏ Select a business name; check the phone book to make sure no one else is using it.
- ❏ Print your business cards and stationary.
- ❏ Write a marketing plan.
- ❏ Select your phone service and begin operating your business number.
- ❏ Begin marketing with letters and phone calls.
- ❏ Order subscriptions to newsletters and memberships in trade groups you decide to join.
- ❏ Spend some time with your modem. Join an on-line service.
- ❏ Go shopping for all the supplies you need to run an efficient, organized business.

Once you are in business:

- ❏ Periodically review your financial and marketing plans and adjust for growth.
- ❏ Keep marketing.
- ❏ Remember your clients with small gifts, holiday cards, and thank you notes.
- ❏ Keep up with technological trends by reading computer magazines.
- ❏ Keep up with accounting trends by reading bookkeeping and tax newsletters.
- ❏ Consider expanding your business with new employees or new services.
- ❏ Remember to pat yourself on the back now and then for a job well done.

Index

"People are thirsty for specific how-to information that can enable them to earn a living at home," say Paul and Sarah Edwards, authors of *Working from Home* and *Best Home-Based Businesses for the Nineties*.

About the series editors

The Windcrest/McGraw-Hill Entrepreneurial PC series is designed to fill the until-now unmet need for step-by-step guidance for people wanting to make the work-home transition. The Edwards' track the trends that yield opportunities for successful home-based businesses and then find authors to provide the nitty-gritty business-specific information that can spare the home-based entrepreneur months of frustration and costly mistakes.

Paul and Sarah have been working from their home since 1974. It didn't take them long to realize they were participating in what would become a major social and economic trend—the home-based business. That spurred them to want to help others make the transition from office to home and to professionalize the image of home-based business.

Paul and Sarah are contributing editors to *Home Office Computing* magazine and write the monthly column, "Ask Paul and Sarah." They founded and manage the *Working From Home Forum* on CompuServe Information Service, an electronic network with more than 30,000 people around the world who work from home. Paul and Sarah also cohost the hour-long national weekly radio program "Home Office" on the Business Radio Network.

About the author

Linda Stern is an award-winning personal finance writer whose Money column appears in newspapers nationwide. A contributing editor of *Home Office Computing* magazine, she has boundless enthusiasm and practical advice for anyone testing the work-at-home waters. Stern is a frequent conference speaker and talk show guest who claims her own PC has been entrepreneurial for almost a decade.